The Sunday Telegraph

Guide to
Looking After Your Property

WHO IS JEFF HOWELL?

I first worked on building sites during summer vacations from university. I graduated in 1975 with a degree in Nuclear Engineering and the Philosophy of Science, which made me unemployable, so I carried on with the building site work. I did a bricklaying course at a government training centre, and spent most of the next twelve years as a full-time brickie. With my engineering and philosophy education, though, it was clear to me that a lot of what goes on in the construction industry is based more on witchcraft than science.

In 1989 I started teaching part-time at a building college in London, and I was in the right place at the right time when a lecturing job came up at South Bank Polytechnic. And when, shortly afterwards, the polytechnics were rebranded as universities, I was able to boast that I had gone from being a brickie to a university lecturer in two years.

In 1997 I got the chance to write a weekly column in the *Independent on Sunday*. Two years later the column moved to *The Sunday Telegraph*, and the 'Ask Jeff' readers' questions and answers section has made me aware of the many problems that householders have in getting building work done on their homes.

By the same author

Struck Off – the first year of 'Doctor on the House'

The Builders' White Boots and Other Stories

The Sunday Telegraph

Guide to
Looking After
Your Property

Everything you need to know
about maintaining your home

JEFF HOWELL

MACMILLAN

ACKNOWLEDGEMENTS

Many building colleagues have helped me to answer these questions. My special thanks go to Tony Poole and George Bennett of Mercury Plumbing and Heating, Dave Sims of DSE Electrical, Jay Webb of Fenestration Associates, Steve Bradford, Mike O'Leary, Peter O'Shea, Brian Cathcart, David Hewett, Paul Morris, Stephen Boniface and Eddie Bennett.

Thanks also to all the staff on *The Sunday Telegraph* Review who have helped make the 'Ask Jeff' feature such a success, and to Jack Scott, former editor of *Building Engineer*, who was the first person to pay me for writing anything.

First published 2002 by Macmillan

This revised and updated edition published 2004 by Macmillan
an imprint of Pan Macmillan Ltd
Pan Macmillan, 20 New Wharf Road, London N1 9RR
Basingstoke and Oxford
Associated companies throughout the world
www.panmacmillan.com

In association with *The Sunday Telegraph*

ISBN 1 4050 4658 9

Designed by seagulls
Colour Reproduction by Aylesbury Studios (Bromley) Ltd
Printed by Bath Press

CONTENTS

ILLUSTRATION ACKNOWLEDGEMENTS

p15 © Andy Hall

p19 © Society for the Protection of Ancient Buildings

p22 © Dennis Gilbert/View

p31 © BonaKemi Limited

p39 courtesy of www.chimneycare.co.uk

p42 © ARUP

p44 © Everest Ltd

pp50, 51 *Double-glazing units: a BRE guide to improved durability* © BRE

p58 Pictures courtesy of *Professional Electrician and Installer Magazine*

p61 courtesy of F L Patents

pp119, 143, 149, 150 courtesy of BRE

pp93, 97 © Strippers Paint Removers

pp95, 135 © David Hoffman Photo Library

pp103, 136 © Abbey Independent Surveys

p121 *Thermal Insulation: avoiding risks* © BRE

p122 © Kingspan Insulation

p126 courtesy of Selectaglaze Ltd. of St Albans, www.selectaglaze.co.uk

p.127 *Improving Sound Insulation in Homes* © BRE

p131 © Garden Matters

p140 © Ellen Rooney/the Garden Picture Library

p159 © Artex-Rawlplug, www.artex-rawlplug.co.uk

p166 © Bat Protection Trust

p168 © RSPB

All line drawings © Jim Robbins

All other pictures © Jeff Howell

A NOTE ON MEASUREMENTS

The British construction industry has officially used the metric system of measurement since 1970. This puts it in line with engineering and farming, but at odds with estate agents and euro-sceptic politicians. The only comment I would make on this is that the metric system is not a fiendish plot by the European Union, but is the official system in most Commonwealth countries, former Eastern Bloc countries, and much of the developing world. The metric system is an attempt to harmonize a world-wide system of measurement. Although it is not without its faults, it is simpler and less prone to error than the old imperial system. To avoid ambiguity, the British construction industry uses millimetres, rather than metres and centimetres, and on construction drawings you will often find that the comma after thousands, and the 'mm' after all measurements, is omitted. So a town house is 5500 wide, a door opening is 2100 high, and a kitchen worktop is 600 deep. The style used in this book is that where a reader's letter uses imperial measurements, these are left as written, and the metric equivalents are added in brackets. My answers are written using metric. Readers who feel a need to translate metric into imperial are advised to forget about complicated conversion formulae, and instead to compare the figures on either side of a tape measure. You'll soon get the hang of it. For easy reference, the nearest equivalents are:

$$25mm = 1 \text{ inch}$$
$$50mm = 2 \text{ inches}$$
$$75mm = 3 \text{ inches}$$
$$100mm = 4 \text{ inches}$$
$$150mm = 6 \text{ inches}$$
$$300mm = 12 \text{ inches}$$
$$\text{and } 1 \text{ metre} = 39 \text{ inches, or 3 feet 3 inches.}$$

For weights, a kilogram is just over two pounds, and 50 kilograms is roughly a hundredweight. A metric tonne (1000 kilograms) is about the same as an imperial ton.

For temperatures, I have been thinking in degrees Celsius (or Centigrade) for so long that I find Fahrenheit (which is not an English system, but a Prussian one) confusing. In Celsius, water freezes at 0 and boils at 100, 20 is a comfortable temperature indoors, 30 is too hot to go out in the sun without a hat, and 60 is the recommended British Standard temperature for hot water.

INTRODUCTION

Buying and maintaining a home is the greatest single item of expenditure in most peoples' lives, but the average person embarks upon home ownership with surprisingly little idea about how to look after their prize investment.

Until quite recently, most British people lived in rented accommodation, with repairs and maintenance being the responsibility of the landlord – either private or local authority. Those who did buy their own homes usually managed it only after first saving up for years with a building society, so that when they did finally become homeowners, they had already rented for years, and had some idea of the dos and don'ts of property care.

But since the deregulation of the financial sector in the 1980s, it has become easier for anyone with an income to buy a home rather than find one to rent, and many people now buy houses and flats without ever having really thought about the responsibility this carries. And whilst the estate agents and mortgage lenders are keen to tell first-time buyers how much money they can borrow as a multiple of their earnings, they rarely mention that an additional sum of between one and five per cent of the value will need to be spent every year to keep it in good order.

In an ideal world, homeowners would engage the professionals – Chartered Surveyors – to advise them, and to arrange and supervise building work. But most people are unwilling to pay the professional fees involved. Quite often this is because they are so unimpressed by the performance of Surveyors during the first and only contact they have with them, which is during the home-buying process itself. The average surveyor doing a mortgage valuation, or Homebuyer Survey, gives a passable impression of someone who doesn't want to get the knees of his suit dirty, doesn't want to commit himself to saying anything about the property, and simply issues a list of things that should be looked at by other 'experts'.

Into this breach leap the companies and individuals offering 'free' surveys. Homeowners never seem to realize that this is nothing more than a crude marketing trick. And whilst people complain about the difficulty of finding a decent builder, there is never any shortage of advertisements for 'quick-fix' solutions for leaky roofs, draughty windows and damp walls. In fact, the first experience that most homeowners have of this end of the building industry is when their mortgage valuation survey report instructs them to invite estimates for 'treatment' from damp-proofing and timber treatment companies. In reality, rising damp only occurs in pre-1877 houses standing in swamps, most woodworm holes date from before the First World War, and dry rot is cured by mending the gutters. But, given the green light by the surveyor's report, these companies are quick to find 'evidence' of rising damp, woodworm and dry rot, and to specify remedial chemical treatment available from themselves.

There is a clear conflict of interests in having these so-called problems diagnosed and treated by the same companies, but the Royal Institution of Chartered Surveyors (RICS) appears reluctant to do anything to stop its members from directing their unsuspecting clients down this route.

There are many other unnecessary, damaging or bogus building treatments and gadgets mis-sold to the public, ranging from foam roof undercoatings to external wall coverings. Many of them are sold on the promise of 'zero maintenance', by companies interested only in a quick profit. Some of these businesses are even 'phoenix' companies, who offer twenty-year guarantees for their useless products, and then liquidate every year to avoid responsibility for failed work, setting up again with slightly altered company names. Consumer protection legislation being practically non-existent in the UK, there is nothing at all illegal about any of this.

And even if you do know a trained, competent, conscientious builder, then always remember that all building problems are liable to be mis-diagnosed if you turn to the wrong tradesman. After all, a carpenter will usually seek a solution that involves timber; a plasterer will suggest plaster, and a decorator will want to cover it up and paint it.

A recurrent theme in readers' letters is, 'I have been told that my x, y or z needs replacing – what do you think?' The missing information in these questions is, told by *whom*? Because if it was by somebody who was trying to sell you the replacement, then the chances are that their opinion was not objective.

Of particular concern in this respect is the role of the privatized utilities, such as British Gas Services. Many people still refer to British Gas as the 'Gas Board', and assume that if the British Gas Three Star Service engineer tells them that their boiler needs replacing, then he is doing so out of a sense of public duty. But British Gas Services is now a private company, owned by the Centrica Corporation, who also own the Automobile Association and Goldfish Credit Cards.

The most common question that I get asked is, 'How can I find a decent builder?' But in many cases this is the wrong question. What the homeowner should really be asking is, 'What building work does my home need, and what is the best way of getting this done?' This book is for anybody seeking the answers to those questions. Over the past six years I have received over 8,000 readers' questions, and what follows is a selection of answers to the most common ones.

STRUCTURES AND MATERIALS

Most readers' queries about structural matters concern the removal of internal walls, and the difference between a load-bearing wall and a non-load-bearing wall. There is no mystery to this; if an internal wall has something resting on top of it – floor joists, ceiling joists, or another wall – then it is load-bearing, and it would be unwise to remove it or cut holes in it. However, the vogue for open-plan living means that some people will always be determined to buy old houses and rip the guts out of them. Many thousands of Victorian terraced houses have had the central spine wall knocked through at ground-floor level, and this used to be done by leaving two nibs or piers of brickwork at the sides and sliding in an RSJ (rolled-steel joist) to pick up the floor joists above. Rather belatedly it became clear that by concentrating the load on the two nibs there was a chance of settlement, causing cracking damage right up the house, and possibly to neighbouring properties as well. So the preferred method is now to insert a rigid steel frame, which spreads the load right across the original span. There are plenty of cowboy builders around who still prefer the old RSJ trick, though.

Neither should it be assumed that because a wall is non-load-bearing, then it is a good idea to knock it out. Internal partition walls provide soundproofing and thermal insulation, can prevent fire from spreading, and in older houses they may also have a bracing or stabilizing effect on the side walls (see also CHIMNEYS, removing chimney breast).

Also remember that if you turn two rooms into one, then you lose the wall space for bookshelves and furniture. And, because of the strange way in which British estate agents value property, a house with fewer rooms may be worth less.

A rolled-steel joist (RSJ) is often used to support floor joists when a wall is removed.

LOAD-BEARING WALLS 1

Q My flat is the top two floors of a Victorian terrace house, and I would like to knock out the separating wall between two lower rooms to form a through lounge/diner. The partition wall is only timber and plaster, but my builder says it is a load-bearing wall. Can this be true?

A Yes, the wall between the front and back rooms in these types of houses is called the 'spine wall', and, although it is of timber construction, it supports the weight of the floors and the roof above, and contains internal diagonal bracing which strengthens the whole building. If the bracing is cut through or removed then there could be serious structural movement. This type of wall should only be removed or altered under supervision from a qualified structural engineer.

LOAD-BEARING WALLS 2

Q Is there a simple way of identifying a load-bearing wall? I want to remove part of the internal wall between my kitchen and dining room. There is no wall directly above and the joists run parallel to the one I want to remove, which is made of concrete aggregate blocks. Two builders have told me it isn't load-bearing but I just want to make sure.

A If you are confident that there is no load on it, then, by definition, it isn't load-bearing. However, depending on the age of the house, there is a possibility that this wall may be providing a bracing or tying effect on the outside walls, so you really should seek professional confirmation before undertaking any work. Also, this wall will be performing other functions, such as fire-stopping, soundproofing and thermal insulation. You may wish to consider what effect these changes might have on the rest of the house before you knock through.

LOADS ON FLOORS

Q We have a large collection of books spread through most rooms of our house, and anyone who has tried to lift a pile of books will know how heavy they are. In addition, our grandchildren, staying overnight, have recently found that jumping off their beds makes the floor bounce most satisfactorily! What are the normal weight limits for bedroom floors? Our house was built in 1973 with brick-and-block walls.

A Your 1973 house will have been built to the current Building Regulations, and the floors should be able to support at least 150kg per square metre. So a 4m x 5m room will be able to carry a load of 3000kg, or 3 tonnes. If the books are spread across the floor, though, they may cause bending of the joists, and cracking of the plaster ceiling below. It would be preferable to concentrate the load near the ends of the joists; i.e. bookcases against the front and back walls. The same principle applies to the grandchildren.

CHANGING ROOM LAYOUTS

Q 1930 semi-detached houses such as ours have kitchens too small for all mod cons and no room under the stairs for a toilet. The house itself is big enough for our needs and we do not want to build an extension. Is it possible to alter the layout of the ground floor/staircase to provide the areas we need?

A It is always possible to change rooms around, but you need to take care. Non-load-bearing partitions are easy to remove; load-bearing walls are much more difficult – and expensive. Moving a staircase is also usually a fairly complicated procedure, and I would have thought that there is an easier way to install a downstairs WC than moving the staircase. A good architect – preferably one with engineering skills – will be able to advise you on what is possible [ARCHITECTS, SURVEYORS AND ENGINEERS].

REPAIRING FRONT STEPS

Q We own the lower flat of a converted Victorian house. We have the semi-basement and ground floor, and our front door is the old basement entrance below the front steps. Our upstairs neighbours have the top two floors, and enter via the front steps and the main front door. In heavy rain, the steps have started to leak, and the water drips down the walls of our hallway, and is making a considerable mess. The steps have previously been coated with asphalt, but this looks like a bit of a cowboy job, as it is drooping off in places. What is the best way to stop the water coming in, and whose responsibility is it to pay for the work? The steps, viewed from the old coal cellar below, are a kind of soft flaky brown stone.

A The front steps of houses of this type and period are often soft sandstone slabs. When freshly quarried this type of stone is reasonably strong, but after a hundred years exposed to the air it may have become friable and weak, and it is not uncommon for these steps to collapse, causing serious injury. They probably always leaked water to a certain extent, but this was not considered a problem when the only things below them were the coal cellar and the servants' quarters. The cheap roofing-grade asphalt covering was probably applied when the house was converted into flats in the 1980s or thereabouts, and will have done well to have lasted fifteen years. You should engage a structural engineer to investigate the state of the stonework, and if it is in reasonable condition, then it may be worth applying a fresh waterproofing. But this is usually throwing good money after bad, and the best solution is to remove the old steps and cast a new flight of steps in reinforced concrete. Responsibility for the work depends upon the conditions of your lease or joint freehold.

STRENGTH OF JOISTS

Q I would like to make a storage area in my loft. The ceiling joists are 3in x 2in (75mm x 50mm). Would I need to strengthen them or not?

A Many older houses were built with 75mm x 50mm ceiling joists over the upper rooms, and whilst these are capable of supporting the weight of the ceiling, and a few suitcases and boxes of Christmas decorations, they should not be loaded with too much else. (Having said that, many homes have 250-litre water-storage tanks resting across two 75mm x 50mm ceiling joists!) The current Building Regulations require much more substantial timbers. 75mm x 50mm ceiling joists would only be allowed to span 1.4m, and if you wanted to use the loft as a habitable room then you would need to add at least 150mm x 50mm joists, which would allow you to span 3.5m. So the short answer is, it depends how much weight you want to store up there. The Loft

Shop [LOFT CONVERSIONS] supply a free guide to loft conversions and the Building Regulations, and a leaflet answering frequently asked questions.

Deeper joists must be added to turn a ceiling into a floor.

STIFFENING JOISTS

Q I am looking to convert our loft into a bedroom/study for our teenage son, but the quotes I have received are beyond my budget. Much of the work I could do myself, but the main obstacle appears to be the additional floor joists. At present the joists are 6in x 2in (150mm x 50mm) and I have been told the Building Regulations require them to be 8in x 2in (200mm x 50mm). I have no quarrel with this, but I would have thought that placing additional joists alongside the existing ones would put an additional loading on the building. Is it not permissible to enlarge the existing joists by adding 2in x 2in timber on top of the existing joists? I'm sure I saw this done on a TV programme some time ago, but I cannot find anyone to confirm that it is acceptable.

A The strength and stiffness of a joist depends on the fact that it is a solid, homogeneous material. Nailing an extra 2 inches to the top would not give a 6in joist the same strength as an 8in joist, as the added section would still be able to flex independently. The added weight of the new joists would be unlikely to cause a problem, but if it did, you could always use lightweight composite timber joists.

LOFT LADDERS

Q I have heard a couple of horrific stories from friends regarding accidents putting Christmas decorations in the loft when balancing on chairs or inadequate steps. We went to buy a loft ladder this year but our 1960 house has such a mass of trusses that it would need something very neat that folded away, probably onto the hatch itself.

A You are right to be concerned. Most serious accidents are caused by falls, and it is a good idea to install a proper retractable ladder for loft access. The Loft Shop [LOFT CONVERSIONS] do a range of folding loft ladders that are mounted on the door of the hatch. The narrowest is about 540mm, which will often fit into an existing hatch width. But if your roof trusses are at 400mm or 450mm spacing, then it is still relatively easy to enlarge the opening by cutting through one ceiling joist and supporting the cut ends on trimmers to the adjacent joists. With care, this can be done without even damaging the surrounding plasterboard ceiling.

LOFT CONVERSION RULES

Q What are the possibilities of doing a conversion, with flooring, lighting, wall cladding, window, safety ladder, etc., without obtaining planning permission, as 'storage plus study room' and actually using it as a spare bedroom for my three sons, age thirteen, eleven and nine?

A Most loft conversions do not need planning permission. The exceptions are houses in conservation areas, those that involve raising the height of the existing roof, those that have dormer windows facing the road, or if the house has already been extended to the limit of its permitted development (15 per cent of its original size). There is no regulation governing minimum headroom. However, it would be very foolish to allow children to sleep in a loft conversion which did not comply with the fire and access requirements of the Building Regulations.

LOFT CONVERSION IN MODERN HOUSE

Q I own a six-year-old detached villa. It is timber-frame construction with brick outer walls. I need another bedroom but the roof is of modern construction with a 'lattice' of timbers joined together. Am I correct in thinking that this makes it virtually impossible to convert the roof space into a bedroom?

A Doing a loft conversion in a modern roof is by no means impossible, although it is clearly more complicated than in an older house with traditional rafters. Modern roof trusses are designed to make construction cheap and simple for builders, by using thin sections of timber, prefabricated in factories. In order to make space for a bedroom, the crisscrossing struts and ties will have to be cut out and replaced with an alternative load-bearing structure. One method is to strengthen the floor by spanning between the end walls with steel beams, and to use vertical timber studwork to pick up the weight of the rafters. This may sound complicated, but it is a fairly standard procedure, and a loft conversion is usually the most cost-effective way of creating space in a house.

CONCRETE CORROSION

Q My 1960s cavity-wall bungalow has a reinforced-concrete surround to the kitchen window. Some years ago there was water penetration above the window, and the reinforcement has rusted, causing the concrete to split. I regularly scrape out the splits and refill them, with several different types of filler, none of which lasts for more than a season. Is there any combination of treatment of the reinforcement and filler which would be longer-lasting or permanent? I naturally wish to avoid having the window and surround removed and replaced.

A When reinforced concrete is new, the alkalinity of the cement prevents the steel from rusting. But over the years it absorbs carbon dioxide from the atmosphere and becomes acidic. The steel inevitably rusts, expands and splits the concrete. This phenomenon can be seen all over the place on old concrete lamp posts, fence posts, bollards and park benches. Repair is a specialist job (see 'Concrete Repairs' in the Yellow Pages) which involves re-alkalizing the concrete, coating the steel reinforcement with resin and bonding new concrete to the surface. It is unlikely to be economically viable in the case of one window surround.

BRICKWORK AND MASONRY

Brick walls are one of the mainstays of building construction down the ages. The historical principle is simple. If you lived in a part of the world where there were a lot of trees (which included most of Britain until the sixteenth century) then you built your walls with wood. If there was no wood but you had access to broken stone, then you built your walls with stone. If you didn't have either of those, then it was probably because you lived on clay, as in most of Central and Southern England and the Low Countries. These areas have a history of building with raw earth, and many examples survive, such as the cob houses of the West Country and the clay lump buildings of East Anglia.

But it had been known since Greek and Roman times that if you fired the clay in a kiln then you got a more hard-wearing material. At first this was used only to make clay roof tiles, but as kiln techniques got more sophisticated it became possible to produce large quantities of burnt-clay bricks. Following the Great Fire of 1666, the London Building Acts have always required all new buildings to have brick walls.

Brick construction reached its peak in the eighteenth and nineteenth centuries, and many of the surviving brick terraced houses that still make up around 50 per cent of our housing stock were built with a skill and attention to detail that we will never see again. The twentieth century saw the widespread adoption of the cavity wall, first built with two leaves of brickwork connected by wrought-iron ties, and later with an inner leaf of various types of lightweight concrete blocks. These are referred to by lay people as 'breeze blocks' but are actually made from aerated pulverized fuel ash (PFA). God knows how many banned toxic waste materials will be discovered in them in years to come.

The last twenty years have seen the introduction of insulation materials into the cavity. This has made the building of brick walls ever more difficult, and, coinciding with a drastic reduction in the availability of skilled bricklayers, means that modern brick houses are usually built very badly. So, whilst a Victorian brick-built house remains a sound investment, one built since the Second World War may be hosting many problems.

Older brick houses are often spoilt by having the surface of the mortar joints (the 'pointing') replaced with sand-and-cement. This is harder than the original sand-and-lime mortar, and can cause many problems. If there is any movement in the brickwork then the new pointing will be unable to move with it, and this can result in cracking damage to the bricks; and because sand-and-cement is impermeable to moisture, the mortar will be unable to breathe, concentrating moisture evaporation in the bricks, which may then lose their faces through frost damage or salt crystallization. Damaging repointing is a classic example of misunderstanding the nature of traditional building materials. Our forebears understood that the pointing between the bricks was a sacrificial material, which served its purpose by being gradually worn away, and would be replaced every half-century or so. But today, when surveyors or builders see weathered pointing, they see it as a defect, and think it would be better to replace it with a more hard-wearing material.

Lime mortar is easy to make and use. The only problem is trying to find a bricklayer prepared to use it. There is a common myth amongst builders that lime-and-sand mortar will not harden unless cement is mixed into it. This is simply not true, and once you get a brickie to try using sand-and-lime, you will probably have a convert on your hands.

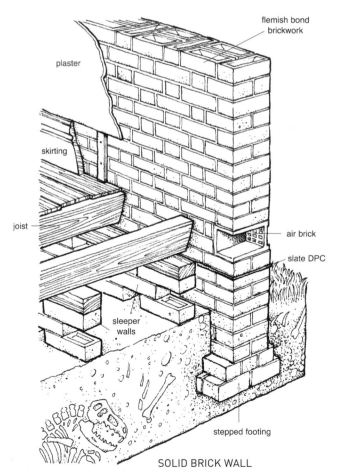

SOLID BRICK WALL

MORTAR FOR POINTING STONE WALLS

Q What is the best mortar mix for pointing old stone walls? A quarrying firm says they find the best mix for the area is 1 part hydrated lime/1 part cement/1 part sand (theirs). This seems much too strong to us. Some pointing on our old stone house has been done with a strong cement mix, which appears to have affected some stones, causing a spongelike appearance full of small holes.

A You are right – strong cement mixes can be very damaging to old stonework. Because the mortar is impermeable, it means that any evaporation must take place at the surface of the stone, causing salt efflorescence and frost damage. A more suitable mix would be 1 part hydrated lime/4 parts washed coarse sharp sand; and absolutely no cement at all.

MATCHING BRICKS

Q I want to have a porch built to shelter the kitchen door of my 1950s bungalow, and would prefer to use the same bricks, to match up for colour and size. But local builders tell me that these bricks are no longer available, and that I will have to have a different type, or have rendered blockwork instead.

A Several brick merchants around the country provide a brick matching service. Some deal with modern bricks, and some specialize in conservation work. For details of the local merchants most likely to solve your problem call the Brick Development Association [BRICKWORK].

EXTERNAL BLOCK WALLS

Q My builder says breeze block is a suitable material for building outer walls, without being covered with render. Is this true? The wall is unseen but open to the elements.

A There is no such thing as breeze block. If your builder means lightweight or aerated blocks (Thermalite, Celcon, etc.) then the answer is no – this type of blockwork will soak up water from the outside, and it needs to be protected from the worst of the weather with a suitable render coat. If he means concrete blocks, then the answer is maybe – it depends upon the type of building. Dense concrete blocks can be used as the outer leaf of a cavity wall, but, as with all cavity walls, they must be built to a very high standard, with wall ties sloping down towards the outer leaf, and damp-proof courses wherever the inner and outer leaves touch.

WRONG MORTAR COLOUR

Q We have put a deposit on a new house and visited the site to check progress. On one of the outside walls there is a strip of approximately twelve courses of bricks where the mortar is a different colour from the rest. The site foreman says that it will weather in time and blend in with the rest. Is he right?

A Different-coloured mortar indicates a different mix, and therefore a lack of quality control by the main contractor. On most newbuild sites the mortar arrives ready-mixed from a specialist supplier. A different colour usually indicates a batch knocked up on site by the brickies' labourer.

This may or may not have structural implications, but is not what most people would expect from a new house.

DECAYING SANDSTONE

Q The sandstone of my 120-year-old terraced house is now very friable. Would painting on a silicone water sealant delay further deterioration?

A No. If anything, it will make things worse by trapping moisture in the stonework and stopping it from breathing. Unfortunately, soft sandstone starts to deteriorate from the moment it is quarried, and exposure to the prevailing weather and traffic pollution speeds up the process. The traditional way of stabilizing sandstone, which was used successfully on churches up until the 1900s, was to apply an annual coat of limewater (the water that separates out on top of a bucket of limewash). This soaks in and binds the stone, but still allows it to breathe.

MORTAR PLASTICIZER

Q The plans for our new extension, currently under construction, specify that the mortar is to be '6:1:1 building sand, hydrated lime, ordinary Portland cement, incorporating a suitable plasticizing additive'. I have seen five-litre containers of 'mortar plasticizer' at the local builders' merchants, but the bricklayer insists on using my washing-up liquid instead. He says it is the same as plasticizer, only cheaper. Is this true?

A Mortar plasticizers work by lowering the surface tension of the water, so that the mortar will 'flow' without it being too wet, and dribbling down the brickwork. Proper plasticizers are based on lignin, an organic substance extracted from wood. Washing-up detergent will certainly make the mortar flow, but it can also contain other undesirable ingredients, such as salt, which will corrode metal wall ties and may emerge as efflorescence on the surface of the finished wall.

SPALLED BRICKS

Q We have a north-facing end wall on our Victorian semi. Numerous bricks have lost their faces, and previous owners have repaired some of these with cement. We have had a visit from a company who would use a fibreglass render and protective top coat. They give a twenty-year guarantee but have quoted £4,500. Someone else has said that ordinary rendering or pebbledash holds the wet in and is likely to break off, so shouldn't be used. What should we do?

A All external renderings and coatings trap moisture behind them and stop walls from breathing. The modern versions are more expensive, more damaging and the twenty-year 'guarantees' are meaningless. Spend your money on repairing the wall properly, by having the damaged bricks cut out and replaced, using lime mortar to match the original. It is likely that recent cement pointing has probably caused most of the spalling damage in the first place.

WHITE POWDER ON BRICKS

Q My 1930s Accrington brick bungalow has always had a white powdery fungus on many of the north-facing bricks, some of which have had their surfaces eaten away. Is there a cure?

It is not a fungus, but efflorescence. This is the deposit of salts on the surface of the brickwork, and indicates the passage of water through the structure. This could be due to wind-blown rain, or water dripping from an inadequate roof detail or perhaps even condensation from inside the house. The situation may have been made worse if the brickwork has been repointed using a hard cement mortar in place of the original lime. Finding out the source of the water can be difficult, and will probably require a specialist investigation by an independent dampness specialist [DAMP-NESS AND TIMBER SURVEYORS].

REMOVING CEMENT POINTING

Q **Having read around about pointing I am still confused about what to use. I have a 1930s semi built from Leamington brick. Previously repointed with cement mortar, some weaker bricks are spalling. The old mortar feels crumbly and is light brown, unlike modern cement mortar. Should I repoint the damaged bits with 1:1:6 (lime:cement:sharp sand)? If I remove the spalled material from the brick face will the brick be OK or has it been irreparably damaged?**

A Old brickwork damaged by hard cement pointing is a real problem. There seems to be hardly a house left in the country that has not already been repointed using this damaging material, and surveyors and builders are continuing to specify and use it. Since some of your bricks have already spalled, it is likely that others will spall in the future, so the best thing would be to remove all the cement mortar and repoint with lime. Cement mortar can be removed cleanly using a diamond-covered 'Easy Raker' [BRICKWORK]. Bricks that are already damaged will have to be cut out and replaced, since, having lost the fire skin from their faces, they will suffer from further weathering. Lime mortar can be made using bagged hydrated lime and sharp sand, both available from

Hard cement pointing can hasten the deterioration of old brickwork.

builders' merchants. Try a mix of 4:1 sand:lime and do a small area first, to check for colour and consistency. Mix it dry, then add the water, cover it over with plastic sheeting (or in buckets) and leave it for at least twenty-four hours before remixing and using.

HYDRATED LIME OR HYDRAULIC LIME?

Q My local builders' merchant has told me that I should use hydraulic lime and not hydrated lime for pointing mortar. My house is 130 years old.

A Hydraulic lime is a kind of natural cement. It sets quickly by reacting with water and, like cement, it is too hard and too impermeable for repointing old brickwork. Hydrated lime, on the other hand, is a semi-slaked version of traditional lime putty. It sets slowly, by absorbing carbon dioxide from the atmosphere, and makes a softer, more breathable mortar, the same as that used to build your nineteenth-century walls. Hydrated lime is the correct material.

REPLACING WALL TIES

Q My surveyor has said that my 1920 terraced house in the Isle of Wight needs new wall ties. My understanding is that cavity walls were not usual until the thirties, so why wall ties?

A Cavity walls were first built in the early 1800s, on the exposed south and west coasts of Britain and Ireland, as a way of keeping out wind-driven rain. So it is quite probable that houses were being built with cavity walls in the Isle of Wight by the 1920s. But just because a house is old, it does not follow that the wall ties are corroded. Your surveyor cannot possibly make a judgement on this unless he has cut out and exposed two wall ties – at high and low level – on each face of the house. The necessary diagnostic and replacement procedures are described in Building Research Establishment Digests 329 and 401 [CONSTRUCTION LITERATURE].

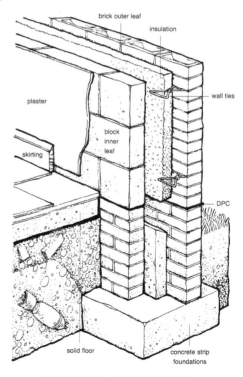

CAVITY BRICK-AND-BLOCK WALL

RECESSED MORTAR JOINTS

Q My 1971 house has recessed mortar joints between the bricks. We have lived in the house for twenty years and during that time the bricks have become chipped at the corners. There are very few bricks not affected. I presume this is caused by weathering because the bricks are more exposed to the elements than they should be. What can be done?

A Recessed mortar joints were popular with trendy architects in the 1970s and 1980s because of their visual effects. But they allow water to accumulate on the exposed top edges of the bricks, which can lead to frost damage. Recessed joints only really work with hard engineering bricks, and even then, the retained water can give rise to moss growth and staining. In your case, as long as it is only the corners of the bricks that have been damaged, and the faces are still intact, then it should be possible to fill the recessed joints with a weather-struck joint that will prevent any further deterioration. Your builder should use a mortar softer than the bricks and the original mortar. A 9:2:1 sand:lime:cement mix should be about right.

FROST DAMAGE

Q After a period of wet weather followed by frost, some of the brickwork on my three-year-old house is flaking. This applies particularly to the bricks with smoother faces, those in brick-on-edge sills and those near ground level, where the rain is splashing up off concrete paving. Is there some way of waterproofing the brickwork with a clear liquid during a warm dry spell to prevent this flaking in frost?

A No. Whatever the manufacturers' claims, external waterproofing compounds are at best ineffective, and at worst can exacerbate the problem, by trapping water in the brickwork. The spalling you describe is really a design problem, because the bricks used clearly are not of suitable quality to cope with the exposure conditions. Badly damaged bricks should be cut out and replaced, using frost-resistant new bricks (they should have an 'F' classification under British Standard BS3921, which means they can withstand freezing even when saturated).

NEED FOR REPOINTING?

Q Our semi-detached bungalow is thirty-four years old. Three neighbours have had their brickwork repointed although there seemed to be nothing wrong with them. When is repointing needed, and should it be an all-over job or done in patches?

A It seems unlikely that a thirty-four-year-old property would need repointing, and your neighbours may have been victims of over-enthusiastic builders or surveyors, who often specify repointing in survey reports. Odd patches of brickwork may sometimes be exposed to extreme weather conditions or water leaks which erode the mortar, and these areas should be repointed, but under normal conditions a house should not need repointing for sixty to a hundred years. The pointing should be considered as a sacrificial medium which gradually erodes away, leaving the bricks intact, and over-enthusiastic repointing with strong mortars is responsible for a lot of damage.

REPOINTING: MODERN MORTAR

Q Most ready-mixed mortars sold in DIY stores dry to a grey colour. Most houses have beige mortar. Which mix (with or without cement) would match this colour? Would builders' merchants sell this mix in small amounts – of 10kg (or less) for instance?

A The grey colour comes from a high proportion of cement, which is probably mixed with a washed sharp sand. This mix is intended for patch repairs to renders and floor screeds, and is not generally suitable for brickwork repairs or repointing. The colour of the 'beige' mortar used in most post-war housing comes from the impurities (mostly clay) in soft 'building' sand, which is used in a 6:1:1 sand:cement:lime mix. You are unlikely to be able to buy this ready-mixed from a builders' merchants, although you may be able to persuade a builder to give you a bucketful.

ROOFS

The roof is the first line of defence against the rain, and leaks can seem very dramatic – although the total amount of moisture entering the house may be insignificant compared with a leaking gutter dripping against an outside wall, or the condensation introduced into the house by daily showers. It's that drip, drip into the saucepan that makes it seem like a desperate situation.

The roofing trade is notorious for providing a refuge for cowboys, which is a shame for the many skilled, conscientious roofers who get tarred with the same brush. So, although I am always loath to recommend trade associations, I do suggest that readers with roofing problems should always use members of the National Federation of Roofing Contractors or the Flat Roofing Alliance [ROOFING]. Membership of these bodies does not mean that a roofing company is 100 per cent wonderful, but it does mean that if something goes wrong, then you will at least have a point of reference to start chasing them. The main things to be aware of are:

- Victorian houses where original slate roof coverings have been replaced with interlocking concrete tiles. These are heavier than the original slate and the extra weight can cause deflection of the rafters.
- Cement fillets around the edges of upstands instead of proper lead flashing.
- Anything sprayed or painted on top of a roof (usually black bituminous stuff, but sometimes red paint).
- Anything sprayed underneath a roof – e.g. insulating foam.

SPRAY-ON FOAM TREATMENT

Q Every year gusts of wind dislodge one or two of my roof slates. The roof is in its original 1920s condition with no underfelt. There are adverts in the papers for a 'foam spray solution' for old roofs. These are guaranteed for twenty or so years. Is this the easiest way forward, or should we look to get the whole roof redone?

A The fact that slates are slipping every year probably indicates that the nails which hold them to the timber battens are rusted through. Roofers refer to this as nail fatigue or nail sickness, and it is definitely time to have the roof stripped off and re-covered. Having foam sprayed onto the undersides of the slates may sound like a wonderful high-tech solution but it is actually a bad idea. It is at odds with the recommendations of the Building Regulations, which require a clear 50mm ventilated gap between insulation and roof covering. The foam sets hard and removes the two vital attributes that allow a traditional roof to last and perform so well for so long – the ability to breathe and the ability to move. The foam completely encloses the timber battens and the top surfaces of the rafters, which might cause them to rot. It also sticks tight to the slates and makes it almost impossible for them to ever be reused. You will also probably find that the cost of the spray-on foam solution will be three or four times that of having the roof re-covered in the traditional way. Try to find a roofer who will remove the existing slates carefully, and reuse as many as possible. Also make sure that the roofer uses a breathable sarking felt, and allows it to sag between the rafters. The ridge tiles and any hip tiles should be rebedded using lime-and-sand mortar to match the original; do not allow the roofer to use sand-and-cement.

FOAM ROOF UNDERCOATING

Q My son and his partner live in a 1930s ex-council property. It has a tiled roof and although it appears to be perfectly weatherproof, he wonders about having the interior of the roof sprayed with foam, which is claimed to overcome almost all roofing problems (slipping tiles or slates, lack of underfelt, leaks and condensation, freezing pipes and tanks, nail fatigue). The company he is considering have BBA approval, are members of the British Urethane Foam Contractors Association, and are BSI registered.

A Firms themselves do not 'have BBA (British Board of Agrément) approval' – BBA testing is paid for by the company, and only tests what they ask to be tested – in this case that the foam sticks to tiles and slates. It does not mean that this is a good thing to do to a roof, and does not prevent possible condensation and rot problems in the enclosed timbers. The British Urethane Foam Contractors Association is a trade association, and again, membership of this does not prove that it is a good thing to spray foam on roofs. Neither can a company be 'BSI registered', although their paperwork may have conformed to BS5750 – which became obsolete in 1996, and was replaced by ISO 9001.

The National Federation of Roofing Contractors (another trade association, but one whose members repair roofs using traditional methods [ROOFING]) publish a technical bulletin on spray-on coatings of this nature, and a spokesman told me that they would only recommend it as a stop-gap measure to extend the life of an old building – a farmer's barn, for example – for another few years. They do not recommend it for use in houses.

FLAT-ROOF COVERINGS

Q The felted flat roof of my rear extension is leaking, and a number of firms are offering apparently foolproof solutions, such as fibreglass, rubber membranes and jointless glass-fibre-reinforced plastic coverings. These systems are all promoted with a variety of impressive-looking glossy brochures and promises of twenty-five-year guarantees.

A Flat roofs in Britain are notorious for leaking, and the problem does not usually lie with the roof-covering material, but with poor workmanship. 'Flat' roofs actually need a fall of at least four degrees, a requirement which is often neglected. And if the timber roof joists are not thick enough, they can sag in the middle, allowing water to pond, and find its way through any minor defect.

The problem with most of the 'instant fix' flat-roof repairs on the market is that they simply cover the existing leaking flat roof with a new waterproof coating, which will not remedy the underlying causes of the leak. This is throwing good money after bad. The GRP (glassfibre-reinforced polyester) and glassfibre flat-roofing systems are often advertised as having 'no joints', as if this was an advantage, but in fact a large flat roof area exposed to sunlight should always have movement joints to cope with thermal expansion. If there are no joints then there may be expansion damage later on. And the twenty-five-year 'guarantees' are usually meaningless. Also, the prices charged by these companies are often greater than the cost of getting the roof re-covered properly using tried and tested traditional methods. Modern high-tensile roofing felts should last for fifty years if they are installed properly.

FLAT-ROOF REPAIRS

Q Where can I obtain information on DIY flat-roof repairs? I am an accomplished DIY enthusiast and am confident that I can carry out the necessary work properly but would like some tips on the correct method to adopt.

A Try the Flat Roofing Alliance, which publishes a free booklet, 'The Householder's Guide to Flat Roofing', and a more detailed handbook for £17.50 [ROOFING].

REPLACING OLD SLATES

Q My roof needs attention because of slipping/cracked slates. Builders have said that, although it would be possible to reuse a lot of the slates and buy in replacements for the damaged ones, it would be very expensive. They have suggested using concrete 'slates', but I have been warned about the increased weight and consequent stress on the supporting timbers. Is there a cheaper product that would not be too heavy?

A Slate roofs should not be re-covered with interlocking concrete tiles, as they are heavier than the original slates, and may cause the rafters to sag, and the walls to be pushed outwards. Artificial slates are an acceptable substitute, although they do not look as good as real slate.

CRUMBLING VERGES

Q The gable end of my house faces into the prevailing wind and nearly every year the high winds loosen the mortar which retains the end roof tiles. There is a danger of the loose mortar and tiles coming down through the conservatory roof. Could you advise a more secure way for my builder to retain the end roof tiles?

A The mortar is not there to 'retain' the tiles – it just fills the gaps. The tiles along the verge should be held in place by being nailed every course (on the rest of the roof they should be nailed every fourth course). Lime-and-sand mortar will work better than cement-and-sand, which becomes hard and brittle, which causes it to shrink and fall out. But most tile manufacturers also supply a 'dry verge' system, consisting of specially shaped plastic sections. Ask at your local specialist roofing suppliers.

ROOF CLEANING AND SEALING

Q I have had a pamphlet pushed through my letterbox offering to clean the moss from the roof of my house, and to reseal and waterproof the tiles. Is this type of treatment a good idea?

A Almost certainly not. Firms or individuals who solicit for building work by putting flyers through letterboxes are always suspect, and the 'roof cleaning and sealing' scam has become particularly widespread in recent years. Although it may look unsightly, moss or lichen growth on roof tiles is unlikely to present a problem, and is usually best left alone, or occasionally scraped off. And several readers have reported damage to roof tiles and flashings after employing these types of cowboy operators Also, tiled or slated roofs do not need 'resealing' or 'waterproofing'; they are perfectly capable of surviving for a century or more without any kind of chemical additive or coating. But the worst aspect of this type of activity is the financial fraud involved; I recently heard of an elderly lady who was persuaded to pay £5,000 to have her bungalow roof covered with red paint, and the police and local trading standards officers were unable to take any action against the perpetrators. Don't let it happen to you.

MOSS GROWTH

Q The moss on my roof is getting more abundant and I am concerned that it may damage the tiles. I have been advised of various remedies including a chemical solution, although warned that it may cause blotchiness to the tiles. Another interesting suggestion is to affix copper wire at various points of the roof. Can you advise?

A Lichen and moss growth on roofs is a totally natural occurrence. Some people find it unsightly; others welcome it as a sign of natural weathering and ageing of a house. The only serious damage is likely to occur on soft old red clay tiles, where the roots of button-type mosses can eat through and eventually create a leak. Even this can take a century to happen. Lichen and moss growth occurs more in country locations than in cities, where air pollution prevents it. The problem with chemical treatment is not just staining, but the fact that it has to be repeated regularly. The idea of copper wire laid along the ridge is that the copper oxide is washed off by the rain and flows down the surface. Again, this can lead to staining, and water running off copper onto other metals can cause severe corrosion – aluminium gutters and window frames are especially at risk. Personally, I'd learn to love the moss, or else pay a roofer to scrape it off every few years.

MOSS ON FLAT ROOF

Q You have commented on the effect of moss on tiled roofs – i.e. that it should be left alone. Are your remarks relevant also to felt flat roofs and, if not, what treatment do you consider might solve the problem? It's difficult enough to eradicate moss from paths and patios, and I hesitate to tangle with a felt roof unless really necessary.

A Moss will always grow on unpolluted shaded surfaces that hold moisture. On flat roofs, excessive moss growth may be a sign of inadequate fall – i.e. the slope is too flat for water to drain off – but I have never seen a case where moss has actually damaged the roofing felt.

SARKING FELT

Q My valuation survey report says that the roof of my 1930s semi has no underfelt, and that it will have to be brought up to modern standards by stripping off the tiles and battens and re-roofing, including felt. The roof seems to be in good condition, both internally and externally, and there are no signs of any leaks, past or present. Is re-roofing really necessary?

A Since the 1960s it has been common building practice in Britain for roofers to drape sarking felt across the rafters before battening and tiling. The term 'sarking' originally referred to close timber boarding laid across the rafters to prevent wind-driven rain and snow penetrating through the gaps around tiles and slates. Sarking is a good second line of defence in areas of high exposure, and the original boarding is still used in exposed areas in Scotland.

But for less exposed parts of the UK sarking felt is less of a necessity, and has generally been adopted simply to make life easier for roofers. When retiling an old roof, roofers used to have to work in sections, stripping and re-covering an area in a day, so as to leave the roof weathertight. With sarking felt they can strip the whole roof covering off in the first day and felt it, and then take their time with the replacement tiling or slating. Sarking felt has two disadvantages:

Fitting sarking felt to an old roof can cut down on ventilation.

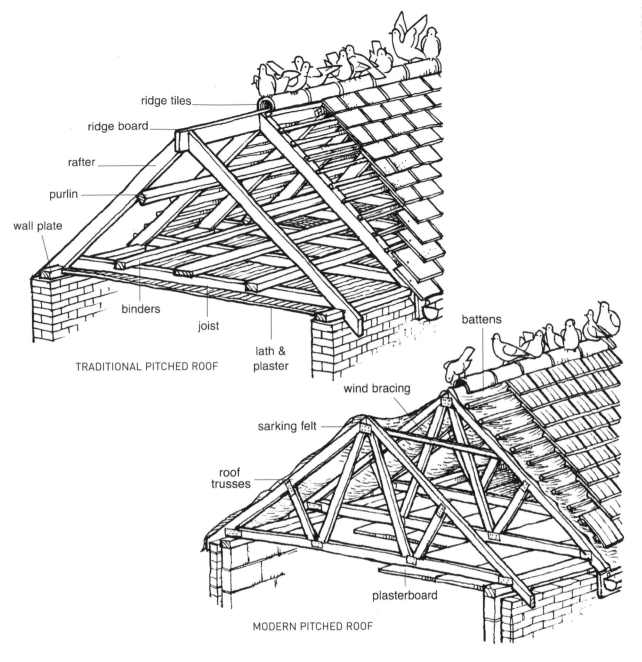

ridge tiles
ridge board
rafter
purlin
wall plate
binders
joist
lath & plaster

TRADITIONAL PITCHED ROOF

battens
wind bracing
sarking felt
roof trusses
plasterboard

MODERN PITCHED ROOF

The idea that it is a fail-safe second line of defence encourages roofers to take less care with the final tiling or slating. This is especially notable with regard to calculating and laying the correct headlap (vertical overlap) to cope with prevailing weather conditions. Tile manufacturers (and the Building Regulations) specify a minimum lap, to prevent wind-driven rain and snow being blown up under the lap and into the roof space. This may be as much as 60mm or 75mm, and if this measurement is adhered to, then no roof should leak. But by shrinking the headlap to 25mm, roofers can save one or two complete courses of tiles or slates (thus saving themselves £50 in materials), and if the water gets in then the sarking felt will catch it – as long as it stays intact – for maybe fifteen or twenty years. After that, the roof will start to leak in severe weather conditions, and there will be no alternative to complete re-roofing.

Sarking felt cuts down on the natural ventilation in the roof space, especially if it is stretched too tight (it is supposed to sag loosely between the rafters) or if it is one of the new plastic varieties. With the current high standards of ceiling insulation, roof spaces are very cold in winter, so the water vapour which finds its way up from the bedrooms condenses against the cold surface of the felt, and can drip down and stain the ceilings. Some readers have reported a steady dripping of condensation from the felt, and have even thought that the roof is leaking. It is notable that other European countries, including those with cold northern climates such as Germany and Denmark, do not use sarking felt, but prefer to keep the natural ventilation that comes from air passing through the gaps between the tiles or slates.

If a roof really needs re-covering, due to a large number of rusty nails and/or a large number of slipped slates or tiles, then it is probably worth letting your roofer use sarking felt as part of the new installation – as long as it is installed properly according to Building Research Establishment standards, and adequate ventilation is provided in the form of special vents at eaves and ridge. But if an old roof is in sound condition and not leaking then there is no need to strip it off simply to install a layer of felt. This recommendation indicates a misunderstanding by the valuation surveyor.

LEAKS BETWEEN TILES

Q In 1985 we built a rear extension onto our 1957 semi. The roof has been leaking since about 1990. The flashing and tiles have been checked on numerous occasions, all to no avail. Last year we bit the bullet, and had the roof completely redone (it turns out the original builder had not used big enough joists for the size of the roof). And now it is leaking again!

The roof is a very shallow pitch, covered with Redland concrete tiles. The leak comes through the ceiling towards the edge of the pitch, and towards the outside wall. This only happens when it rains heavily, so we have ruled out a leaking pipe. Any ideas?

A I suggest you call Redland and ask them the minimum headlap they recommend for that particular tile for the given pitch. My guess is that there isn't sufficient lap, and the rain is either getting blown in, or tracking back under the edges by surface tension.

THATCHED COTTAGE

Q Please could you advise on the implications of buying a semi-detached thatched cottage, some parts of which are believed to date back to the seventeenth century. We have always lived in up-to-date houses so have no experience of life in such a property.

A Thatch is an attractive traditional roofing material and very good for insulation – both thermal and sound. People who live in thatched houses have nothing but praise for the material. Its insulation properties are second to none, keeping a home warm in the winter and cool in the summer. And estimates of longevity are actually greater than you might think. Norfolk reed thatched roofs (the best quality material) have been known to last for over a century, with sixty years being a reasonable minimum, and even a straw roof can last a good forty years. All thatch needs reridging every fifteen to twenty years, and localized damage needs prompt repair, on the 'stitch in time' principle.

For details of qualified thatchers contact your local authority building conservation officer, or call the National Council of Master Thatchers' Associations [ROOFING].

FLOORS

Readers' floor problems tend to fall into two main categories: solid concrete ground floors, and creaking upstairs chipboard floors. Both can be equally troublesome.

Solid concrete ground floors were introduced into Victorian houses in a big way from the 1960s onwards. The rationale was that the original suspended timber floors could be affected by rot, and many surveyors, architects, housing associations and even private owners decided that it would be a good idea to do away with the timber and replace it with a slab of good old solid concrete, poured onto a polyethylene damp-proof membrane (DPM). This may have removed the possibility of wood rot, but at the same time it deprived a house of the sub-floor ventilation which had kept it dry for decades. The perceived wisdom was that the DPM would keep the floor dry, and a chemical injection damp-proof course (DPC) would stop the ground moisture being diverted into the walls. The fatal flaw in the scenario was the blind faith in the idea that chemical injection DPCs actually worked. They don't. So tens of thousands of Victorian houses have had perfectly serviceable dry, ventilated, timber floors torn up, to be replaced with cold, hard concrete, and with the added disadvantage of damp walls. It is still being done.

Creaking chipboard blights the lives of many people who live in 'modern' homes – by which I mean mass-produced, speculatively built houses and flats of 1970s vintage onwards. Some estate homes of this period were built with proper timber floorboards, but not many. Like concrete ground floors, chipboard upper floors were built on a misconception – that, being a man-made board material, tongue-and-groove chipboard was more stable than pesky old-fashioned real wood, and that it would therefore have none of the disadvantages of traditional floorboards (i.e. shrinking, swelling, twisting, splitting, creaking). What was not appreciated was that chipboard suffers from a phenomenon called 'creep', which means that over time it sags between the joists, and in the process becomes distorted, so that it creaks when it rubs against the joists, and it squeaks when it binds against adjacent boards.

Both of these problems are examples of what can go wrong when builders fall for the idea that old-fashioned construction materials and methods must be inferior to new ones. It is a problem of the modern age.

MATCHING OLD FLOORBOARDS

Q I have been thinking about sanding and sealing the floorboards in my dining room. However, some sections of the floor have been ruined by successive plumbers and electricians, and need replacing. The problem is, the modern 6in x 1in (150mm x 25mm) floorboards from builders' merchants are narrower and thinner than the original boards. Where can I buy suitable matching replacement boards?

A The timber sold at the builders' merchants will be PAR (planed all round), sometimes called PSE (planed square edge), so the 150mm x 25mm sawn size is reduced to about 140mm x 20mm. You could try to find second-hand boards at auctions or from architectural salvage firms (or keep an eye out for boards dumped in builders' skips). These will provide a good match in colour and grain. But new sawn boards of the right size should be available from specialist timber merchants, and any sawmill will cut boards to order. Victorian floors were often laid with rough-sawn boards which were then planed and sanded in situ. For a perfect fit buy the boards slightly over-size and allow them to acclimatize to the room conditions for as long as possible before fixing.

WIDE FLOORBOARDS

Q **We have bought a redundant farm building to renovate as a house. The floor is dirt at the moment and we intend having a suspended timber floor. I would appreciate your opinion on our using scaffold boards instead of standard floorboards. They were used on a recent *Changing Rooms* programme on TV. We like the idea of wider boards.**

A You can have floorboards any width you like. But if you buy scaffold boards you will just be paying extra for stress-graded timber with metal reinforcing strips fixed to each end. Any local timber merchant or sawmill will supply you with boards cut to size.

CURLING FLOORBOARDS

Q **My 1930s semi has suspended wooden floorboards throughout. Over the last few months I've noticed that some of the floorboards feel through the carpet as if they are 'curling' up at the edges and coming away from the supporting joists.**

This 'curling' or lifting is accompanied by the obligatory squeaky floorboard sound which is expected on a seventy-year-old house. Now I would like to pull back the carpets and secure the floorboards back to the joists but am unsure as to what means to do this is best. Should I (a) screw the boards to the joists; (b) hammer standard nails in; (c) use special nails?

One concern I do have is what is causing the floorboards to curl/lift on both the ground and first floors? Is it normal to do so, or are there any other possible reasons lurking around?

A The nails to use are called floor brads, which are 60mm square-cut nails with a one-sided head. These provide a good grip into the joists, the heads are easily 'lost' in the surface of the board without splitting it, and, like all cut nails, it should be relatively easy to work them loose if the boards need to be lifted for access to the sub-floor void. (Round-head, or 'wire', nails cannot be 'lost', and leave bumps on the surface of the floor. Round-heads and ovals both grip tight into the joists and cannot be worked loose, so when the boards are lifted the nail heads rip through the boards and split them.)

Screwing floorboards is often done to cure squeaking, but it can create difficulties. Not least that if the boards have to be lifted, it is difficult to locate all the screw heads and remove the screws. And it takes only one screw to be missed and the board will split, making it unfit for reuse.

The sudden curling of the floorboards can only be due to rapid drying shrinkage. The house in question must have just experienced a marked increase in heating and/or ventilation.

GAPS BETWEEN SANDED FLOORBOARDS

Q **What is the best way of sealing gaps between old floorboards? We have sanded and varnished the floors, but in some rooms wind blows cold through the gaps between the boards. We have tried doing an area with wood filler, wiped off with a damp cloth, but this takes ages, and does not always bridge the gap. Is there a better way?**

A The main point to note is that floorboards in Victorian/Edwardian houses were not intended to be left exposed, and would usually have been covered with loose rugs or mats. Sanding softwood floorboards is very much a recent fashion, and is a poor substitute for tongue-and-groove hardwood boarding. Having said that, it is possible to make a good job of sanding old floorboards (although bear in mind the noise problems that bare timber floors can have, especially for downstairs neighbours (see SOUNDPROOFING)).

The gaps between the boards are due to drying shrinkage, which is accelerated in most cases by central heating, which is good, because it means that the boards are well seasoned and unlikely to shrink any further. If you want to do a really good job then you should consider lifting the boards, cleaning off the edges, and refitting them, wedging them up tight to each other as you go. You will probably find that tightening up all the gaps leaves you room for almost one extra complete board across the width of the room. This sounds like a major upheaval, but if it can be combined with rewiring or central-heating work, or fitting insulation below ground floors, then it is probably worth it.

If you decide to leave the boards in their original state, and the gaps are large – 2mm to 3mm – then you could ask a local joinery workshop to cut you tapered strips to glue into the gaps, which you then trim and sand flat. Otherwise you should save the dust from the sanding machine (collected in the vacuum bag), mix it with PVA adhesive or a proprietary resin adhesive [TIMBER FLOORS] and work it into the gaps with a filler knife. Sand it flat when it has dried.

Not all floorboards are suitable for sanding and sealing.

TIMBER FLOOR IN BATHROOM

Q I want to put new flooring in my bathroom, and would like to put down a wooden floor. However, I'm worried this will be a problem due to moisture. Is it advisable to put wooden floors in bathrooms, and are there any special measures I should take?

A Timber floors can look good in bathrooms, and provided they are fitted properly and kept dry, they can provide an easily cleanable surface. The problem is always going to be moisture movement – timber expands when it gets wet and shrinks when it dries. The worst-case scenario would be shrinkage gaps between the boards followed by a sudden spillage – water could leak through and damage the ceiling below. The first thing to do is ensure that your bathroom has a fairly stable internal environment. A large bathroom with good ventilation could be suitable for a timber floor; a small one where condensation runs down the walls every time you have a shower may not be. Bamboo is a hard, resilient flooring material (e.g. the charmingly named Pandafloor from Pioneer Woodfloors [TIMBER FLOORS]).

DAMAGED TEAK-BLOCK FLOOR

Q Our teak-block floor, laid in 1949, is causing concern. A few of the blocks have become loose and can lift out. What would you suggest as the best substance to reseat and secure them?

A Hardwood-block floors were originally laid in hot bitumen, so you need a special solvent-based adhesive which will melt the bitumen and enable the blocks to be pushed back down into it. Lecol adhesive is available from Victorian Wood Works [TIMBER FLOORS].

SQUEAKING CHIPBOARD FLOOR

Q Our house is only twenty years old, but we suffer from creaky floorboards in one particular area. Is there a practical solution that does not involve major work?

New houses have chipboard floors which can sag and squeak.

A Many houses built since the 1980s have chipboard flooring rather than the traditional solid-timber floorboards. Over time the chipboard sags between the joists, and the edges rub against each other, which is what causes the creaking. The first step is to lift up the carpet and look to see if there are any obvious signs of movement – it may be that one or two screws have worked loose, and tightening these may effect a cure. If this doesn't work, then you may need to use some extra screws. Avoid under-floor pipes and cables by checking with a metal detector, and use screws that are twice as long as the thickness of the boards, which are probably 18mm. If this still fails to cure the squeaking, then you could try the old stagehand's trick of sprinkling French chalk or talcum powder into the gap between the boards.

TIMBER ON CONCRETE 1

Q We have just laid a concrete base in our new extension and would like advice on the best way to lay tongue-and-groove floorboarding over this. The concrete is not completely level with some bumps and hollows.

A The best way would have been not to have a concrete base in the first place. Timber ground floors are better constructed using the traditional method of supporting them on honeycombed brick sleeper walls, and ventilating the space below using airbricks in the outside walls. Your options now are to either bed some timber battens in mortar to take out the unevenness, and fix the boards to the battens, or to try to level the floor with a screed, and lay the boards onto a sheet of polystyrene – known as a floating floor.

TIMBER ON CONCRETE 2

Q The ground floors of our seventeen-year-old house are concrete which, in turn, is covered by chipboard tongue-and-groove panels. My wife would love to have 'real' floorboards in the living room, despite the fact that we do not have a suspended floor. We've used laminate wood-effect flooring in some rooms, but is it possible to lay real floorboards over concrete, and what special measures should be taken when laying them, such as some sort of under-lay to give some 'spring'?

A This is perfectly possible, and quite common. The most authentic effect will be achieved by fixing timber battens to the concrete, and laying solid timber boards (either pine or hardwood) across them. The boards can be nailed to the battens, just as they would be to the joists in a conventional floor. The boards will spring, and have all the feel of a suspended timber floor. However, the combined thickness of the battens and boards will be greater than the existing chipboard, so the doors, door linings, architraves and skirting boards will have to be cut to accommodate the extra depth, and there may be a notable step down into the adjacent rooms.

Alternatively, you could fit a 'floating' floor, where the boards are laid onto a thin foam-rubber underlay, and not fixed to the concrete. This will also be comfortable to walk on, although not quite as springy, but will not raise the floor level as much. The boards are tongue-and-groove, and are glued together. They can be either solid timber or real wood laminate, with a hardwood veneer on a softwood base, similar to parquet flooring.

CRACKED TILED FLOOR

Q We bought a new flat three years ago and two of the kitchen floor tiles are cracked. I have been informed that this is due to the movement of the building. The floors are concrete and we are on the second floor. As these tiles are no longer available do we have any redress against the builder, and should this have happened after three years? We feel that spares of these tiles should have been kept if this problem was likely to arise, considering the flats were sold as luxury apartments.

A The theory that your tiles have been cracked by building movement may or may not be true; this could only be confirmed if the alleged movement was measured. It is certainly common for new buildings to move, through settlement or drying shrinkage, and it is good practice to allow for this by bedding floor tiles on a flexible material such as asphalt rather than a rigid one like sand-and-cement. However, the ultimate reason for the cracking will almost certainly be that the tiles are too thin for the job. The term 'luxury' often refers only to the surface appearance of a new property, and not to the quality of the materials used. Since the tiles are no longer available, you could justifiably claim that the builder should relay the whole floor, but you may have to take him to court to achieve this.

BRICK FLOOR

Q We have recently bought an old cottage and when we took up the carpets we found that all the downstairs floors have brick pavers, presumably with bare earth underneath. Surprisingly, the house didn't smell damp, and the carpets weren't damp either; they were protected in one room by what looked like roofing felt between carpet and floor, and in the others by a thin layer of polythene sheeting. Although the pavers were slightly damp, there was no sign of mould.

Presumably what we should do is take up all the bricks and put down a damp-proof membrane before relaying the bricks. But what is the difference between stopping any damp below brick level or, as had been done, above? We want to avoid the rigmarole of taking up the bricks if we can.

A My advice is not to mess around with it. You are lucky to have found an old cottage with a brick floor in original condition, and if you put in a membrane now then you'll upset the moisture equilibrium, and could even make the walls damp. I'm not sure why you would want to have carpets anyway – one of the beauties of an old brick floor is its appearance. If you must have a floor covering then use loose sisal mats, which will still allow the floor to breathe.

CHIMNEYS

In these days of central heating, it may seem strange that fireplaces, flues and chimneys should cause problems for so many readers. But most weeks my postbag contains two or three chimney queries. In many cases, the problem is due to the fact that the chimney is no longer in use. Rain landing on the chimney stack or falling into the flue via the chimney pot will always percolate down and may appear as dampness further down inside the house. When fireplaces are regularly used for their original purpose, then the heat of the fire will constantly dry things out, but when there are no fires then other steps need to be taken. It is important to maintain a drying flow of air through the flue, and if the fireplace opening is bricked up in the room, this is best achieved by venting the flue at ceiling height. This allows a flow of warm air from the top of the room to enter the flue and flow upwards by natural convection, and also helps to ventilate the room. It is also a good idea to stop excess rain from entering a redundant flue by fitting a terracotta cowl, either into the top of the existing chimney pot, or in place of it.

Leaks at high level often manifest themselves as staining on the chimney breast within the loft space. This may look alarming but is probably not a problem as long as there is sufficient ventilation within the roof space. Regular leaks on the prevailing (windward) side of the chimney breast may be caused by inadequate flashing allowing rainwater to flow straight down the side of the brickwork, which is usually apparent from the staining pattern. Flashing round chimney stacks

Chimneys are a traditional feature of British housing.

has to be applied with great care and attention. It should always be in proper lead (not stick-on 'Flashband' or similar), and tucked a good 25mm into the brick joints.

Isolated damp patches that appear further down the breast, often with a brown stain, could be caused by rainwater dripping down inside the flue and hitting an obstruction or bend. If this occurs near an inside ceiling level, then the stain sometimes spreads out across the ceiling, especially if this has been repaired or replaced with plasterboard.

In neglected, unvented flues, it is not uncommon for rainwater to find its way right down to the ground-floor fireplace, and over time the soot and tar can be leached out into the surrounding brickwork, where it is often misdiagnosed as 'rising damp'. The soot contains hygroscopic salts, which, apart from giving very high readings on electrical moisture meters, also absorb moisture from the atmosphere, so where a property has a condensation problem, this can concentrate moisture in the flue, and cause staining on the surface of the chimney breast, even when there are no rainwater leaks.

Another problem concerns the removal of part of a redundant chimney breast. Victorian terraced houses were built with large chimney breasts, often back-to-back on the party walls. These contain a huge number of bricks and probably weigh twice as much as the wall itself, so they provide a buttressing effect which stabilizes the building, as well as providing ventilation to the rooms. Chimney breasts are often partially removed to provide extra space within rooms, and the brickwork above is supposed to be supported by spanning across the room to the wall opposite with rolled-steel joists (RSJs). It never is. The danger is not of the bricks falling down into the room – because they are bonded into the party wall itself. Rather, it is that the centre of gravity of the wall has been shifted, and over the long term, this may result in movement of the whole terrace.

Readers in houses whose chimney breasts have been removed also report being troubled by their neighbour's noise, and even their smells. So the removal of a chimney breast is not something to be undertaken lightly.

The other common problem with chimneys concerns using an old flue as a vent for a gas fire or boiler. This is a very dangerous thing to do unless the old flue has been prepared with a purpose-made flue liner (see Using Chimney as a Gas Flue on page 39).

STAINING ON CHIMNEY BREAST

Q Two of the fireplaces in my 1937 house (bedroom and dining room) are closed off and vented at grate level. The front-room fireplace is still in constant use during the winter with coal and log fires. There is now staining and dampness on the chimney breast in the bedroom upstairs. Is this because the vents are in the wrong place?

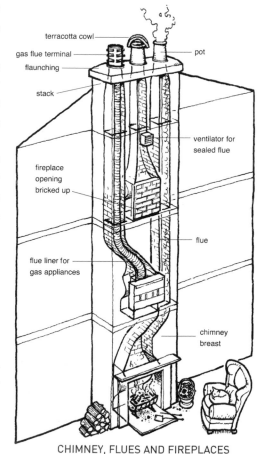

terracotta cowl

gas flue terminal

pot

flaunching

stack

ventilator for sealed flue

fireplace opening bricked up

flue

flue liner for gas appliances

chimney breast

CHIMNEY, FLUES AND FIREPLACES

CHIMNEYS

A It is more likely to be due to a build-up of tars and salts from the smoke of the downstairs fire, whose flue will pass to one side of the breast in the bedroom. These deposits are hygroscopic – i.e. they absorb moisture from the atmosphere – which gives rise to the phenomenon of 'chimney damp'. Staining on upstairs chimney breasts is especially common with log fires – these burn at a lower temperature than coal, and produce more tar. Get the flue swept regularly, and if the problem persists, then you may have to get it relined.

SMOKE IN ROOM

Q **I have lived in my house about thirty years and have always had open fires. I never had much trouble until the last eighteen months, when I have had smoke returning down the chimney into the living room. It seems to come in puffs. I've had a cowl put on top of the chimney and had it swept, but the smoke still comes back down. The chimney sweep said the cowl might be too low. I do have some tall trees about 15ft (3m) away from that side of the house and I wonder if they are causing a downdraught.**

A All sorts of environmental factors can create bursts of positive pressure, which cause the smoke to be blown back down the flue. Internal draughts and kitchen extractor fans can also sometimes draw air down the flue. Are you sure you haven't carried out any draught-proofing measures in the past eighteen months – such as having replacement windows fitted? A fire will not work in an airtight room – it needs an incoming draught to feed the flames and carry the smoke up the flue. If the doors and windows are all draught-proofed, then you may need a separate air supply for the fireplace, ducted in under the floor to a vent next to the fire.

If all these factors have been accounted for, then it may be worth trying an aerodynamic cowl, which uses the wind to create an uplift. Colt make a range of these, with different models suitable for different exposure conditions. For further information call The Loft Shop [LOFT CONVERSIONS].

SMOKE IN OTHER ROOMS

Q **My 1898 semi has a living room with an open coal fire, a dining room with a gas fire and a kitchen with an extractor fan. If I light the coal fire, and have the extractor fan working in the kitchen, the dining room fills with smoke! The chimneys have been swept and smoke pellets in each fireplace indicated that there is no problem.**

A It sounds as though there is insufficient ventilation in the kitchen, so the extractor fan is drawing air in through the nearest inlet, i.e. down the dining-room chimney. Not only is this annoying, but it is potentially dangerous, as when the gas fire is lit, the fan will be sucking in carbon monoxide from the flue gases. You urgently need extra permanent ventilation in both the kitchen and the dining room – either airbricks or floor vents – and you should keep the kitchen door closed when the extractor fan is running.

REMOVING CHIMNEY BREAST

Q **I own a two-bedroom mid-terrace Victorian house. The bathroom, upstairs and at the back of the house, has a chimney breast; the kitchen directly below it does not. The chimney** breast appears to be supported with 6in x 3in (150mm x 75mm) timber, taken to the supporting walls. Should I reinstate the chimney breast in the kitchen, or at least replace the timber with an RSJ?

A For many years builders and DIYers removed fireplaces and chimney breasts in downstairs rooms without giving it a second thought, supporting the breast above by bolting a couple of steel gallows brackets to the party wall, or, as in your case, inserting some extra timbers into the floor. It is now accepted that this is not the best thing to do to an older house, and surveyors usually comment on removed chimney breasts in homebuyer's reports. This does not mean that the brickwork above is liable to come crashing down, because it will be bonded into the party wall or flank wall. But it is a warning that the equilibrium of the structure may have been altered by the removal, and that in the future some kind of movement or settlement may occur. So when chimney breasts are removed nowadays, the preferred method is to insert rolled-steel joists (RSJs) to transfer the load across to the opposite wall. Unless there is obvious movement or cracking, there is no immediate need for you to do this now, but it could be part of any future building work in the kitchen. Alternatively, you could consider taking out the breast in the bathroom as well, thereby giving you more space, and putting the supporting RSJs in the roof space. You should seek advice from a structural engineer about this.

REMOVING PART OF CHIMNEY BREAST

Q You have referred to the potential damage caused by removing a chimney breast from a downstairs room. Does the same problem apply to a top-floor room?

A Yes, the problem is one of removing any section of the breast and failing to support the remaining brickwork above it. In a top-floor bedroom this would mean the part of the breast remaining in the loft space, and the chimney stack above the roof line. This situation can be especially dangerous, as in smaller bedrooms the bed is often situated against the wall from which the breast has been removed. There have been several instances of chimney stacks being blown over in gales and crashing through roofs. Remember, there is a very large amount of weight in a chimney stack.

INSTALLING A CHIMNEY

Q We live in a house with no chimney. What are the options for putting in a fireplace? One hears such horror stories of potentially lethal chimney/flue installations.

A Constructing fireplace openings, flues and chimneys used to be a standard part of the bricklayer's craft, so if you can find a bricklayer of the old school, he should be able to sort you out. The least disruptive option is to cut a fireplace opening in an outside wall and construct an external chimney breast. If the chimney breast has to be on the inside then it will require cutting through floor and ceiling timbers, and making sure they are adequately fire-protected.

An easier option may be to install a solid-fuel stove with a cast-iron flue pipe up to ceiling height, and a twin-walled insulated flue liner through upper floors and roof space. Ask your local authority building control department for guidance.

Readers in smoke-controlled areas will need to buy stoves with catalytic converters, or resort to 'coal-effect' gas fires. The regulations for these are the same as for any gas-fired appliance, and

CHIMNEYS

they must be installed by a CORGI-registered gas fitter (see the CORGI block advert in the Yellow Pages under 'Gas Installers').

USING CHIMNEY AS GAS FLUE

Q We are about to have gas fires installed in our 1934 house and our installers have said that flue lining is not necessary, but you have mentioned that flues in older houses should be lined. Is the potential danger due to age, or to the materials that were used in a particular period?

A In 1934 the chimneys will have been built with bricks and lime mortar, and whilst probably being structurally sound, will not be airtight enough to contain the exhaust fumes from gas fires. The problem is the carbon monoxide in these fumes, which is a deadly poison; if it leaks through the brickwork into the bedrooms above, then it can be fatal. Even houses built with purpose-made concrete flue liners in the 1960s and '70s are now thought to be inadequate for this purpose, and therefore metal flue liners must be inserted in all older flues before they are used to vent gas fires or boilers. You should use only CORGI-registered gas fitters, as they will be up to date with all the necessary safety regulations.

Inserting a stainless steel flue liner.

OPENING UP FIREPLACES

Q We want to recommission the downstairs fireplaces to use open fires. One is currently fitted with a gas fire and the other blocked off. Are there any pointers you can offer as to the best way to do this?

A As long as the flues are still open – i.e. not capped at the top or lined with gas flue liners – then you will probably just be able to open them up and use them. Get a local chimney sweep round to sweep them and give his opinion. The only problem is likely to be that if the parging (the mortar lining the flue) has broken down you may, in time, get staining on the breasts above.

SMELLS FROM NEXT DOOR THROUGH FLUE

Q How can we deal with smells from a bathroom next door coming into our bedroom? There is a chimney breast in the party wall, and we wonder if the neighbours have used it for venting. The noise is bad enough, but the smell is quite another matter.

A If there is a bathroom vent going into a redundant flue then it should be lined with a flexible flue liner or plastic ducting. This is to vent not just the smells to the outside of the building, but water vapour too – otherwise there could be condensation occurring within the chimney breast. It is always better for bathrooms to be ventilated directly through to an outside wall, and this can usually be achieved by ducting through the ceiling void.

CRACKS

Cracks cause householders a lot of unnecessary distress, usually because of the fear that they might signify serious problems. This is largely a result of the publicity given to subsidence damage, and stories about huge insurance claims for underpinning and other structural work. Most internal cracks are actually harmless, and their only drawbacks are cosmetic. And in reality subsidence is a hugely over-diagnosed and overrated problem.

Subsidence first hit the public consciousness following the dry summer of 1976, and a little-noticed change in the wording of buildings insurance policies that enabled owners to claim for the repair of cracking damage caused by ground shrinkage. Once one owner down a street had had their house underpinned at the insurer's expense, everybody else wanted it too, and almost overnight a huge army of 'specialist' underpinning contractors sprang up ready to cash in on this lucrative insurance-financed work. Underpinning is hugely expensive and disruptive, and very often unnecessary, as when the drought ends the ground swells again, and the cracks that opened up in the summer close themselves. The insurance industry belatedly realized this, and they are now more reticent about agreeing to fund underpinning work.

What many people fear as 'subsidence' is actually just minor differential settlement. The main causes are shallow foundations below front bays – which can cause cracks to open up between the bay and the main house – and softening of the ground due to leaking drains – this often occurs where drains run along alleys between houses, and so are close to the walls. The former is often curable by tying the bay back to the house with traditional brick stitching (or resin-bonding in serious cases), and the latter by lining or replacing the damaged drain. Old houses built with lime mortar and plaster can often cope with this sort of movement quite easily, which is why you can see brickwork above windows looking decidedly lopsided, but with no evidence of serious cracks. Modern materials are much more brittle and can withstand very little movement. So cement mortars and renders, and gypsum plasters, tend to emphasize movement by opening up into cracks. It's like the difference between icing and marzipan.

Most cracks in internal plaster occur in gypsum-plastered surfaces. On walls they are often nothing more than drying shrinkage, and on ceilings they usually follow the lines of the joints between sheets of plasterboard. It is also a surprisingly common practice by cowboy builders to plaster over wallpaper – this looks fine for a few weeks, but then lots of cracks open up, running in all directions. I know of a house in London where a structural engineer specified £30,000 worth of structural repairs based upon such cracking, and the buyer duly got that sum knocked off the price.

The situation in which cracks can result in serious problems is where they occur in external rendering. Most external renders are cement-based and are much too strong for the wall below. So they crack, and allow rainwater to penetrate. And once the water is behind the render, it is trapped, because strong sand-and-cement plaster is impermeable.

CRACKS IN EXTERNAL RENDER

Q My forty-year-old bungalow is rendered and I have several vertical cracks, mostly under the window sills. In the past I have Sandtexed the whole of the rendering after filling the cracks with Tetrion. This lasts for a couple of years and then the cracks show again. How can I get a lasting solution?

A Cracks below window sills are sometimes an indication of structural movement, rather than simply shrinkage of the surface render. You need to hack off the render in the offending areas and investigate what is happening underneath it. If there is cracking in the brickwork then this will need to be repaired by stitching-in with new bricks. The exposed area should be reinforced with expanded metal lathing and primed with a dilute PVA solution, before rerendering with a 6:1:1 washed sharp sand:lime:cement mix. Use a mortar plasticizer to reduce the amount of water in the mix and prevent drying shrinkage.

CRACKS IN RENDER ON LIGHTWEIGHT BLOCKS

Q My Victorian house has a two-storey back addition built of lightweight blocks and rendered. The rendering has many fine cracks and one large one. Rain has penetrated through the cracks and the lightweight blocks act like a sponge, causing the internal plaster to crack and 'blow'. I bought the property eight years ago and despite having a full survey, no damp problems were found!

A External render on lightweight block walls often cracks, due to the differential movement between the hard cement-based render and the softer lightweight blockwork. Where the blockwork forms the outer leaf of a cavity wall this is not such a serious problem, but when, as in your case, the wall is solid, then it can present serious difficulties. Unfortunately, there are no easy answers. The fault lies with the original builders, who did not understand the need to provide movement joints in the blockwork, or to use a soft lime-based render. The only long-term solution would be to hack off the render and replace it with the correct material (a 6:1:1 washed sharp sand:cement:lime mix), with the provision of a movement joint where the addition joins the main house.

CRACKS IN PLASTERBOARD CEILING

Q The plasterboard ceiling in my 1976 house suffers from cracks. I have tried many types of fillers without a successful permanent cure. Apart from rejointing with scrim, or Artexing, do you have any suggestions?

A Plasterboard ceilings very often crack. The cracking is worse in upstairs rooms because the plasterboard is fixed to the underside of the roof trusses, which will always move around in response to changes in temperature and moisture. In order to cope with this movement, 1 per cent of the ceiling is supposed to consist of joints between the boards (so a 4m-wide ceiling should have at least 40mm of joints). Plasterboard manufacturers produce special narrow 600mm 'plank' sizes to allow for this, but most builders prefer the convenience of larger sheets, which means there are always too few joints. The best thing is to open up the existing cracks to around 5–10mm, and cut extra joints, if needed, to reach the 1 per cent figure. And then fill the joints, and replaster,

Hairline cracks often occur along the joints between sheets of plasterboard.

with a soft plaster such as 'universal one-coat'. Even then, it may not work perfectly. The problem lies with the modern materials.

CRACKS IN ARTEXED CEILING

Q Our bungalow roof is made of preformed trusses and there is a large crack running across the living-room ceiling, along the joint in the boards. We had the ceiling professionally Artexed ten years ago, where the workmen sealed this crack with scrim and Artex before applying the textured coating to the whole ceiling. Needless to say the crack has returned. I have considered reinforcing the cracks from above using timber or plasterboard, but I presume I would have to get the Artex coating removed and have the ceiling recoated with either Artex or plaster, or is there some way of repairing a crack in Artex?

A Plasterboard ceilings fixed to roof trusses often crack, as the ceiling joists move in response to temperature and moisture changes within the roof space. You could try opening up your ceiling crack to around 5 to 10mm and fill it with a soft filler such as one-coat plaster, reinforcing from above with plasterer's hessian scrim. Matching the original Artex pattern will be difficult, although the manufacturers suggest using flexible decorator's filler, blended into the existing pattern with a wet cloth or brush. But it may be better to plaster over the whole lot with a smooth finish, using Artex Ceiling Finish – then it will be easier to repair next time the crack opens up.

CRACKS IN LATH-AND-PLASTER CEILING

Q Two lath-and-plaster ceilings in my Victorian house are cracked and sagging. My builder proposes removing the plaster but leaving the laths, and then fixing plasterboard over them. Will this not make it difficult to level the plasterboards and thus make for an uneven ceiling, or is this normal practice?

A Fixing plasterboard on top of laths is not a very professional way of working. But then plasterboard is an inferior material to lath and plaster anyway. Why not simply repair the cracks and damaged areas, using lime:sand:hair plaster to match the original? (Or universal one-coat plaster if that's all your builders can manage.) Finish with two layers of heavy-grade (1000-gauge) lining paper.

CRACKS – SUBSIDENCE CAUSED BY LEAKING DRAIN

Q The property we want to buy has been underpinned due to subsidence caused by a leaking drain. The repair work was carried out by the insurance company. I would be happy if I could be sure that this is a one-off problem that has been fixed and that it is not ongoing. Or should I be aware of other factors concerning this?

A As long as the offending drains have been completely renewed there is unlikely to be any further problem. My usual advice to people in cases like this is that if you like the house then buy it – there's nothing that can't be fixed later. Your main problem is likely to be getting buildings insurance on a property on which a subsidence claim has already been made. Make sure this is sorted before you incur any further expense.

These minor cracks in the brickwork would not be noticeable if the correct mortar had been used to repair them.

PVC-U

PVC-U roofline products.

All materials are subject to decay, but this is not something that is much discussed by salesmen, who prefer the idea that their products will last for ever. Adverts for PVC-U replacement windows and cladding, for example, often give the impression that the material is 'maintenance free', and, for the scientifically uneducated, this must sound like a wonderful thing. Unfortunately, it is simply not true.

A recent reader's letter describes a typical scenario. The reader lives in a fairly modern purpose-built block of flats, and someone on the residents' committee has decided that, in order to 'reduce maintenance costs', all the windows, fascias and soffit boards should be replaced with PVC-U, at an estimated cost of over £100,000. The current annual amount they are spending on exterior maintenance is, of course, zero, because the windows, fascias and soffits have not actually been painted since 1976.

Imagine if we adopted the same approach to our clothes. Or teeth. Don't bother to clean them or look after them. Just let them rot away and then buy some plastic ones. Society would judge anyone who behaved like this as foolish, or deranged, or both. They would be sent for psychiatric counselling and their children would be taken away from them. But when it comes to the buildings that we live in, it seems to have become socially acceptable to allow them to rot.

The PVC-U salesmen exploit this inertia by reassuring us that it really is all right to neglect our homes. It is not our fault that the windows have rotted, they say; it is because they were made from that pesky old-fashioned stuff called wood. Time to get modern and use space-age materials that will last for ever.

Only they won't. PVC-U inevitably becomes discoloured, and brittle, and, because of its high thermal-expansion coefficient, it can even crack. This last problem is especially common in PVC-U replacement fascias and soffit boards, which need very careful fixing and – dare I say it – maintenance? – if they are to remain intact for more than a few years.

DISCOLOURED WINDOWS

Q Our white PVC-U double glazing is turning brown. Is it possible that the steam from cooking is affecting what may be recycled material?

A Brown or yellow discoloration in PVC-U occurs because of faulty manufacture. There is an imbalance between the amount of titanium oxide in the formulation and the heat or speed of the extrusion process. Steam has nothing to do with it. The only cure is replacement. The installers may try to tell you they can strip off the top layer and apply lacquer, or paint them, but this will only be effective for a few years.

PAINTING PLASTIC

Q We had an extension built and now have exposed white plastic windows and waste pipes, a brown pipe going into the drain, a grey plastic soil stack, and black plastic gutters and down pipes. Would the life of all this plastic be prolonged if painted, and is there a special paint for the job?

A All plastics become brittle through exposure to u/v light, but not at the same rate. This will depend upon the type of plastic, the colour and the amount of u/v stabilizer used in manufacture. Your white internal waste pipes are probably polypropylene, and the windows, brown and grey drainage pipes and black guttering are PVC-U.

The biggest maintenance requirement for PVC-U (the 'U' stands for 'unplasticized') products is to keep them clean. The plastic surfaces seem to attract dust and pollutants – possibly by electrostatic attraction – and white PVC-U can quickly become dirty. So all PVC-U windows and roofline products should be washed with detergent at least once a year – more frequently in towns or areas close to the sea. All plastics will last longer if painted. ICI/Dulux make Weathershield PVC-U paint – for use on weathered PVC-U windows – which will need rubbing down and recoating every few years, like all paintwork, but ordinary spirit-based undercoat and gloss can also be used.

ROOFLINE PRODUCTS

Q I live on an estate of houses with much white boarding – soffits, fascias, etc. Firms come around offering maintenance-free white PVC. Some firms cover the surfaces of the existing wood soffits with thin plastic boards; others insist it is better to remove the original wood and replace entirely with PVC. Few of us still have the original woodwork, which, of course, has the disadvantage of needing repainting at intervals. Which is the best option?

A 'Maintenance-free' PVC-U is a myth. It won't last for ever. It becomes brittle through exposure to sunlight, and discoloured by airborne pollutants. PVC-U must also be fixed using slotted holes to allow for thermal movement. If this is not done then the boards can buckle and split. Fastening PVC-U boards over existing timber is a real bodge job, as it will trap moisture underneath, and the timber will rot. Why do you think there are so many of these firms around touting for work? It's because they are making a fortune for doing not very much. For the money they charge you could pay to have the woodwork maintained and painted for fifty years.

JOINING DIFFERENT TYPES OF GUTTERING

Q We live in a semi-detached bungalow. We have the rainwater downpipe for the front of the two properties discharging at the front corner of our bungalow, and our neighbour has the corresponding pipe for the rear. He is going to have his original wood fascias, guttering, etc., replaced with PVC, and wants us to do the same. Ours is quite sound, and we do not care to replace with PVC in any case. What do we need to be aware of with regard to jointing, etc., and what redress would we have if there were problems in the future?

A The main thing to be aware of is that most of this kind of replacement PVC-U work is carried out by unskilled, unqualified cowboy companies, who are unlikely to still be trading in twelve months' time, when the gutters start leaking. You should make it clear to your neighbour in writing that you will hold him responsible for any problems caused to your property as a result of his actions. You should also commission a condition survey from an independent surveyor, which should include a photographic record of the guttering as it is now.

Q My guttering is the standard half-round plastic, and my neighbour has had his renewed with a square shape. His fitter joined up to our gutter with a big wedge of silicone mastic, which has now started leaking. Is there an actual fitting which will couple half-round to square gutters?

A There are various adaptors for connecting different shapes of plastic guttering together, and for connecting plastic to cast iron. The best place to ask is in a specialist plumbers' merchant, where they will have all the different manufacturers' catalogues. It will help if you find out the brand names of the two types of guttering, which should be written or stamped somewhere on the guttering, downpipes and clips. In the event that you cannot find a suitable adaptor, you will have to fit stop ends to the two lengths of guttering, and adjust the fall of the higher section so that the rainwater drains back to the nearest outlet and downpipe.

This PVC-U guttering has been melted by the heat from the boiler flue below it.

WINDOWS

Most people who have double-glazed replacement windows fitted to their homes do so under the impression that they will last till the end of their days. Unfortunately this is often not the case. Sealed double-glazed units have a limited lifespan, and the seal will eventually fail, resulting in misting up between the two panes of glass. In the highest-quality installations this may not happen for thirty years. Some experts say twenty years is a reasonable life expectancy. But poorly installed windows can fail much sooner – sometimes within a year – which can come as quite a shock to people who swallowed the sales pitch that their new windows would be maintenance-free for ever.

The sales techniques used to flog double glazing are much the same as those for any other building gimmick, except that double glazing is now apparently approved by the world's leaders. The Kyoto Accord on reducing carbon emissions committed nations to cutting down fuel consumption, and the British government is amongst those concentrating on reducing home heating energy in order to reach their Kyoto targets.

The only problem is, double glazing requires energy to manufacture and install, and the payback period, in terms of both energy and money, is very long. Taking the average British home, and replacing its existing windows with new double-glazed units, it would probably take around a hundred years of reduced heating bills to cover the cost of the installation. So the salesman who recently persuaded a ninety-five-year-old man that new windows would save him money in the long run surely deserves some kind of award.

In any case, there is no way that new, sealed double-glazed units are going to last a hundred years. They are doomed to eventually fail because of the way they are made. The two panes of glass are joined at the edge with a polymer compound, which by its very nature is slightly vapour-permeable – i.e. it will always allow a small amount of water vapour to enter from outside. So to keep the glass from misting up, each double-glazed unit also incorporates a desiccant – a drying agent – housed within a perforated alloy strip running around the edge. This desiccant absorbs the invading moisture and prevents misting. But eventually there will come a day when it can absorb no more. It will be saturated, and then there will be free water between the panes, which will form as mist on the glass. How long this takes depends upon the quality of the materials and workmanship.

In ideal circumstances the sealed glass unit will be mounted in drained and ventilated recesses in the window frames, positioned on special setting blocks and with spacers at intervals around the edges to support it when the window is opened or subjected to wind loads. When this is not done – which is very often – the resulting stresses on the glass can break the seal. Units fitted into timber windows using ordinary putty or oily mastics can also fail quickly, as these dry out the sealant and cause it to crack.

When the seal is broken, any water collecting at the bottom edge of the glass will find its way through and saturate the desiccant. And once these double-glazed units mist up inside there is nothing – but nothing – that can be done to remedy it. Thousands of windows in hundreds of homes already have this problem, and the numbers are set to grow.

Do the boffins at the Department of Trade and Industry know about this – the ones who are madly promoting the use of replacement double glazing in existing buildings? I very much doubt it.

REPAIRING DAMAGED FRAMES

Q **Can you offer advice regarding dry rot in the bottom transom of window frames? I am thinking in particular of the use of fillers or even splices as a repair.**

A Windows are unlikely to suffer from dry rot, as this requires high humidity and so only occurs within enclosed spaces. Your windows are more likely to have been damaged by wet rot, caused by water running down the glass and getting in behind poorly maintained paint and putty. If the transoms, bottom rails or sills have rotted badly, there is really little point in trying to patch them up with filler, especially if the joints have been weakened, and it is better to engage a skilled carpenter to cut out and replace the damaged sections. Surface damage on otherwise sound sections of timber is best filled with a two-part epoxy filler such as Nickerson Chemical's Timbabuild, a specially formulated repair paste. Nickerson can put you in touch with people who do the repair work [TIMBER REPAIRS].

New timber windows, or new sections, should be given two good coats of primer before glazing, and the paintwork should be inspected annually and, if necessary, touched up to cover any damaged areas. The life of timber windows can be greatly extended by opening them at regular intervals to release water trapped between the sashes and the frames.

SLIDING SASH PROBLEM

Q **I have a flat in a Victorian house with sliding sash windows. These all work well, apart from one in the kitchen, which will not stay open. The cords on both sides are intact, but the window falls shut unless it is propped open with something. How can there be a fault with this one window?**

A The most likely cause is that the sliding sash in question has had a glass breakage, and been reglazed with 4mm glass in place of the original 3mm. On a large pane, this can represent a significant weight difference. On a top sash, it will result in the window refusing to stay shut, and on a bottom sash, in its refusal to stay open. You should be able to spot a new pane of glass by looking at the putty and paintwork. Your options are to have the offending pane reglazed, or to add extra weights to the sash weights hanging inside the box frame. They are almost equally troublesome.

REPAIRING SASH WINDOW

Q **My flat in a converted Victorian house has a large twelve-pane sash window which is rotting at the bottom. It won't close properly so I have a permanent 2in gap at the top. Does the whole window have to be replaced and what is the likely cost? I am on the first floor so I would expect it to involve scaffolding if it had to come out. Also, being in a conservation area, I would need to replace it with a wooden window, which I would prefer anyway. I have no idea who to contact for what needs doing.**

A Your course of action depends on the actual state of the window, its age and whether it has any important historical features that are worth saving (even crinkly panes of glass have a value). The total replacement scenario might not be as expensive as you fear – maybe only a few hundred pounds for the sliding sashes, depending on who you find to do it. No scaffolding is involved; sashes are easily removed and replaced from the inside. A local carpentry workshop should be able to make you a close copy, glazed and primed. Repair might also be an option, but would require an older traditional sort of carpenter.

METAL WINDOWS

Q My 1930s-style bungalow has steel windows, manufactured by a firm called Crittall. They have stood up fairly well through the years but now they are difficult to open and close, and some of the smaller panes have cracked. Would you advise on the best way of rectifying this problem – would it be best to approach a double-glazing salesman or a blacksmith?

A Nobody should ever approach a double-glazing salesman of their own free will, as they are interested only in selling new windows, not repairing existing ones. Neither would a blacksmith be the right person. Crittall windows are still being made by the original firm, and if you call their technical services department on 01376 324106 they will give you a list of regional distributors who provide a repair and refurbishment service. As you point out, Crittall windows have performed well over the years, and it is worth keeping them if at all possible. Steel windows are also supplied by other members of the Steel Windows Association [WINDOWS AND GLAZING].

DOUBLE GLAZING – LEAKING VENTS

Q I know that replacement double-glazed windows should always have ventilation slots at the top, but we had windows replaced two years ago and unfortunately when it is very windy, the wind howling through the closed vents produces a noise like elephants trumpeting! At times the noise drowns out the TV. Is there something wrong with our windows' vent system or is this inevitable with window vents?

A Other readers have complained of wind noise, and also of rain being blown in through window vents, even when they are shut. The idea of these 'trickle vents' is to provide a gentle flow of ventilation, to make up for the fact that the replacement windows have probably sealed off all the natural ventilation that was occurring before. But trickle vents should always be designed to cope with the prevailing weather conditions, and if they are noisy, or leaky, then this is because they are simply poor quality and not fit for their designed purpose. Your installers have an obligation to rectify this. A soundproof trickle vent is available from Renson, and Glazpart claim to supply a weatherproof vent [WINDOWS AND GLAZING]. Both can be fitted to existing windows, although this may be more than a DIY job.

DOUBLE GLAZING – MISTING UP

Q Several years ago I had my windows replaced with double glazing. After a few years, the south-facing ones became subject to occasional, unsightly internal misting. As there was a ten-year guarantee I claimed for renewal of the windows. The insurance company claimed that the condensation was normal and therefore refused the claim.

A One of the great unspoken truths of sealed double-glazed units (SGUs) is that eventually they will all mist up. The timescale should be twenty-ish years in a perfectly made and installed window. But in poorly made ones it can be a lot less. Five months has been reported.

Double-glazed windows will all mist up eventually.

So, in a way, the condensation is 'normal', in that it will happen eventually in all windows. But I would have thought you could expect that a ten-year guarantee would reasonably cover you against misting within that time. It depends on the insurers' small print, I suppose.

MISTING UP

Q Is it possible to have misted double glazing repaired rather than replaced? Can the two glass panes be separated, cleaned, new desiccant added, and reassembled again, or is the cost of this not significantly different to new units?

A No, it is not possible. Nobody has yet found a way to remove the spacer bar and its sealant, and leave a clean surface able to take a new spacer bar and sealant. Any attempt to do so will cost far more in man-hours than making a new sealed unit with fresh clean glass. Some 'experts' suggest a repair trick of drilling two small holes in the outer pane, allowing the misting to clear, and then sealing the holes. This may work for a few weeks, but the glass will soon mist up again because it has not remedied the actual cause of the misting, which is water getting in through the seals and saturating the desiccant inside the spacer bar. Drilling holes and leaving them unsealed has also been suggested, but this removes the thermal-insulation benefit of having double glazing. This is why it is so important that double-glazed units are installed correctly in the first place, using a drained, vented dry-glazing system, that prevents water coming into contact with the edge seals.

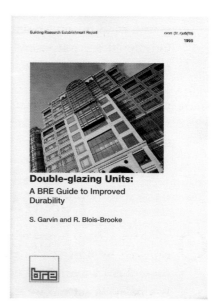

Building Research Establishment Report   case (3).(poб)(8в)
                                                        1995

Double-glazing Units:
A BRE Guide to Improved Durability

S. Garvin and R. Blois-Brooke

bre

DRY-GLAZING SYSTEM

Q You have advised against fitting double-glazed units in timber windows using putty or mastic, because of the problem of internal misting. Our property was built in 1987, and soon after we bought it in 1993 we had to replace ten units which had misted up. Two different glaziers said our units could be installed only with putty, the recesses not being deep enough to accept timber glazing beads. In 1994 we installed sealed

Pilkington K units in a new sun lounge, which were fitted with beads but reinforced with mastic because of the local wind-driven horizontal rain. All of these have now acquired internal misting. We would dearly love to get twenty years' use out of replacements, rather than the seven to eight years we have had so far, but how can we get a glazier to use the dry-glazing method you recommend?

A Sealed glazed units (SGUs) installed with putty or mastic can mist up within a short time because the oils in the putty or mastic dry out the edge seal, causing it to crack, and because these sealants also trap water, allowing it to penetrate the edge seal, saturate the desiccant and cause condensation between the panes. A drained, vented dry-glazing system overcomes both of these problems and should help to give SGUs a mist-free life of twenty years or more.

Any competent glazier or carpenter should be able to adapt a timber window to a dry-glazing system. In the unlikely event that the existing glazing rebates are too shallow, they can easily be deepened using a router, plane or oscillating shear. The replacement SGUs should be mounted on plastic setting blocks to hold them clear of the rebate, and the bottom glazing bead should have 5mm x 35mm slots cut in the lower edge to allow water to drain away. This technique is described in British Standard BS6262 and in the Building Research Establishment book *Double-glazing Units: A BRE Guide to Improved Durability* [CONSTRUCTION LITERATURE]. Alternatively, a patent dry-glazing system which can be used to convert existing timber windows, and which includes self-adhesive security gaskets, is supplied by Reddiseals [WINDOWS AND GLAZING].

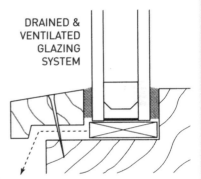

DRAINED & VENTILATED GLAZING SYSTEM

SECONDARY GLAZING – FOR SOUND REDUCTION

Q My brother-in-law and I are seeking to fit secondary glazing to our houses for different reasons. My requirement is to bolster the soundproofing effect of my existing double-glazed units because of road noise. He wishes to improve the heat insulation of single-glazed windows on a north-east-facing wall. What are your views regarding secondary glazing for these purposes? Do you have recommendations regarding glass thickness or aluminium versus PVC?

A Secondary glazing is best for noise reduction, double glazing for heat insulation. But secondary glazing will also help to keep the heat in, by cutting out draughts, and your brother-in-law may achieve good results by using a single pane of 'low-E' glass from Pilkingtons. Alloy frames are better than PVC-U as they are less obtrusive and longer lasting.

SECONDARY GLAZING – FOR WARMTH AND SOUND REDUCTION

Q We have a 1910 house with its original windows. Most of our neighbours have had theirs replaced by horrible-looking plastic double glazing. We do not want to do this. On the other hand we would like some of the benefits of double glazing such as more warmth and less noise. What can we do?

A You should fit secondary glazing on the inside of the original windows. This is better for cutting down sound than sealed double-glazed units, and the greater the gap between the two sets of windows, the greater the sound reduction. It will also cut down the draughts. Aluminium-framed sliding secondary glazing can be made to match the fenestration pattern of the original windows, and is unobtrusive.

DIY SECONDARY GLAZING

Q Some years ago secondary glazing kits appeared to be widely available at most DIY shops, but they no longer seem to be on the market. Is it possible to purchase these for installation as a DIY project, or are they only supplied and fitted by specialist manufacturers?

A Aluminium secondary-glazing kits are still available for keen DIYers. For example Selectaglaze supply kits to builders, and also have a network of approved fabricators and installers. Many local replacement window firms will also be able to supply made-to-measure secondary glazing, and you may find that these are cheap enough that you will save very little by making them yourself. Try looking up 'Window frame and accessory manufacturers' in the Yellow Pages. The Monarch secondary-glazing system is also available from a network of local fabricators and installers [WINDOWS AND GLAZING].

GEORGIAN LOOK?

Q I'm forever replacing putty and repainting our mock-Georgian window frames. Not only is it a constant battle against leaks, but single glazing means pools of condensation throughout the winter. You've described the pitfalls of PVC-U but my wife is adamant that she wants to enjoy the comfort of double glazing and I don't want to continue with high maintenance. Can I satisfy both of us and still maintain a 'Georgian' look?

A Yes. Modern sealed glazed units can be as thin as 14mm, so this makes it possible to double-glaze your existing timber windows, or new timber replacements. Timber windows can achieve minimal maintenance if they are painted with high-build microporous paint, which needs a rub down with steel wool and a single recoat every seven to ten years. And this gives you the warmth of timber, which is superior to PVC-U reinforced with aluminium. You need a vented and drained dry-glazing system (no putty or mastic bedding) to keep the SGUs from misting up prematurely.

LEAKING LEADED LIGHTS

Q My 1930s house has small leaded windows. When it rains heavily, some of the windows leak. I have tried putting putty or wood filler on the horizontal sections but it is a very protracted job and I have had little or no success. Is there a product on the market to insert between the lead and the glass or is the answer to have new sections made?

A Leaded lights can be repaired using traditional leadlight cement, which requires the windows to be taken out and laid flat on a bench. Scrape out areas of loose old cement, and make sure that none of the soldered joints have corroded, as these can also be points of leakage. The joints are resealed by brushing in fresh cement. Small areas can be resealed without taking the window out, using black putty. For professional restoration look under 'stained glass suppliers' or 'leaded lights and windows' in the Yellow Pages. James Hetley supply books on leaded-light work [WINDOWS AND GLAZING].

PVC-U DOOR WON'T OPEN

Q I had replacement PVC windows and back door fitted to my small semi in June 2000. The supplier and fitter went out of business soon afterwards. In the summer of 2001 I had difficulty turning the key in the lock of the back door and called in a locksmith, who said the lock was not at fault, but that the door needed rehanging. This summer the same thing is happening again. It seems to be a heat-related problem. First thing, in the cool of the morning, the lock functions easily enough, but later in the day when the temperature goes up, I can't turn the key in the lock and have to go out the front way to get to the back garden. Short of replacing the door, can you suggest a way of solving this problem?

A PVC-U expands in heat a lot more than other materials – nearly 1mm per metre per 10°C. Dark colours absorb more heat than white, so expand more. The clearances around the door should be a minimum of 5–6mm all round if the PVC-U is white (7–8mm if any other colour). The rollers can be adjusted up and down to accommodate the expansion, and the lock clearances can also be adjusted separately, but it needs someone familiar with the mechanisms who can make the adjustments while leaving the door secure. Unfortunately most PVC-U replacement window firms do not have this expertise, and are only after your money. For independent advice on finding someone to solve your problem call Fenestration Associates [WINDOWS AND GLAZING].

PUZZLING BREAKAGE

Q Neighbours had a stone thrown at their double-glazed PVC-U door. Strangely, the outer sheet of glass didn't break but the inner one shattered, looking like a spider's web. How is this possible?

A It sounds as though the outer pane was toughened glass, which would be able to withstand the impact of the stone, but which would deflect momentarily, to transmit a pressure wave across the air space. This pressure broke the inner pane, which was laminated glass. Both materials qualify as 'safety glass', which is required in doors.

So – you ask – why weren't both panes made of toughened? Well, it's tough, but it's not that tough. It can be broken by impact from a sharp instrument such as a pickaxe, and when it does break, it disintegrates and falls out of the frame. Laminated, on the other hand, while it shatters more easily, still hangs together in one piece. So they each have different security advantages.

NEW WINDOW REGULATIONS

Q I am shortly to embark on an extension to my 1935 property and wish to install single-glazed wooden window frames similar to the originals. Architects have informed me that since 2002 all new windows have to be double-glazed to comply with Building Regulations. This means I shall have two new double-glazed windows in the drawing room along with the three original single-glazed windows. It is most unlikely the new windows will match the old ones, and the whole issue of two types of glazing in one room seems a nonsense. Is there any way to overcome this?

A This is a typically absurd result of the new Part L of the Building Regulations that came into force on April Fool's Day 2002. All windows in new houses, and replacement windows in existing houses, are supposed to be double-glazed with low-emissivity ('low-E') glass. Exceptions apply only to listed buildings, houses in conservation areas and buildings of architectural or historical interest. However, in your case, since the new walls of your extension will presumably be built to the current Building Regulations, you could argue that you are in fact improving the thermal insulation of the room overall, and that you should therefore be allowed to trade this off against the thermal value of the new windows. Your local authority building control department does in fact have the discretion to consider the thermal value of the whole construction, and not simply the windows in isolation. There is much confusion over this amongst architects, surveyors and builders.

SCRATCHED GLASS

Q **We recently moved house and it wasn't until we moved in that we noticed scratches on the double-glazed patio doors. They are surface scratches obviously made by the previous owner's dog. Is there any remedial treatment, in order to avoid the expense of having new doors fitted?**

A The traditional way to do this is with jewellers' rouge and much elbow grease. Rouge can still be bought from glass-processing suppliers, and even some old-style builders' merchants. You wet it, apply it to the scratch and rub and rub and rub. Eventually, depending upon how deep the scratches are, they will disappear.

Alternatively, find a glass merchants in Yellow Pages – not a double-glazing supplier or leaded-lights maker, but one who really cuts and supplies pieces of glass. Most of these now have a high-speed electric buffer which can be brought along with some of the new buffing pastes, which make scratches disappear very quickly.

REMOVING OLD PUTTY

Q **My architect-designed house was built forty-three years ago with wooden Georgian sliding sash windows. The original nineteen windows have been regularly painted with good-quality paint, but over the last few years cracks have appeared in the glazing putty – typically 30–50mm apart. The painter who has painted the windows several times now says that were he to try to remove the putty, not only would the pane on which he was working be broken, but also the one next to it would be at risk. I have bought a 'Prazi putty chaser' from the USA, but I have found it unsatisfactory for extensive use. Is there any solution other than replacement PVC-U windows in 'heritage' style?**

A You should certainly not think of replacing your timber windows with PVC-U, as they will be unlikely to give you anything near forty-three years' service. Any competent glazier should be able to remove your cracked putty without breaking the glass, but if you or your painter want to do it yourselves then the tool to use is the Fein MultiMaster [WINDOWS AND GLAZING]. This is a power tool with a patented oscillating action and a selection of blades which will get into all sorts of tight corners. It is excellent for window refurbishment, and also good for cutting out old grout and sealants.

ELECTRICS

'Electrics' is the name given by builders to anything in a house that is connected to the main power supply. So it covers the nests of hidden wires that run all around the house, and anything that has one or more of these wires permanently attached to it.

I have always tried not to get too closely involved in electrics, because (a) electricity is dangerous and (b) the regulations and the equipment are constantly changing. But there are basics that everyone should know, such as the position of electrical cables under wall plaster and floors.

Wall-mounted power sockets and light switches are the way in which we use and control electricity in our homes. In winter, we may use the kitchen light switch twenty times in a day, but we never stop to think about the cable route which carries the electricity from the consumer unit to the switch and then on to the light fittings. The cables are run under floors and up and down walls behind the plaster. It is useful to have an idea of where they might be, if for no other reason than to avoid drilling through them when we put shelves up.

Under timber floors, electrical cables running parallel to the joists should be clipped in place along the mid-axis of a joist. This is mostly the case with houses built since 1960. Houses older than that are likely to have been rewired since their birth, which means that new cables will have been poked or dragged into place beneath already fixed floorboards. So the chances of the cables having been carefully clipped in place are slim. They are probably just lying on top of the ceiling plaster. Nothing wrong with that, but bear it in mind if you ever decide to drill a hole in the ceiling.

Cables which have to run perpendicular to the joists should go through holes drilled as close as possible to the vertical centre of each joist. This is the section of the joist which is in neither compression (the top half) nor tension (the bottom half), so drilling a 25mm hole through the centre of a 180mm floor joist does not, theoretically, affect its strength. Let's hope not. And make sure your electrician understands what is meant by 'centre'. (The reason these holes are usually hit-and-miss is that you can't fit an ordinary electric drill down in the space between the joists, in order to drill square, so the holes are drilled at a downward angle. Only the most dedicated electricians carry special drills with right-angle attachments.) But as long as the cables are running through holes somewhere near the centre of the joists, at least they won't be hit by nails hammered into the floor from above. Unlike copper plumbing pipes which, because of their stiffness, have to be laid into notches cut in the tops of the joists.

Behind wall plaster, cables are supposed to be run vertically to and from power sockets and light switches. This is basic good practice, in order to give other people a rough idea of where they might be. So light switch cables will almost always drop down vertically from the ceiling. Power cables usually run below timber floors, and vertically up to the sockets, but in houses with solid concrete ground floors, they may drop down vertically from the ceiling above. Bear in mind, also, that unqualified electricians and DIYers may not always have been completely diligent about having vertical cable runs, and that cables can sometimes be found running at all angles around rooms.

This is especially likely in kitchens or rooms that have previously been used as kitchens, where power circuits for above-worktop sockets may have been run horizontally behind tiled splashbacks.

If in doubt, or when drilling into walls close to sockets or switches, it is a good idea to trace cable routes using a metal detector or cable finder. These are inexpensive and can be bought from builders' merchants or DIY outlets.

Another common question concerns light bulbs. Is it true, as some people say, that lamps blow more easily in cold weather? The only logical reason for this might be that the greater temperature difference between the 'on' and 'off' states of the light causes more stress on the filament – the thin wire inside the bulb that glows white hot and gives off the light. But since the tungsten filament of an incandescent bulb glows at around 2,500°C, the fact that it starts off at ten degrees rather than twenty, say, would appear to be neither here nor there. Neither is there any evidence that failing bulbs are a sign of faulty wiring. We must face the fact that light bulbs break more often in the winter months because there are more hours of darkness to eat up their 1,000-hour average lifespans. Since this is equivalent to only three hours per day over a year, it is hardly surprising that bulbs in heavily used rooms such as kitchens should need replacing on a fairly regular basis.

As incandescent bulbs glow white-hot, tungsten molecules evaporate from the filament and get deposited as a black residue on the inside of the glass, until the filament becomes so thin that it burns through. So a blown but thoroughly blackened bulb will be one which has served its time well; a clearer one is more likely to have failed due to impact or vibration.

A more significant factor in bulb life is which way up it goes in the fitting. Bulbs are designed to hang downwards, and if they point upwards or sideways they don't last as long. This is because, as the filament becomes thin and brittle with use, if the bulb is pointing upwards or sideways the filament can eventually collapse under its own weight. The filaments in downward-hanging bulbs are subjected to less stress and will usually only break before their time if you bash them.

Another disadvantage of upward-facing bulbs is that when they do blow, they tend to short out the whole circuit, blowing the fuse or MCB (miniature circuit breaker or 'trip switch') on the consumer unit, and plunging the whole place into darkness. This is because bits of the broken filament fall across the two bulb terminals and cause a surge in power. If the bulb is hanging downwards then the broken bits land harmlessly in the glass.

Lately, however, even downward-hanging bulbs have started to trip circuits, because of a lowering in manufacturing standards. Light bulbs used to have a little built-in fuse – a very thin strip of wire in the bayonet cap – which would burn out first, leaving the rest of the filament intact. But now, pressure on costs from overseas manufacturers has meant that most modern bulbs are unfused, and can blow at any point along the filament. So you can now buy light bulbs for 20p; but they won't last as long and they'll blow your fuses. You never, ever, get something for nothing.

Nowadays we are all supposed to be using energy-saving light bulbs, which are claimed to last for 10,000 hours. I have been a keen user of these ever since they were first introduced, but I have yet to own one which has lasted anything like that length of time. Their price has come down in recent years, but they still cost up to ten times more than incandescent bulbs. They are claimed to use only one-fifth of the electricity, but this still means they need to last at least 1,000 hours before they start saving you money, and it is not unusual for them to break before reaching this age. When you put one in, write the date in felt-tipped pen on the side of the plastic base, so you can keep a check.

Energy-saving bulbs are more accurately called 'compact fluorescents', and the latest versions consist of two or three fluorescent glass loops attached to a mounting block containing the electronics needed to keep it working. This means they cannot always be used directly in place of incandescent bulbs. The light quality is cold, as with most fluorescent tube lighting; they cannot be used with normal dimmer switches; and they are too bulky for some light fittings and shades. The packet advertising which states 'interchangeable with an ordinary bulb' does not seem to mention any of this. Like all fluorescent lamps, they have a high initial rate of electricity consumption until they have warmed up, so they only save energy in situations where a light would normally be left on for long periods. They lose light intensity with age, and their life is shortened by regular switching on and off. Readers have also pointed out that they may be dangerous if used on dark stairways, because of the time taken to warm up and give full illumination.

And, like all fluorescent lighting tubes, the compact fluorescents contain mercury and need to be disposed of as hazardous waste since, if crushed as landfill, the mercury may find its way into the water supply. Local authority waste sites are supposed to be equipped to deal safely with fluorescent tubes, and householders should be allowed to deposit a maximum of six tubes at a time (this being the number used in a sunbed, I am told).

Electricians are obliged to dispose of redundant fluorescent tubes via specialist contractors – a service for which they have to pay a fee. This is why so many tubes are dumped illegally in builders' skips, and why anyone driving through a city centre early in the morning will have noticed forests of fluorescent tubes apparently sprouting out of litter bins. Any government worth its green credentials would obviously provide free recycling for such a hazardous material. Ours appears keen to persuade us to use the bulbs, but doesn't want to think about the consequences.

REWIRING 1

Q We have lived in our 1961 semi since it was built. Over recent years a number of neighbours have had their houses rewired. As far as I am aware this has been done because the owners felt it was time to do so, rather than as the result of any specific problems. Should ours be rewired?

A It depends upon the type of cable. The 1960s saw the changeover from rubber-sheathed cable to PVC. The rubber (usually black) had a life expectancy of around twenty-five years, so it would almost certainly be needing replacement now. PVC-sheathed cable (either white or grey) has no known life expectancy, and should still be perfectly serviceable. However, up until about 1970, lighting circuits were usually wired in twin PVC cable with no earth wire, and whilst this is still acceptable for plastic light fittings, anything metal (such as some types of wall light) would need an earth cable running to it. Also, in the same period, it was usual for one 30A ring main to supply power for the whole house, whereas now, with the increased number of electrical appliances, it is normal to have one ring main for downstairs and one for upstairs. Upgrading does not necessitate a complete rewire, as the circuit can be cut in half and reconnected to provide two separate rings.

It would also be advisable to replace an old fused consumer unit with a modern one with circuit breakers (trip switches), and incorporating a residual current circuit breaker (RCCB) – sometimes also referred to as a residual current device (RCD).

You may also consider having your old light fittings replaced, as these become brittle with age

Rewiring.

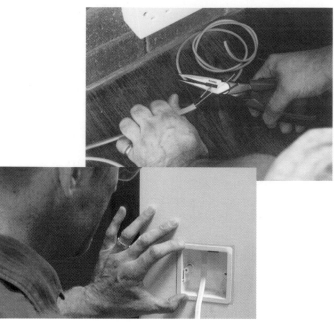

and heat, and having your power points inspected and replaced if necessary. The NICEIC recommend that household electrical systems should be inspected at least every ten years.

REWIRING 2

Q My Victorian house needs rewiring, and I read somewhere that modern regulations do not permit new electric cables to be inserted in lath-and-plaster walls, but that they must be surface mounted in plastic conduit tubes. I am worried that this will spoil the character of the house. Is there any way of getting around these regulations?

A There is no regulation that replacement electric cabling in old houses must be surface mounted. It is perfectly acceptable to run cables in chases (slots) cut into old plasterwork. The new cables are normally protected by hard plastic sheathing before being plastered over, to protect them from accidental damage – when someone is nailing a picture hook into the wall, for example. But lath-and-plaster partition walls in old houses are even easier – the new cables can usually be fed down in the hollow core of the wall, and fished out into the light switches or power points. An NICEIC-qualified electrician should be able to rewire your Victorian house with minimal surface wiring.

CORRODING CABLES

Q I have lived in my house since it was built in 1967. The wiring is of the twin-and-earth type (for lighting and power), covered in grey PVC. There are two separate lighting circuits. Recently I have noticed a green tenacious substance seeping out from a number of light switches (particularly on the two-way circuit to the hallway). On closer inspection this seems to be coming from out of the cable itself. Is this a chemical reaction between the copper and PVC, or caused by something else?

A This happens to some cable installed in the 1965–1970 era. Although the outer sheathing is PVC, the inner red and black sheathing on the conductors was a different plastic, known as 'capathene', and it does seem that it reacts with the copper wire to produce a green runny liquid. It is likely to be happening on all the cabling, but will be most noticeable on the light switch cables, as these drop down from the ceiling. You should get the cabling checked by an NICEIC-registered electrician.

SENSITIVE CIRCUIT BREAKERS

Q **My friend, who is eighty-eight years old, lives alone and is registered blind. He has had numerous instances of a 'trip switch' operating when a light bulb blows. This means he has to grope his way to the consumer unit, open it and feel along the switch knobs for the one that needs to be reset. Is this not evidence that these switches are excessively sensitive, and is there any way of overcoming the problem?**

A Miniature circuit breakers (MCBs) in the consumer unit, and the even more sensitive residual current circuit breaker (RCCB) next to the meter, are there for one main reason, which is safety. When a light bulb blows, pieces of the broken filament can fall across the conductors, causing a surge of power which may cause overheating and a fire risk in some other part of the circuit. It is worth noting that light bulbs are designed to hang down, from ceiling fittings, in which case the pieces of filament usually fall harmlessly into the bottom of the bulb without tripping the circuit breakers. The problem is far more likely to occur with wall lights and table lamps in which the bulbs face upwards. Also, good quality British Standard bulbs have built-in fuses, which should burn out at a lower current than that which trips the circuit breaker; cheap imported bulbs do not have these fuses, so the only protection is the circuit breaker.

If these suggestions do not solve the problem then your friend may consider having an emergency lighting circuit installed, which would come on when the main circuit fails. Seek advice from an NICEIC-registered electrician [ELECTRICS].

EXPENSIVE LAMPS

Q **About a year ago I installed three sets of lights in my house, each with nine bulbs. These are the 240 volt version of the halogen-type lights that are so fashionable. The advantage of the 240 V version was quick installation and no need to put a transformer in the ceiling. The disadvantage has become apparent in that the bulbs blow frequently and cost £8.99 a go. In fact it is cheaper to buy a complete new light fitting with three bulbs included than to buy one replacement bulb! Could you advise me where I might buy 50 watt, 240 volt GU10 bulbs wholesale?**

A My local electrical wholesalers sell GU10 bulbs for £3.50 each plus VAT (£3.25 each if you buy a pack of fifteen). Look in the Yellow Pages under 'Electrical Supplies Wholesalers'.

Any out-of-the-ordinary type of bulb will sell at an inflated price in a supermarket or high street retailers. I have seen screw-in 40W reading-lamp spots on sale for £2.85 (packed in individual blister packs) when I know they can be bought for around 60p at an electrical supplier. Similarly, 15W screw-in 'pygmy' lamps for cooker hoods and under-worktop fittings cost 99p in the shops, but 25p from electrical suppliers. The trick is to buy in bulk, and not to be afraid to ask advice from the guys at the trade counter. It also helps if you know the trade parlance – for example you want 'lamps', not 'bulbs' (lamps are for lighting; bulbs are for growing). Screw-in Continental lamps are called ES (Edison screw – either large or small), and conventional British-style lamps are called BC (bayonet cap).

And anyone contemplating fitting halogen lighting from scratch should consider the cost of the replacement lamps – the low-voltage variety are usually cheaper, which makes up for the extra initial cost of the transformers. (Plus, low-voltage lights can be used safely in showers and bathrooms.)

DOWNLIGHTERS AND CONDENSATION

Q I have recently had a new shower room built (en suite to the top-floor master bedroom) and was dismayed to find, after only a week, water stains appearing on the plasterboard ceiling. Upon going up into the loft, I found the whole space dripping with condensation. There is white mould growing on the rafters, and water is literally dripping off the felt between the rafters. A surveyor friend says that the shower-room ceiling should have incorporated a vapour barrier to stop water vapour getting into the loft, but it seems likely to me that the moisture is rising up around the bulbs of the downlighters, and it says in the instructions for these that they should never be covered. Is there any solution to this problem, or does it mean that downlighters are not suitable for bathrooms?

A It would have been a good idea to incorporate a vapour barrier but, as you point out, this would be pretty ineffective if the water vapour was able to escape around the downlighter bulbs. There are special sealed downlighters made specifically for wet rooms, but ordinary downlighters also come in a wide range of styles – some of them are open around the bulb, like yours, notably the 'eye ball' type with a moveable directional spot bulb. In this case, the heat of the bulb is likely to create a convection current and actually draw moist air up into the loft, like a flue. In other types of downlighter the bulb fitting is integral with the surround and these will present less of a gap for the water vapour to escape. With luck, you may be able to find some of the latter which are a similar size to the ones you have to replace, and so avoid having to make new holes. In any event, it sounds as though you need much more efficient air extraction in the shower room (see CONDENSATION), and you will also need to look at the ventilation in the roof space (see ROOFS).

DOWNLIGHTERS AND CEILING FIRE RESISTANCE

Q I have discovered another problem with downlighters – that cutting the holes in the plasterboard apparently compromises the fire resistance of the ceiling. I am in the process of converting a house into three flats, which means the separating ceilings must have a one-hour fire rating. The building-control officer says that cutting holes in the plasterboard for downlighters weakens the integrity of the ceiling, and he will not permit them.

A Low-voltage downlighters cut into ceilings are all the rage with interior designers and architects, but few of them consider the implications for fire safety (or noise or moisture transmission) of cutting 65mm holes all over the ceiling to fit them in. Fortunately, some manufacturers are grappling with the problem. Electro-Technik's 'Fire Safe' downlighters, for example, have been tested and found to preserve the required half-hour fire resistance in houses and one-hour fire resistance between flats, and are also claimed to stop sound and moisture transmission through ceilings [ELECTRICS].

Downlighters are very popular but they can compromise fire safety and sound insulation.

DOWNLIGHTER FIRE HAZARD

Q Low-voltage downlighters can actually start fires. In old houses, the space between ceiling and floorboards is often liable to periodic inhabitation by rodents. The material that they use for their nests – scraps of paper, hair, dried vegetation, etc. – is highly flammable. When shown a low-voltage downlighter by the designer revamping my kitchen I was alarmed enough to carry out a test. It did not take long before smoke was rising from the scraps of rodent bedding with which I had covered the (normally concealed) top of a downlighter. Needless to say, I refused to countenance their fitting.

A You are right to be concerned. Low-voltage downlighters are currently in vogue and they are being fitted in their thousands in every conceivable situation. But few people realize just how hot they get in the part of the fitting that is hidden above the ceiling, and that this may create a fire risk. Where downlighters are fitted in top-floor ceilings the loft insulation should be removed from at least a 150mm radius around them, and care should be taken that stored goods do not come into contact with them. Where loose granular (vermiculite) insulation has been poured between the joists, the top of the downlighter should be covered with a fire-proof enclosure (inverted terracotta flower pots are one answer). In downstairs ceilings similar precautions should be taken; if it is not possible to access the ceiling void by lifting floorboards from above, then there are flexible downlighter fire-protection covers that can be pushed up through the hole from below (e.g. Tenmat [ELECTRICS]).

But obviously many downlighters are just pushed up into ceiling voids without any precautions and, as you have pointed out, they can get very hot, and present a fire risk. I am afraid it will take a few disasters before anything is done to regulate the use of these trendy light fittings.

MODERN LIGHT FITTINGS

Q We live in a modern house with loop-in lighting circuits, i.e. all wiring connections take place in ceiling roses or batten holders. We want to replace the batten holders in our kitchen with spotlights, but every spotlight assembly I have looked at has only live, neutral and earth connections, but no terminals to connect the loop-in, loop-out and switch cables. What is the best way of wiring these spotlights? I have been told by some to use a terminal block, but this doesn't sound very safe to me, as it would just be hanging in space, i.e. connections would not be in a fireproof enclosure. I cannot alter the cabling easily as it is not readily accessible.

A Most modern homes are wired in this way – called three-plate wiring – where all the connections are made at the lighting point. Yet very few manufacturers consider this in the design of their light fittings. So the new fitting comes with connectors for the earth, neutral and switched live conductor, to operate the light, but no provision for terminating the permanent live conductors which, although they do not connect to the light fitting, must all be connected together to carry the supply on to the next lighting point.

Regulations and good practice require that all connections are made in an 'appropriate enclosed accessory', which is often not easy, given that there is very little space in the mounting. Some fittings come with strip connectors and instructions that clearly encourage the installer to push them up into the ceiling void above the fitting, which is not advisable. Strip connectors (or 'choc block', as they are known) may be used provided they can be enclosed in the housing or mounting of the light and that they are of good quality – i.e. either Bakelite or self-extinguishing PVC (you can always check this with a match). But if there is insufficient room, then you will have to fit a small four-terminal joint box in the ceiling void. These can be as small as 50mm in diameter, which means they can be pushed through the hole made for a downlighter, for example. With some types of fittings, it may be possible to adapt them by screwing them to a circular-type pattress (like you get on a pull-cord switch) to house the connections.

HALOGEN LIGHTS

Q What are the advantages and disadvantages of mains halogen and low-voltage halogen lamps?

A Halogen lamps give a very white light and come in mains voltage or low voltage, usually 12V. The main differences are cost. The low-voltage lamps are cheaper, but you have the initial additional cost of a low-voltage transformer. There is a wider variety of fittings to choose from in the low-voltage range, and if the transformer is fitted remotely then they can be used in more situations where mains voltage would not be acceptable, such as bath/shower rooms or saunas. As far as lamp-life and running costs are concerned, I suspect there is little difference.

FUSE ALWAYS BLOWING

Q We have a peculiar problem with our downstairs lights. Every twelve to fourteen weeks the 5 amp fuse blows on the lighting circuit. We replace it, but it blows again, several times on the same day. On two occasions when this has happened we have engaged a qualified electrician to locate the fault. He has put his meter on the fuse box and told us that there is no fault indicated. He says it may be due to condensation or dampness entering one of the lights or switches, and this is the reason why the fault is only occurring every twelve to fourteen weeks.

A The first thing is to do a rough calculation to check that the lighting circuit is not overloaded. The formula watts = volts × amps indicates that a 5A circuit on a 240V supply should be able to carry 1,200W – equivalent to twelve 100W lamps or twenty 60W lamps. If you are at or near this limit, then the fuse wire will be getting hot, and gradually burning out. If the fuse wire is tarnished and dull looking, and if, when it blows, the ends remain intact, but a little blob burns out in the middle, then overloading is very likely the cause. If, however, the fuse explodes with a bang, and burns out along its whole length, then a localized electrical fault is probably to blame.

Dampness or condensation could well be the cause, and you will have to do a bit of detective work by inspecting the fittings in the bathroom and kitchen, and outside lights. Any fitting that is faulty will usually show evidence of scorching, or a black carbon trace where dampness has allowed the electricity to short-circuit between the terminals. Obviously you should isolate the circuit at the fuse board before you open up any electrical fittings.

EMERGENCY POWER SUPPLIES

Q We are told that flooding, gales and blackouts may become more common. What are the practicalities of installing some form of generator-based emergency light and power supply that would enable family life to go on – albeit in a reduced way – until proper power is restored?

A Petrol-powered generators have become remarkably small and quiet in recent years, and if you live in an area prone to power cuts then it may make sense to keep one in the garage for emergency lighting using extension cables. Prices start at around £400 for a 1kW model. The other main 'essential' is to power the fridge and freezer, which may need more power (the compressor on a chest freezer may use only 500W, but it needs a higher surge of power every time it kicks in). It would also be useful to be able to power the central-heating pump and boiler (without which the gas or fuel oil are of little use) but this would require wiring-in to the existing house electrical system. You should consult a qualified electrician for advice about installing the necessary switching gear. At the upper end, a 10kW diesel generator with automatic start which will power the whole house could cost between £6,000 and £10,000. The market leaders are Honda [ELECTRICS].

PLUMBING, HEATING AND DRAINAGE

In a temperate climate like Britain's, homes need heating for three-quarters of the year. And since over 70 per cent of us own our homes, or are responsible for the heating in the homes we rent, it is no wonder that when the heating goes wrong, we are prone to being held to ransom by the trade. The fact that almost every house or flat has its own central-heating system – with boiler, radiators and controls – is one reason why Britain is so inefficient in its use of energy. Other European countries make much better use of energy, with blocks of flats and even whole streets sharing heating systems.

The majority of us use natural gas as a fuel, which heats water in a boiler, to be pumped round a wet radiator circuit. Oil, solid fuel and LPG (liquefied petroleum gas, or propane) are also used to fuel the same type of heating system. The principles are very simple, but the equipment gets more complicated by the year. It's very similar to cars. The first few cars I owned were noisy, dirty and not particularly efficient. But when they went wrong – which was often – I could usually open the bonnet, spot the problem and fix it with a screwdriver and a pair of pliers. My current car is quiet, clean and hardly ever goes wrong. But when it does, I open the bonnet and I haven't a clue how to fix it. It has to be towed into a garage where they plug it into a computer which diagnoses the fault, and the remedy is often the wholesale replacement of a huge chunk of electronics, costing hundreds of pounds.

Where old central-heating boilers differ from old cars, though, is in the fact that they don't wear out as quickly. A boiler consists of a cast-iron vessel with a burner underneath it. The water is circulated through it and around the radiator system by a separate electric-powered pump. So there are no moving parts in the boiler itself, and nothing much to go wrong. The old pilot lights were pretty infallible and cost maybe £40 per year to run, but this was deemed to be wasteful, so electronic ignition systems were introduced. When these go wrong the parts have to be replaced, at a cost of maybe £200, or five years' worth of pilot-light fuel.

Nevertheless, the industry is geared up to 'upgrade' the nation's boilers, which means selling new, complicated boilers with lots more electronic circuitry, rather than keeping the old ones going. At the forefront of this sales push are British Gas Services, formerly known as the Gas Board, but now privately owned by the Centrica Corporation. British Gas Services operate the

Three Star Service contracts, whereby customers pay an annual fee as a kind of insurance against breakdowns. Except that many readers report that when they call the engineers in, they are told either that their problem is not covered under the terms of the Three Star Service contract, or that the boiler is beyond repair because parts are no longer available. An increasing number of readers report being told this in the course of their annual Three Star boiler-safety check.

This idea that boilers can become 'obsolete', or that 'parts are no longer available', is disputed by some independent gas engineers, who point out that just because a particular manufacturer no longer supplies original catalogue-numbered parts, this does not mean that equally effective replacement spares are not available from other sources. Pressure switches, pumps, fans and timers, for example, are all pretty much standard components which will fit a variety of appliances. Potterton may no longer supply a cut-to-length section of asbestos rope for the door seal of a 1969 floor-standing boiler, but the equivalent modern material is available by the reel from plumbers' merchants.

Going back to the car analogy, it's like saying that a 1975 Ford Escort is beyond repair because Ford no longer manufacture replacement gear sticks. There are always replacement parts that will fit the bill – witness the huge number of Ford Escorts still being driven around.

The prices that British Gas Services quote for supplying and fitting a new boiler are in the region of £2,500 to £3,000 for a boiler whose trade price is nearer £600 (plus labour for fitting). The latest Building Regulations also stipulate that any new boiler must be accompanied by new efficient controls, including zoning controls, which pushes the price even higher.

So if you have trouble with your boiler, or are thinking of upgrading, then it is always best to get two or three estimates from independent CORGI-registered gas engineers before coming to a decision.

Apart from central-heating problems, most readers' queries concern poor water pressure, noisy plumbing systems, toilets that won't flush and leaking shower enclosures. These are all things that should be within the remit of any half-decent plumber, but unfortunately there are lots of guys calling themselves plumbers who don't seem to have a clue.

What to do if you are a Three Star Service customer, and you have had a letter from British Gas/Scottish Gas, telling you that the 'manufacturer has stopped making some of the spare parts'. Most boilers are put together using standard parts from a variety of third-party manufacturers, and these parts are usually easily available from specialist spares suppliers, if not from the boiler manufacturers themselves. In some instances, the only part that is 'unique' to a particular model is the boiler casing with the manufacturer's name stamped on it. (Note, however, that the casing can sometimes be important. 'Positive pressure' boilers, such as the Potterton Netaheat, can leak fumes into the room if the casing corrodes.)

If British Gas has told you that a particular part is unobtainable, the first step is to check this with the boiler manufacturer. Some of them are still carrying large stocks of spares, especially for models less than ten years old. Next, get a second opinion from an independent CORGI-registered gas engineer (look in the CORGI block advert under 'Gas Installers' in the Yellow Pages). An experienced gas engineer should know where to obtain parts anyway, but, more importantly, should advise you on whether your boiler is *worth* repairing. For example, if £250 worth of repairs will keep a boiler running for another ten years, then this works out at £25 per year, and is worth doing, but if a £100 repair is needed on a boiler that will only last another year or two, then it may be wise to think about a replacement, since a decent new boiler can now be bought for as little as £600.

If your gas engineer cannot find a particular spare part, then try the local spares firms that advertise under 'Central Heating Services' in the Yellow Pages, or the following companies, which operate mail-order services:

- Curzon Components, 0870 510 3030
- FMT Ltd, 01245 357993
- HRPC, 01772 819671 (parts availability can also be checked on their website, www.hrpc.co.uk)
- Thermagas, 01257 275080
- In addition, Peter Porter Electronics Ltd (01920 871711) sell refurbished components, which they will exchange for your old components, at a considerable cost saving. They will also repair damaged components, including electronics and printed circuit boards.

If you order parts yourself, then you will need to give the supplier as much detail as possible, i.e. the exact boiler model and Gas Council number (GC:—:—-:— on a data plate somewhere on the casing). You should not attempt to fit parts yourself, but should always engage a CORGI-registered engineer to do the work.

What to do if your boiler really needs replacing. If you have decided that you really want a new boiler, or if a trusted independent gas engineer has convinced you that your existing boiler is not worth repairing, then you should think carefully about which replacement model to choose. The government (through the Energy Saving Trust) is promoting new condensing boilers, and the manufacturers are making some outrageous claims about these – '15 per cent more efficient' is a common one. These figures are almost certainly over-optimistic, and based upon the manufacturers' own best-case laboratory test results, rather than actual use in people's homes.

The official test results can be found on the website www.sedbuk.com (Seasonal Efficiency of Domestic Boilers UK), and the difference between the lower end of the condensing boilers list (83 per cent) and the most efficient of the conventional boilers (82.1 per cent) is negligible. And what the list omits to measure is the poor reliability of condensing boilers, and the frequency of repairs needed to keep them running. Some independent gas engineers who have installed condensing boilers say they have had to return three or four times in the first few months to attend to breakdowns and replace parts. As one of them said, 'Every time I go back to fix it, driving my diesel van, and stopping for a bacon sandwich on the way, it does more damage to the environment than their old boiler did in five years.'

Condensing boilers are only more efficient if they run at 54°C, which is cooler than the 60–80°C of a conventional boiler. So to distribute the same amount of heat around the house, they need bigger pipes and larger radiators. Once the reliability problems have been sorted out, condensing boilers may be something for the future – if they are built into new houses, with new radiators, as part of a designed heating system. But they are definitely not something to be added on to an existing central-heating system as a replacement for a conventional boiler.

Combination or 'Combi' boilers are also heavily promoted. These are basically glorified versions of the old 'geysers' or instant gas water heaters. Most Combi systems do not have sepa-

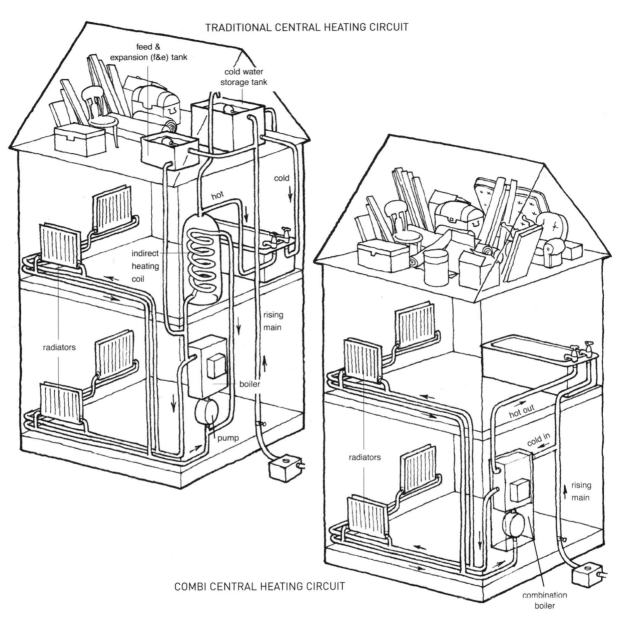

TRADITIONAL CENTRAL HEATING CIRCUIT

feed & expansion (f&e) tank

cold water storage tank

cold

hot

indirect heating coil

rising main

radiators

boiler

pump

COMBI CENTRAL HEATING CIRCUIT

radiators

hot out

cold in

rising main

combination boiler

rate hot-water storage tanks, but rely on heating the mains cold water as it flows through the boiler. In winter, when the incoming mains water is very cold, it can take a long time to run a bath. Combis can be useful in one-bedroom flats, or where there is no loft space for water tanks, but they are not generally suitable for larger flats or houses. There *are* new Combi-heated systems with higher outputs, and various forms of pressurised hot water storage tanks, but they are expensive. If you have an existing conventional system with a tank in the loft, there is usually nothing to be gained by replacing your boiler with a Combi.

My independent gas engineers recommend traditional gas boilers, and amongst the models they prefer are the Glow-Worm Micron, Potterton Suprima, Ideal Classic and (for a floor-standing model) the Ideal Mexico. These all come in a range of sizes, and you need to choose the one that will match the size of your house and the number of radiators.

PLUMBING
MAGNETIC/ELECTRONIC LIMESCALE INHIBITORS

Q We live in a hard-water area, and a plumber has recommended that we install a device which he called a limescale inhibitor. We understand it is fitted to the mains water pipe and by magnetism it causes the lime particles to separate out, thus giving us softer water. It sounds like a good idea – or are we being conned?

A Instead of installing a proper ion-exchange water softener, which requires plumbing in and the monthly application of a dose of salt, manufacturers of these devices advocate cutting into the mains pipe and inserting a chrome tube containing a magnet. There are also electrical versions which involve wrapping coils of cable around the pipe.

The companies who market this equipment produce lots of glossy brochures with artists' impressions of pipes, water, wires and coloured blue and red arrows showing how their patented electromagnetic waves will save your immersion heater. They are not so keen on producing independent research supporting their inventions, though, because there isn't any. Well, perhaps – in anticipation of the abusive letters that the manufacturers of these devices will be writing to me – I had better qualify that.

Work at Cranfield University has shown that, under certain conditions, some magnetic water conditioners do reduce limescale formation. The bad news is that nobody knows exactly what these conditions are, or why the devices work when they do work. There are theories, but none of them tells the whole story, and no experiments have stood up to the test of scientific repeatability.

What is known is that the devices can be made to work in closed industrial processes – i.e. where the same water is recirculated at a known flow rate and constantly remagnetized. These conditions do not exist in the average home's plumbing system, where the device is fitted to the incoming pipe, and the water passes through it once only, and at a varying rate of flow.

The manufacturers' literature does not make this clear. And it often makes selective use of the research by reproducing data from the experiments which worked, but omitting the data from those which did not. On the other hand, those who market the devices claim that British Water, the trade association, is dominated by companies which sell ion-exchange water softeners, and there are even dark mutterings that favourable research is being deliberately suppressed by the salt manufacturers. Skulduggery indeed in the murky world of water treatment.

Many readers ask whether these magnetic or electrical water conditioners actually work, and the answer has to be . . . maybe. But since they cost between £50 and £150, and since proper ion-exchange softeners now cost as little as £200, it would seem sensible to pay the extra and buy something that is proven to work. And, as a footnote, some readers have suggested that in cases where electromagnetic water conditioners do stop limescale formation, they may do this by causing the inside of the copper pipe to gradually dissolve. This would have the twin effects of gradually weakening the pipes – causing possible leaks – and raising the level of dissolved copper in the drinking water. Since raised copper in tap water has recently been linked with Alzheimer's disease, this is possibly not a risk worth taking.

If your only concern is to stop limescale forming on your immersion heater element and bath taps, then the simplest option is to dose your water with phosphate by suspending a bag of Fernox Limescale Preventer in the cold-water tank. These cost around £8 and last for six months.

WATER SOFTENERS – BLUE STAINING

Q Since we installed a water softener, water drops left in baths and sinks have been tinged with blue, which we understand is due to copper sulphate being leached from the pipes. We have slightly reduced the hardness setting on the softener, but this has not solved the problem. Is there a solution apart from bleeding untreated water into the system (as recommended by the manufacturer), which rather defeats the object, one would have thought?

A Soft water dissolves salts, which is why rainwater (soft) extracts calcium and magnesium salts from the ground it passes through to become hard. So if you have corrosion within your pipe system – possibly due to reaction between mixed metals (copper and steel, or copper and zinc) – then the softened water will be washing it out and depositing it on the bath and basin. It sounds as though your water may be *too* soft, and the manufacturer's suggestion is the correct one – to increase the hardness by mixing a proportion of unsoftened water into the supply. This does not defeat the object, but adjusts the hardness/softness to a suitable level, where you get the advantages of softened water, but not the blue staining problem. It is simple to bleed unsoftened water into the supply, by opening the bypass valve a little. You should aim for around 50mg/l hardness, and the manufacturer should advise you on how to test for this.

The trade association British Water publish ten free fact sheets on all aspects of domestic water treatment [PLUMBING, HEATING AND DRAINAGE].

NOISY PIPES

Q We recently moved to a refurbished 1930s house with polished floorboards. When the heating is on, we hear a high-pitched ringing noise, presumably from the pipes. Can we remedy this by carpeting the room?

A Central-heating systems make noises for a lot of reasons, but bare floorboards should not be one of them, and whilst carpeting the room may muffle the sound, it would be better to fix the problem at source. Noise can be caused by thermostatic radiator valves, or may be due to the circulating pump being on too high a setting. If either of these is the cause, then a replacement variable-speed pump may be the answer. Ringing noises can also be caused by a small blob of loose solder running up and down inside the pipes when the pump is circulating the heating water.

Pipes can also be noisy if they are not clipped securely enough to the joists, or if they are clipped too securely. (Pipes need to be supported but also allowed to expand and contract.) A common problem occurs where pipes have been run across shallow notches in floor joists, and the floorboards have been screwed down tightly on to them. So it would pay to do a bit of under-floor investigation before you pay for that new carpet.

NOISY CISTERN

Q Is there such a thing as a silent-filling domestic lavatory cistern? My twenty-year-old model needed a new valve and ballcock. The old one filled through a silencer tube, but the plumber fitting the new valve told me that it was designed not to take a silencer tube, and that this was illegal anyway – something to do with back-siphonage. The new system is much noisier. Is there any legal remedy?

A Silencer tubes direct the incoming water below the surface, rather than allowing it to splash down from a height. The problem with back-siphonage is that should there be an interruption to the mains supply, then it is theoretically possible for the water in the cistern to be siphoned back through the tube, down the rising main and thence to emerge through next door's kitchen tap. However, there are ways of getting around this problem, either by using a collapsible polyethylene tube, or by having a small hole drilled in the tube above water level. Examples are the Torbeck and the Fluidmaster, which both comply with the Water Regulations, and are available from plumbers' merchants.

COWBOY PLUMBING FIRM

Q After a week away during freezing weather, I came home to find water cascading down from the loft. I called an emergency plumbing company from the Yellow Pages. The plumber charged me £180 plus VAT and said he had replaced two sections of split pipework and two tank connectors. But when I went up to check, I couldn't see anything that looked as if it had been replaced. It looks as though I have been 'had'. But the leak was real enough – how has this con man repaired the split pipe, and should I be expecting fresh leaks any time when his bodged repair fails?

A It is unusual for pipes to 'split' or 'burst' when the water freezes, although these are common expressions. Water expands as it freezes, and what usually happens is that the expansion pushes the copper pipes out of the compression fittings connecting them to the water tanks. It is often possible to push them back into place and retighten them, and it sounds as though this is what your plumber has done. You should contact your local authority trading standards officer to complain about the fraud, and in future remember not to pay for any new parts or materials unless you have actually seen the old ones removed, and been given an itemized receipt.

WATER HAMMER

Q I live in a semi-detached house, and have started to suffer from water hammer at various times of the day which seems to affect all the pipes in the house. We are not using the water when this occurs, but find that if we turn on the cold-water tap for a few minutes it stops. The main water supply comes from across the street to a stopcock under the pavement and a spur then goes to our house and the neighbour's house by separate pipes. My neighbour says she does not have any problems but I am doubtful of this.

A Water hammer can travel along any interconnected pipework. It is quite possible that you are hearing the effects of a faulty ball valve in your neighbour's property, which should really have its own stop valve and service pipe. It could also be due to a loose 'jumper' in a stop valve somewhere along the system. If the source of the noise cannot be traced, a skilled plumber can insert an expansion vessel or a 'dead' vertical length of pipe, containing air, in order to absorb the pressure fluctuations causing the water hammer.

NOISY WASTE PIPE

Q My kitchen sink, when the water is let out, makes a loud 'glug glug glug', which goes on and on. Could anything be done to stop that?

A This usually happens when the waste pipe to the soil and vent stack is too long, or at too steep an angle. (The maximum length is 1.7m, and the slope no more than one in ten.) Or maybe the soil and vent stack has been blocked at the top by a bird's nest. What happens is that the water flowing out through the waste pipe acts like a piston, lowering the pressure and drawing air in through the trap (the 'U' bend) under the sink. It is also possible that a length of unsupported plastic waste pipe has sagged, allowing water to pool in it, and the noise is caused by air being drawn through this.

POOR WATER PRESSURE

Q We have very poor mains water pressure, which means that only one cold-water tap can be used at a time. In addition, since we live in a bungalow, the pressure from the storage tank in the loft is minimal. It takes twenty-five minutes plus to fill a bath, and showering is interfered with if someone turns on a kitchen tap. Plumbers have suggested raising the storage tank in the loft, and/or a complicated system involving a series of electric pumps and thermostatic shower controls. Is there nothing more straightforward that could improve the water pressure?

A Poor mains water pressure results in a limited flow, which means that only one tap can be used at a time. This situation can be improved by using a water-pressurized storage system. Combined with an unvented direct hot-water cylinder, this can improve the flow to both cold and hot taps without the need for raised header tanks or electric booster pumps. For further information contact Dualstream [PLUMBING, HEATING AND DRAINAGE].

POOR WATER FLOW

Q I have had the water company and plumbers out to try and find out why the flow of water from cold taps reduces when more than one tap or appliance is being used. The standing pressure from the mains supply measures 5 bar. It has been suggested that the problem is that we are supplied from the mains by a half-inch copper pipe.

A 5 bar is a very high pressure for a mains supply, so it certainly sounds as if the problem is with flow rather than pressure – i.e. the bore of the pipe is too narrow. Whilst this will not affect the standing pressure reading, it means that there is simply not enough room inside the pipes for the water to get through quickly enough to feed more than one outlet at a time. It may be caused by scaling, or other obstruction in the pipes.

LOW FLOW FROM NEW TAPS

Q I recently changed my kitchen taps from the conventional 15mm pipe single hot and cold to a mixer tap with smaller bore supply pipes, and the hot-water pressure is now much lower. Cold-water supply is from the mains, and the hot water is from a header tank in the loft. The hot-water pressure has remained good to the bathroom basin tap, which has a 15mm supply pipe. I do not understand why having a different-size pipe should lower the pressure. Is there any way of overcoming this problem?

A Many kitchen mixer taps are of European origin and have 10mm or even 8mm feeds, soldered on to 15mm tails for the British market. Reducing the pipe diameter does not lower the pressure, but it does lessen the flow, which is especially noticeable with the small vertical head of pressure that you will have from a roof tank in a bungalow. There is no solution, short of an electric booster pump.

SHOWERS – PLASTERBOARD

Q I am having a shower cubicle built in a corner of my bathroom, the internal walls of which are constructed of plasterboard on timber studding. Thus two of the cubicle sides would be of plasterboard (suitably tiled) and two of glass (side and door). But from your comments it seems this is not a good idea, so could you please let me know why plasterboard is unsuitable and suggest how this problem might be overcome?

A Ordinary plasterboard consists of a slab of plaster of Paris sandwiched between two sheets of paper. Both of these materials absorb water readily and so are unsuitable for shower cubicles. The water will always be absorbed through the grouting between the tiles and will wet and soften the plasterboard underneath. After a couple of years the tiles will fall off, exposing spectacular outbreaks of mould growth. Shower cubicles are better lined with one of the proprietary brands of lining boards (Knauf Aquapanel or similar). The only plasterboard suitable is British Gypsum's moisture-resistant (MR) board.

NOISY SHOWER PUMP

Q Some time ago we had our bathroom modernized and, because of poor water pressure, had a power shower installed. We now seem to be getting continual noise from the shower pump; there is a whirring and knocking noise as though it is trying to function although not in use. The refurbishment is now out of guarantee and the company that did it do not want to look into the problem. Can you offer any solution?

A Shower booster pumps are activated by flow switches which detect water running through the pipes and complete an electrical circuit to start the pump. If the pump is situated higher than the hot water cylinder, then convection currents ('parasitic circulation') can sometimes fool the flow switches into trying to turn the pumps on.

ONE-PIECE SHOWER ENCLOSURE

Q We stayed in a mobile home in France this summer. It had a shower with a one-piece plastic interior lining – wall, floor, ceiling. It didn't look at all bad, and the long-term advantages of cleaning and maintenance must be tremendous when compared with tiles, grouting and caulking. Is this kind of product available for domestic use here?

A Leaking showers are a perennial problem. The typical British version has a shower tray set into a corner, with two sides enclosed by a glass or plastic door system and the other two sides tiled and grouted. The weakest point is always the joint between the tiles and the shower tray, and the usual thin smear of silicone mastic is unable to cope with the movement when an adult stands in the shower.

One-piece shower enclosures are available in the UK – enquire at any plumbers' merchants – but they are expensive, starting from around £700. Self-assembly shower cubicles with three walls and a door are also a good design for avoiding leaks, and cut out the need to tile the walls. I have never seen them on sale in the UK, although a US model can allegedly be ordered from B&Q warehouses, again for around £700. They can also be bought in European DIY stores from around £300, including tray, enclosure and shower taps. You can easily bring one back on a roof rack.

SHOWERS – SILICONE SEAL

Q **You have said that the weakest point in a shower is always the joint between the tiles and the shower tray, and that the usual thin smear of silicone mastic is unable to cope. Is there nothing that one can use that will do the job satisfactorily or is there a particular mastic or method of applying it that would give optimum results?**

A Silicone mastics will absorb around 20 per cent movement, and the weight of an adult on a plastic or resin shower tray on a timber floor may move it by 3–4mm, so the mastic joint has to be at least 20mm deep. The mastic joint should be as thick as it is deep, so you need a 20mm-square bead of mastic all round. The joint should be clean and dry before application and, if necessary, treated with the manufacturer's recommended primer. Shower trays and enclosures should be thoroughly cleaned with methylated spirits before application. Very few builders follow these basic principles.

RE-ENAMELLING BATHS

Q **I was intending to replace my large cast-iron bath, but have heard that it might be re-enamelled. Does this work, and what would be a reasonable cost?**

A Enamelling is a factory process which involves heating the metal to a very high temperature and melting a new vitreous surface on to it. This cannot be carried out in situ, although some firms claim to be able to use a heat process to re-enamel small areas, to repair chips and cracks. What is usually advertised as 're-enamelling' is the application of a two-part epoxy resin coating over the whole bath. It will never be as good as the real thing, but if you like your existing cast-iron bath and would like to keep it in place, then it may be worth considering. Prices are from around £150. Try Renubath [PLUMBING, HEATING AND DRAINAGE].

MOULD ON SHOWER SEALANT

Q **I have resealed round my shower tray and bath with a silicone sealant which incorporates a fungicide. Nevertheless black mould has reappeared. The tray and bath are both made from plastic. Is there any proprietary treatment, safe to use on plastic, which will remove it and prevent further invasion?**

A Mould will always grow on shower sealants. It can be killed with strong bleach, e.g. HG's mould spray, from plumbers' merchants. Once white silicone has been stained, though, it is very difficult to clean up.

HEATING

HEATING – ELECTRIC

Q Is there such a thing as electric-fired central heating? Not Economy 7 or storage heaters but something that does exactly the same as a gas-fired system?

A Electric-flow boilers do exactly the same job as gas- or oil-fired boilers, heating primary water which is pumped round a conventional wet radiator circuit. It is claimed that this is more efficient, and more controllable, than other forms of electric heating, and allows conventional central heating to be easily installed in homes with no access to mains gas. One supplier is Electroheat, whose boiler prices start at around £500 [PLUMBING, HEATING AND DRAINAGE].

RELATIVE COSTS OF FUELS

Q We heat our house by a modern conventional oil-fired boiler and, up to now, our domestic hot water too. However, the price of oil has increased from 10.5p to 22.7p per litre in the past three years. Standard rate electricity has remained constant at 6.4p per unit. Would we be better off heating our water by electric immersion heater or is it still better to use oil, given that the boiler is already working to heat the house?

A Relative costs of heating by different fuels are difficult to work out, as the suppliers' invoices record their calorific values in different ways. Prices also vary in different parts of the country, and between different suppliers. The standard 'unit' of electric power is the kilowatt-hour (kWh), which will heat a one-bar radiant electric fire for one hour, and costs around 6p. Off-peak electricity (e.g. Economy 7) costs between 3 and 4p per kWh, but usually with a higher standing charge, and is used with night-storage heaters, which many people find inconvenient. Natural gas piped into the house costs around 1.3p per kWh, but gas boilers may be only 65–75 per cent efficient, giving a truer cost of nearer 2p. Heating oil and LPG (propane), which are delivered by tanker and stored in tanks outside the house, provide roughly 10 kWh per litre, so at current prices this is around 2.3p per kWh (say 3p allowing for boiler efficiency), still slightly cheaper than off-peak electricity and half the price of standard-rate electricity.

Anyone thinking of switching from one fuel to another, or considering upgrading to a new boiler, needs to calculate the payback period for the costs of the new installation. In most cases installation will cost thousands of pounds, and this will take many years, or even decades, to show a profit. So it is usually better to stick with the system you've got, unless you have a very large house and/or very high heating bills, and can accurately calculate that a new installation will start saving you money within five years.

COMBI BOILERS

Q After twenty trouble-free years with a 'bog-standard' indirect gas-fired central-heating system we are about to have a change, in order to recapture the efficiency of our system when it was younger. All we hear is combi – combi – combi, extolling the virtues as being 'you only pay for the gas you use, the radiators heat up quicker and no need for a hot-water tank'! But we cannot get any real advice regarding the advantages of the traditional

Combi boilers are only suitable for small flats, not bigger properties.

indirect system, apart from the fact that you can use a power shower off an indirect system but not a combi system. What are the pros and cons of the indirect and combi systems?

A Combination, or 'combi', boilers normally allow hot water to be drawn from only one outlet at a time. So if you are taking a shower and someone else turns on the kitchen tap, then you are in trouble. Also, in winter, when the incoming mains water is colder, you will get less of a flow of hot water, and it can take ages to run a bath. There should be no difference in the speed with which the two different types of boiler heat up the radiators. Some heating engineers try to sell combis because they are easy for them to install, but in your case you already have a cold-water storage tank and hot-water cylinder, so I can see no advantages in a combi boiler at all. And before you rush out to buy a new boiler, it may be worth asking a CORGI-registered gas installer for an opinion on the existing one.

COMBI BOILER – SLOW BATH FILLING

Q **I have recently had a new central-heating system installed, using a combination boiler instead of the ordinary type used previously. I have now found that the water pressure is extremely low (it takes ages to fill a bath). The plumber says this is because a combination boiler takes its water directly from the mains and the mains pressure is low (although, apparently, within the guidelines). Is there anything that can be done to increase the pressure?**

A Check that your plumber has used 22mm pipe for the gas supply, rather than 15mm, and check the gas rate at the meter. Combi boilers need a bigger flow of gas for heating the hot water than they do for the central heating. But apart from that, there's not much you can do, unless you buy a bigger boiler. Combi boilers rarely provide a good flow of hot water, and they are only really suitable for small flats with showers, not bigger properties with baths.

COMBI BOILER WON'T FIRE

Q The central-heating radiators in my one-bed basement flat were hot at the bottom but cold at the top. Following a friend's advice I bought a 'bleeding key' from a plumbers' merchants and bled the air out of them. They are now completely cold and the boiler refuses to fire up under any circumstances. What have I done wrong?

A Combi boiler systems do not have a header tank but rely on mains water pressure. What has probably happened is that there is a slight leak in one of the radiator valves which has allowed the pressure to drop. This is not unusual, and is not a disaster. You have done the right thing in bleeding the air out of the radiators. Now all you have to do is recharge the boiler up to working pressure. There should be a flexible metal hose somewhere around the pipework feeding the boiler, and opening up the valves at either end of this will allow mains water to flow into the system. Make sure you locate the water-pressure gauge before you start and turn the valves off when you reach 1 to 1.5 bar pressure (or whatever the manufacturer's instructions say).

CENTRAL HEATING WON'T WORK

Q We have just turned our central heating on for the first time since May, and the radiators stay cold. There does not seem to be any fault with the gas boiler, which is firing up and heating the hot water as usual. Is there likely to be a simple problem we could fix ourselves, without the expense of calling in a heating engineer?

A The fact that you have hot water indicates that both the boiler and circulating pump are probably OK. The most likely culprit is the motorized valve on the radiator circuit. These often get blocked with sludge during the inactivity of the summer months. Turn the boiler on, and find the motorized valve, which is a rectangular metal box about 75mm x 50mm x 50mm, usually somewhere near the pump. (If the pipes are hot either side of the valve, then it will be the one that controls the hot water – you need to locate the other one, which controls the radiators.) There should be a manual over-ride lever sticking out of the end, and if you slide this to one side or the other then the valve should open and there will be a gurgling noise as the water flows through. This is usually all that is needed to clear the blockage, but at some stage you should have the system drained down and refilled, using a corrosion-inhibiting additive.

CENTRAL HEATING WON'T TURN OFF

Q I have a baffling problem with my central-heating system, which my regular plumber is unable to diagnose. Whilst the heating usually switches on and off as ordered by the programmer, and usually responds to adjustments on the room thermostat, there are times when the boiler fires up for no apparent reason (e.g. in the middle of the night, or when the temperature is too warm for the thermostat to switch on). When this happens, the only way to stop the boiler running is to turn off the electrical switch which supplies it with mains power.

A The most likely cause is a defect in one of the motorized valves. These are fed with electric current via the programmer, and open up, or close off, parts of the system to allow hot water to flow through them (to heat either the hot-water cylinder, or zoned parts of the heating circuit), turning the boiler on in the process. Sometimes motorized valves can get jammed in the 'open' position, and feed current back to the boiler, which makes it fire up, even though the programmer is set to 'off', and the room thermostat is below ambient temperature. If your motorized valves are more than ten years old, then it is probably worth getting them replaced (about £40 each plus labour), rather than trying to fix them.

OVERFLOWING HEADER TANK

Q My boiler is regularly serviced by a qualified gas engineer, but the header tank has been gently overflowing for some months. The ballcock and valve assembly has been renewed, to no effect, and the engineer says he is mystified as to the cause.

A If there have been no other changes, then this may be caused by a blockage of either scale or sludge in part of the system. Overflowing also occurs if there is a corrosion hole in the secondary heating coil inside the hot-water cylinder. The head of pressure from the cold-water cistern will be pushing water through this hole into the central-heating circuit and causing an overflow from the 'f&e' (feed and expansion) tank. Check by turning off the mains feed to the cold-water cistern, leaving all the taps off, and seeing if the water level falls by the same amount as the water coming out of the overflow. The answer is to fit a new hot-water cylinder.

CORROSION INHIBITOR

Q How can I tell whether enough (or any) corrosion inhibitor has been added to my central-heating system? A British Gas saleswoman ran some water from a radiator into a glass and told me she thought that because the water was black, the system was sludged up, and that I would need to pay extra for a powerflush. But I am sure that the system was drained down, and a corrosion inhibitor added, when we had a new radiator installed in our bathroom two years ago.

A You cannot tell the condition of the system, or diagnose the presence of excessive sludge, from looking at the colour of the water. Even in a clean central-heating system, with corrosion inhibitor added, the water can still appear dark from dissolved oxides and residues. The presence of an inhibitor in the system water can be tested for by any heating engineer (e.g. by using a Fernox Protector test kit, which costs £15 to £20 for fifty tests, or a Sentinel X100 test kit, around £1 for two tests). Both can be used to test the concentration of the inhibiting chemical (sodium molybdenum), by collecting a little water from a radiator bleed valve, adding tablets and noting the colour. Betz Dearbon also offer a complete analysis for system water and mains water for around £10, which involves sending samples away for a laboratory report. Test kits can be bought from Plumb Center or Plumbase, or call 0151 420 9595 for stockists. Alternatively, a simple DIY test is to bleed some system water into a glass jar and drop in a couple of steel nails and a 1p coin (to simulate the metals in the heating system). If, after a month, the nails have gone rusty, then that will be what is happening to the inside of your radiators, too. If the nails remain clean, then the system has enough corrosion inhibitor in it.

PUTTING ADDITIVES IN COMBI SYSTEMS

Q I understand that in central-heating systems where steel radiators are connected by copper pipes it is advisable to add inhibitors to the water to slow down corrosion. How is the inhibitor fluid added to the combi boiler system?

A The corrosion is a result of electrochemical reaction between the two different metals. This corrosion is also responsible for the formation of sludge in the system, which can block radiators and clog circulating pumps. In a conventional wet central-heating circuit, inhibitor is poured into the feed-and-expansion tank ('header' tank) in the loft. A combination boiler operates on a sealed system with no header tank. The easiest way to introduce an inhibitor, or any other additive, into a combi system, is to inject a concentrate into one of the radiator vents. These are available from plumbers' suppliers, or for further information call Fernox [PLUMBING, HEATING AND DRAINAGE].

RADIATORS COLD AT THE BOTTOM

Q My twenty-year-old central-heating system has nine radiators, all with thermostatic valves. The circulating water contains Fernox inhibitor, which I have tested for using the copper coin and steel nails and which seems to be working well. The problem I have is that in the fifteen years I have lived here, some of the radiators, one by one, have gradually run cooler from the *bottom*, so it is not an air problem.

A The thermostatic radiator valves (TRVs) are probably jamming in a near-closed position, and allowing only a trickle of water to flow through the radiators. This is a common fault, and one which the government's 'energy saving' advice never mentions when it encourages us all to fit these troublesome gadgets. When cold, the pin on a TRV is held in the open position by a strong spring. When it gets warm, the expansion mechanism pushes the pin closed. Over the years, the spring will get weaker, and the pin will corrode, and it will gradually fail to return to a fully open position. You may be able to strip your TRVs down and free them up (after draining down the central-heating system).

To avoid the problem recurring, TRVs should be opened and closed once a month, to keep them working freely, and left in the open ('hot') position over the summer months, or whenever the central heating is left unused for a period. Readers have also suggested freeing jammed TRVs by taking off the valve head, squirting WD40 around the pin, tapping it with a hammer or rotating it with a pair of pliers. It is certainly worth trying this, if it avoids having to drain down the whole system. Heating engineers tell me that the latest TRVs are less prone to sticking than some of their older counterparts.

If you can feel a distinctive cooler 'triangle' at the bottom of the radiator, between the two valves, then it may be due to severe deposition of sludge. In this event, it is often easier to fit a new radiator than attempt to clear the blockage.

RADIATORS ALWAYS HOT

Q When my hot water is on, but the central heating is switched off, some of the upstairs radiators get hot anyway. The engineer who serviced the boiler said that this is the problem with gravity-feed systems and there was nothing I could do about it. Is this so? Is there not a valve or something that could be fitted to prevent it?

A The problem is one of pipe geometry, and affects lots of systems, including those where both the central-heating and hot-water circuits are fully pumped. It is a simple matter of hot water, being less dense, rising to the highest part of the system. In some cases the water flowing to the hot-water cylinder passes a 'T' joint connected to the radiator circuit, and is able to divert up it. In other cases the 'flow' side of the pipework is laid out properly, but hot water still gravitates upwards along the 'return' side. The answer can be to insert a loop at the problem point, so that the water has to flow downwards before it goes up – then it will only take this route when it is pumped. If this doesn't work, then a check valve or non-return valve can be fitted, but the first solution is more elegant. Any experienced plumber should be able to rectify the situation for you.

CONDENSING BOILERS 1

Q I am considering buying a condensing oil boiler for our house, which we are in the process of renovating. I would be interested to hear your comments on condensing versus conventional boilers.

A Condensing boilers – both gas-fired and oil-fired – are promoted as being hugely efficient converters of fuel into heat. Efficiency gains of 15 per cent are commonly claimed by manufacturers and retailers, but this is actually a myth. They would only achieve this sort of advantage if they were constantly running in fully condensing mode, which would mean an operating temperature of 54°C (as opposed to the usual 60–80°C for a conventional boiler). In practice, in a domestic central-heating system, a condensing boiler will be firing up from cold, running for two or three minutes, and then turning itself off again, just like a conventional boiler. It will thus only be running in condensing mode for a few seconds in each on/off cycle, and this is the period when a plume of steam can be seen shooting out of the flue (a phenomenon known as 'pluming'), which some owners and neighbours find alarming. Energy efficiency savings will be slight, and the industry has yet to produce any reliable independent figures to support its claims.

In return for this theoretical efficiency, condensing boilers are more complicated, need more regular servicing and have many more parts to go wrong and be replaced.

So condensing boilers are really only worth installing if you have a very big house, or a hotel, and very high fuel bills. And it is worth noting that if the boiler does actually run in fully condensing mode (54°C), then that is as hot as the water flowing from it will ever get, which means radiators will be cooler, and may need to be replaced with larger-sized models in order to emit the same amount of heat to the rooms. The domestic hot-water supply will also only reach 54°C, which is, incidentally, below the British Standard recommended minimum of 60°C.

CONDENSING BOILERS 2

Q All the hype I read about condensing boilers led me to believe that I should tear out my twenty-year-old conventional boiler and install one of these gizmos. Being a sceptic, I asked if there was any downside. After some waffling, I was told that my system would need to be chemically cleaned every three or so years at a cost of up to £200 a time. Surely this will eliminate most of my savings?

A Maintenance and servicing on condensing boilers is certainly more extensive, and expensive. Neither the manufacturers nor the government's energy-saving promotional literature make this clear. If your conventional boiler is giving no trouble after twenty years, then it is highly unlikely that replacing it would save you any money, or save the planet any energy.

CONDENSING BOILERS 3

Q I bought a condensing boiler, and after two years I returned home one day to find it leaking very badly. Investigation revealed that the aluminium heat exchanger was completely corroded, which the manufacturers said was due to 'overcondensing'. They said this happens when the flow/return temperatures are not controlled to within 11°C. I argued that this was impossible to achieve when a boiler is installed in an existing radiator system, and that I had not been told that the boiler would only work properly with new radiators, etc. Unable to obtain any recompense, I replaced it with a conventional boiler, which has given me no trouble and is, interestingly, just as efficient as the condensing boiler in terms of gas consumption.

A The condensate produced within a condensing boiler is acidic, and the boiler therefore requires regular (six-monthly) servicing to clean out the drainage tubes and prevent corrosion. It is also true that condensing boilers work best as part of a new, specially designed heating system with aluminium radiators, and that they often fail when fitted to existing systems. Word in the trade is that there are many more technical problems to be solved before condensing boilers will become worth buying.

BOILER VENTILATION REGULATIONS

Q As a small landlord, I regularly have the gas boilers in my properties checked. One – a Potterton – has been in a property for about ten years and has not had any problems, but this year the engineer said that, whilst the boiler and its components were satisfactory and passed all the tests, the air vents in the room were too small. When I queried why this had only surfaced this year, he said it was because there had been a change in the regulations. I had assumed that the regulations in force when the boiler was fitted remain in force until the boiler needs replacing or a safety hazard arises.

A This is a common situation, and some unscrupulous gas engineers are using the diagnosis 'not to current standards' to pressurize customers into having extra ventilation fitted. But, as you rightly suggest, as long as the boiler was originally installed to the manufacturer's specifications, then there should be no reason to alter it. However, boiler ventilation is an important and complex subject, and you should always get a second opinion from a CORGI-registered engineer.

FREE-STANDING BOILER

Q During the annual British Gas Three Star service for my free-standing boiler, the engineer told me that after 2004 no more free-standing boilers with chimney-type flues will be allowed, and that I will have to install a wall-mounted condensing boiler. He also said, 'You cannot get parts for these boilers now.' My concern is that my kitchen layout will not accommodate a wall-mounted unit. Should I buy a new free-standing boiler now, using the existing flue, before the new regulations come into force and the boiler needs spare parts, etc.?

A It is not true that existing free-standing boilers will not be allowed after 2004, but the Building Regulations due to come into force will require all *new* boilers to have a certain minimum efficiency, and at present none of the manufacturers is making a floor-standing model that complies with this.

There is nothing to stop you keeping your existing floor-standing boiler, and having it serviced and repaired for as long as you like.

HEATING CONTROLS

Q My central-heating radiators all have thermostatic valves, apart from the one in the bathroom, which is supposed to provide a safety outlet in case the boiler overheats. The thermostatic valves have a 'frost' setting, which I intended to use when away from home in the winter, but as the bathroom radiator is uncontrolled, it stays hot all the time, even if I turn the temperature control on the boiler to its lowest setting. The bathroom is too hot, and I am wasting gas. What can I do?

A Your central-heating system is missing one vital component – a room thermostat to turn the boiler off when the house has reached the desired temperature. Thermostatic radiator valves on their own will not control the boiler; they simply shut down the radiators, but the boiler will continue to pump hot water around the rest of the system. When you are away from home you should leave the thermostatic valves on full, the boiler heat setting turned down to '1', or 'min', and the room thermostat on the frost setting. Contact a CORGI-registered gas installer to have a look at your system.

INSENSITIVE THERMOSTAT

Q What would you advise for a central-heating system that blows either hot or cold, but nothing in between? The wall thermostat has to be turned to 24°C to activate the boiler but then lowered to 20°C to turn it off. Any setting between these two levels has no effect. Three different thermostats have all produced the same result.

A A four-degree differential (or 'hysteresis') is about what you'd expect on a normal cheap room thermostat wired as an on/off to the boiler. However, you may find that the thermostat can be persuaded to perform better by changing the wiring so that the small 'accelerator heater' in it is brought into the circuit. Plumbers often use only three-core cable ('twin and earth') to wire up room stats, whereas they really need four-core ('triple and earth'), with the live and switched-live conductors routed through the thermostat, and a spare neutral connected to the accelerator heater. The current through this, when the thermostat is 'on', keeps the thermostat closer to room temperature, and can reduce the hysteresis to plus or minus 1°C. If rewiring presents a problem, and if your room thermostat has no exposed metal parts (and the air grilles are proof against small fingers), then you may be able to sacrifice the earth wire and use it as the neutral connection to the accelerator heater. This is probably not a DIY job. For totally accurate control you will need a more expensive digital thermostat, such as the Honeywell CM67.

THERMOSTAT POSITIONING

Q **In most houses the central-heating room thermostat is mounted in the hall next to the kitchen door. Why? I have been doing some work in a bungalow with a narrow hall and the family kept arguing about the setting on the thermostat. I went through the sequence of their life – cooking with or without the kitchen door open, lounge door open or not, etc. They have now asked me to move the thermostat into the lounge.**

A The usual reason for siting the room thermostat near to the kitchen is that the boiler is in the kitchen, and the installing engineer wants to use the minimum amount of cable. More rationally, the hall is often chosen because when the front door is opened, cold air enters, and the thermostat will turn the heating on to counter the cooling effect that this cold air will have as it circulates around the house. Of course, this can lead to the lounge and kitchen becoming hotter than required. But the problem with having the thermostat in the lounge is that when the lounge reaches the required temperature, the heating is shut down in the whole of the rest of the house, leading to condensation problems. The only real answer is a zoned heating system, with separate thermostats controlling different areas.

QUICKER HOT WATER

Q **When we want hot water in our kitchen, we waste a sink full of cold water before it runs hot. Is there a relatively unobtrusive instant water heater we could have fitted?**

A This is a common problem, especially annoying for people who pay for their water via a meter. If you have a conventional system with a hot-water cylinder, then the problem is that the pipe run from the cylinder to the kitchen is too long. If you have a combi boiler, then it doesn't matter how long the pipe run is – a whole boiler-full of water always has to be run off before the water runs hot. The simple answer is to get a small unvented under-sink electric water heater. These are simple to plumb in, and can be powered from the nearest 13A socket. They are usually 10 litre capacity, which means they heat up quickly, and supply enough hot water for washing up (but not enough for a bath or shower). Manufacturers include Ariston and Heatrae Sadia [PLUMBING, HEATING AND DRAINAGE].

UNDER-FLOOR HEATING

Q **What are the advantages of under-floor heating as against radiators? If you had to choose from either one (to go with a condensing boiler) to go into a new bungalow which we hope to get built within the next few months – what would you choose, and why?**

A I have never lived with under-floor heating, but people who have it seem to be very evangelical about it. The advantages are that you don't have radiators taking up wall space and getting in the way of furniture placement, the floor is nice and warm to walk on and the heat is spread evenly throughout the room.

Disadvantages are that under-floor heating works best on solid floors – concrete, brick or tiled finish – which have their own disadvantages. It also needs fitting in conjunction with under-floor insulation, and so means a lot of excavation and building work. Of course, if you are building from scratch then this is not a problem. UFH can be used under timber floors, and there are various systems involving metal plates to spread the heat around. But obviously you would have to make sure that the floorboards were totally dry before fixing, to stop shrinkage gaps opening up. And then, if the heating was left off for any great time, the boards could absorb moisture and swell and buckle.

Because the floor itself becomes the emitter, rather than radiators, then it may take some time for the house to warm up and cool down – i.e. response times are slow. Obviously the under-floor piping has to be installed to a very high standard, as it would be very disruptive to take up the floor to repair leaks. But the biggest difference between UFH and radiators is that the water temperature from the boiler has to be lowered, otherwise the floor would be too hot to walk on. The water temperature is adjusted by using valves to mix cooler water from the return pipes with hot water in the flow pipes – another complication. Many installations have UFH below a solid ground floor, and radiators upstairs.

KETTLING NOISE IN BOILER

Q My five-year-old boiler is making increasingly loud 'kettling' noises, and I have been told that this is due to lime scale, and that the whole system needs to be 'Powerflushed', at a cost of £550. My local plumbers' merchants tell me that for £600 I could buy a new boiler. Is it worth paying so much to descale the present one, especially since the problem will presumably recur?

A 'Kettling' may well be caused by lime scale on the heat exchanger. This traps steam bubbles which expand and explode, causing the noise. Powerflushing will only clear out the lime scale if descaling chemicals are introduced into the system first, and if the scale is removed by chemicals then it may be possible to drain the system down manually without the expense of the Powerflush. Sentinel or Fernox descaler costs around £20 from plumbers' merchants and can be added to the system and left to act slowly. These must be used with care, as they are acidic, but may be worth a try before embarking on the expense of either a Powerflush or a new boiler.

POWERFLUSH OR BALANCING?

Q Some of my central-heating radiators get very hot, whilst others are barely warm, even after bleeding. I have heard that the radiator system should be balanced, but the British Gas Service engineer does not seem keen on this, and recommends that the system is 'Powerflushed' instead. Can you tell me how to try balancing the system myself, before I incur unnecessary expense?

A Powerflushing is rarely needed. Balancing the system will often direct more heat to sluggish radiators, but it is a time-consuming process, and engineers and plumbers often cannot be bothered to do it. But it is a relatively simple DIY operation. At its most basic, balancing involves restricting the flow through the radiators nearest to the boiler, so that more heat reaches those further away. Each radiator has two valves – the on/off valve (usually, but not always, on the right-hand side), and the balancing or 'lockshield' valve at the other end. The balancing valve is shielded by a loose cap which can be removed by undoing a screw, and the valve can then be adjusted using a small adjustable spanner.

Open all the on/off radiator valves fully and then, starting with the radiator nearest the boiler, turn the balancing valve right off and then open it one-quarter turn. Do the same with the next radiator, opening it three-eighths of a turn, and so on down the line, until the last radiator has the balancing valve fully open. Further 'fine tuning' may be needed to ensure that the heat is evenly distributed around the whole system.

A more sophisticated approach is to use a pair of clip-on thermometers on the flow and return ('in' and 'out') pipes either side of the radiator (e.g. Brannan pipe thermometers from B&Q – about £12 per pair). Again, starting nearest the boiler, adjust the balancing valve until you get a temperature drop of 11°C across the radiator, and then move on to the next one.

FLUSHING RADIATOR SYSTEM

Q **There are four radiators in my one-bedroom flat. The two situated closest to the boiler are working but the two at either end of the flat are not. It is not an airlock problem. I think the system needs flushing through. Is there any way I can do this myself?**

A First try turning the two hot radiators off and see if that forces some hot water through to the others. You may need to turn the pump speed up a notch. If that does the trick, then it's just a case of balancing the radiators. If not, then the next step is to try draining the system down to see if that removes the blockage. If that fails, then use Fernox or Sentinel Central Heating Restorer to clean the system out before draining down and refilling [PLUMBING, HEATING AND DRAINAGE].

LEAKING PIPES

Q **A reputable firm of plumbers has told us that our central-heating and hot-water problems are caused by a leaking pipe somewhere in our concrete floors. If they found the leak and dug up the floor to repair it, then another leak could occur at any time. They say the solution is to fit new pipes for the ten downstairs radiators, running down the walls from the ceiling above. Won't the pipes exposed look awful, or is there some way to disguise them?**

A Copper pipes buried below concrete-floor screeds are corroded by the cement. This was not fully appreciated until the 1980s, and many systems installed before this are prone to sub-floor leaks. Copper pipes should only be used below solid floors if they are sheathed in plastic, or laid in open ducts. Dropping new pipe runs down from the ceiling above is a good solution, and the new pipes can be situated in the corners of rooms or behind curtain drops, and disguised by trunking ot boxing in.

AIR IN RADIATORS

Q **I have a conventional central-heating system with boiler, pump, etc., and thirteen radiators. Of these, two have to be bled regularly to release air and no matter how often I bleed**

them, within a week or two they need bleeding again. There is no sign of any water leak. How can the air be getting into the system?

A The two problem radiators are probably on the return, or suction, side of the pumped circuit, and it is quite likely that there is a leak in one of the radiator valve joints. On the flow side of the pump, a leak would result in water dripping out, but on the return side it can draw air in, with no sign of water leakage. The only cure is to remake the joints in turn, making sure they are thoroughly sealed with jointing compound. Start with the first joint on the flow side, i.e. 'upstream' of the two problem radiators. Then it's a trial-and-error process of elimination until you find the guilty joint. (If the bled gas smells like rotten eggs, then this is a sign of hydrogen sulphide – a gas produced by metal corrosion within the system. It may also burn with a yellow flame, although this is not a recommended way of testing.)

MACERATOR TOILET

Q **A builder has told me that you are allowed to install a macerator toilet only if you have another, conventional toilet in the house as well. Is this strictly true? I would like to do away with the huge bathroom/WC in the downstairs room of my (Victorian conversion) flat, in order to use the space. I would instead create a smaller shower/WC in a corner upstairs. But the distance from the drains is apparently too far to have a normal WC. Is there any way round this?**

A Building-control officers do not like macerator WCs because they are unreliable, and they are right to insist that you have a proper toilet as well. Macerator WCs use an electric-powered mincer to chop up the contents of the bowl and pump it through a 40mm waste pipe. They were originally marketed for basement conversions below the level of the main drain – in which case they represent the only possibility for installing a bathroom. But they are notorious for breaking down, particularly as the macerator teeth are easily snagged by cotton fibres – plumbers say that women should not be allowed near them! Macerator toilets are also very noisy, which can lead to disputes between neighbours.

But there are very few situations where a normal 100mm WC waste pipe cannot be installed in an older house. The pipe needs a fall of one in forty, which can usually be achieved within the ceiling space of a Victorian house. And if not, then the pipe can usually be raised at the bathroom end or lowered at the outlet end to achieve the required fall. Ask an experienced architect or surveyor to design your new bathroom for you.

DRAINAGE
SOAKAWAYS

Q **I understand that there is the possibility of a rebate from my water company if my rainwater goes into soakaways and not into the main drain. Is there any easy way to tell if surface water runs off to a soakaway, without digging big holes in the garden?**

A Find the inspection chamber where your waste water joins the main drain. Lift the lid and check that you have the right inspection chamber by getting an accomplice to flush the toilet or run the kitchen tap. Then get the accomplice to pour a bucket of water down a yard gully. If the water ends up in the inspection chamber then you are connected to the main drain; if not, then it may be going to a soakaway.

(Rebates vary between different water companies, roughly between £15 and £35 p.a. This rebate is available to consumers who pay a fixed annual charge for water and drainage – those who pay by water meter will have their bills reduced by a percentage figure. In order to qualify for a rebate in any particular year, the application must be made before 31 March.)

NEW SOAKAWAYS

Q I suspect that my soakaways are nearing the end of their life and would appreciate your opinion on the best way to renew them. Access to the back garden for machinery, etc., is difficult. I have heard that agricultural land drains can be used for this purpose.

A The traditional soakaway is a hole in the ground filled with rubble or stone, and covered with a sheet of corrugated steel to stop the earth washing into it. In time these silt up or collapse and are no longer able to accommodate the rainwater, or allow it to percolate away into the soil. Also, many 'soakaways' are nothing more than the rainwater downpipes from the roof being stuck into the ground right next to the house. A more modern solution is to use a purpose-made perforated plastic box, wrapped in a geotextile to stop soil from getting in through the holes. These can be used individually or in groups to provide the required drainage capacity. Details from Hoofmark [PLUMBING, HEATING AND DRAINAGE].

SMELLY SEPTIC TANK

Q All sewage from our house runs into a set of underground brick chambers, with concrete tops and inspection/access covers. There is often a quite strong sulphurous/sewage-works smell. Concerned that the system wasn't working properly, I sought advice. A salesman explained that the levels and quality of final effluent could not be improved with the existing system, and that the only solution would be a 'packaged sewage treatment system', which could be installed for £7,863 plus VAT. Am I being sold something that I don't really need?

A A considerably cheaper option for your problem would be to install a pumped aeration device in the last chamber downstream. But be warned, all these systems pong a bit when the wind is in the wrong direction.

If you do decide to go for a new system, then it is still quite permissible to install a plain septic tank, costing around £500, and have the run-off filtered through the ground using 'Y'-shaped rubble-filled drainage channels. Reed beds are also quite the rage, being environmentally friendly and all that. See Building Research Establishment Good Building Guide 42, 'Reed beds' [CONSTRUCTION LITERATURE].

EMPTYING SEPTIC TANK

Q Since moving in sixteen years ago, we have never had our septic tank emptied, and neither had the previous owners. It has two covers, and is situated on a slope below the house. We have never used bleach or biological detergents. My question is, now I have recently extended the property, can I safely divert rainwater from the new roof (approx 8m² area) into the septic tank, and should I have it emptied?

A Septic tanks have two chambers. The first one collects the solids, or 'sludge', which is broken down by anaerobic bacteria. The second one holds the liquid run-off, or 'liquor', which is purified by aerobic bacteria – either by bubbling air through it, or allowing it to percolate into a soakaway in the ground. Eventually the first chamber will fill up, and should be 'desludged'. Depending upon the size of the chamber and the amount of waste, this should be done every three to five years.

When a septic tank is established, and in equilibrium with the waste flowing into it, then the bacteria should break everything down with the minimum of smell. Septic tanks should not be used for rainwater drainage, as this will dilute the contents, and interfere with the bacterial activity.

RAINWATER COLLECTION

Q I have tried to obtain details from local builders' merchants of tanks suitable for installing underground for collecting rainwater. At present the roof water and surface water run to a rubble soakaway. The only suggestion so far has been for a septic tank. I have also contacted the manufacturers of plastic oil tanks, but they inform me that they are only suitable for installation above ground.

A Most people who install DIY rainwater collection systems use recycled orange juice tanks. These hold 1,500 litres, and can be purchased from Tank Exchange [RAINWATER COLLECTION/RECYCLING]. Two or more can be linked together to provide extra storage.

Recycling rainwater does not just save on water-company drainage charges, but if you pay for your water via a meter, then by using rainwater or filtered 'grey' water (bath and shower waste) for garden irrigation, flushing WCs, etc., you can save even more. Advice on partial or complete systems can be obtained from Aquarius Water Engineering [RAINWATER COLLECTION/RECYCLING].

DRAIN SMELLS IN CONSERVATORY

Q I have had a conservatory built at the back of my terraced house, and find that at times it is unusable because of the drain smells emerging from the vicinity of the manhole cover. Does this mean there is something wrong with the drains, and is there any solution short of relocating the manhole?

A Even the best-constructed and ventilated sewer will be smelly on occasions. It sounds as though your conservatory has been built over an existing manhole with a loose-fitting cover. Now that the manhole is inside, it needs to be fitted with a special double-sealed cover, which is screwed down onto a rubber gasket. These are also available with tray-type lids which can be tiled to match the surrounding floor finish.

UNBLOCKING DRAINS

Q Having previously paid £80 call-out fee to a plumber to unblock a drain (when it turned out to be caused by food in the sink outlet) I feel I should learn how to do this myself. But I really haven't a clue what to do, and I am afraid of flooding the floor, which is the ceiling of the flat downstairs. Any tips for a complete idiot?

A Clearing blocked kitchen waste pipes is easy. There is a U-bend below the sink where the offending detritus collects. This is known as a trap. Not because it traps solids, but because it forms a water-seal to stop foul air from the sewer rising up into the house. To clear a blockage, you put a bucket or bowl underneath, unscrew the two plastic collars holding the 'U' to the inlet and outlet pipes, and wriggle it free. It will be full of grease, hair, rice and unidentifiable black sludge, which you scrub off into the bucket and flush down the toilet.

This is not a pleasant job, but it's better than paying a small fortune to someone else to do it for you. If, instead of a U-bend, you encounter a bulbous plastic object, this will be a bottle trap, which you remove by unscrewing the whole thing. In both cases, once you have scrubbed everything clean, reassemble in reverse order and run some clean water through while you check for leaks.

POOR FLUSHING WC

Q I have an oldish low-level cistern lavatory. When it is flushed, the solid waste swirls around the bowl but does not disappear up and over the U-bend. The lavatory has to be flushed several times before it clears. I am assured by my plumber that there is no blockage anywhere, and he admits defeat. Because of a leak under the bathroom floor some years ago, the lavatory was taken out and then reset in the floor; could this be significant?

A Poor-flushing lavatories can be infuriating, and the worst culprits are usually low-level cisterns, which naturally do not deliver the same force of water as high-level cisterns. The first thing to do is to check that there is sufficient water in the cistern – i.e. to adjust the ball valve so that it fills up to the line marked. If you live in a hard-water area, it is possible that the siphon and/or flush pipe may have become partially blocked by scale, so get your plumber to take the whole thing apart and clean it. The other possibility is that when the lavatory was moved, the flush pipe may have been pushed too far into the housing in the pan – it should be seated firmly within the rubber connecting sleeve, but not pushed tight into the porcelain socket, as this can restrict the water flow. If all else fails, replace the siphon assembly with a Continental-style flush valve, such as the Pacific Dual Flush Valve from Polypipe [PLUMBING, HEATING AND DRAINAGE].

REPAIRING CAST-IRON GUTTERS

Q My generally solid house was built around 1930 and has cast-iron gutters and pipes. My builder has advised replacing the gutters – which he has just painted inside and out, and resealed the joints – with plastic ones in due course. He says that if the cast-iron ones are to be renewed they will have to be taken down, cleaned and reinstalled, and he thinks this would cost more than new plastic ones. Is he right? My neighbour is already on his second set of plastic guttering, the first evidently not having stood up to the weather. **Replacement would, of course, detract from the originality of the house.**

A I think you should learn from your neighbour's mistake, and stick with the original cast-iron guttering. If it is carefully overhauled and replaced, it should last another seventy years, whereas the plastic replacement is unlikely to last more than fifteen. You are lucky to have a builder who at least understands the nature of the material, so you should try to persuade him to do a proper overhaul job – rubbing each section down with a wire brush, priming and painting, and reassembling with new bolted joints sealed with linseed-oil putty. It will be cheaper and more reliable in the long run. Cracks can be repaired by conventional electric arc welding, using cast-iron welding rods. Replacement sections from J. & J. W. Longbottom Ltd [PLUMBING, HEATING AND DRAINAGE].

REMOVING VENT PIPES

Q **In our bathroom we have a boxed-in section running from floor to ceiling and out through the roof that encloses the stench pipe from the bathroom toilet and the downstairs toilet. We are considering having a new bathroom fitted and have been told by one of the salesmen that the stench pipe can be cut off and capped with a valve that redirects the gases back down the pipe. Is this feasible, safe and wise?**

A Vent pipes serve two purposes. One is to allow air to enter the system from the top whenever toilets are flushed or basins are emptied – this stops the outflowing waste water from drawing the water out of the drainage traps (or 'U' bends), and this function may also be served by an air-admittance valve. The other purpose of the pipes is to ventilate the entire sewage system, preventing the build-up of harmful gases (which may be poisonous and even explosive). Obviously bathroom salesmen are keen to cut down on internal clutter in order to sell their wares, but the ultimate say on removing the vent pipe will rest with the local authority building-control officer, and you should seek his advice. He will want to check whether your neighbours still have sufficient roof-level vent pipes to keep the whole system safe.

CLEARING RAINWATER PIPES

Q **I have a recurring problem with blocked plastic rainwater downpipes. I have resorted to a long ladder in the past, but with advancing years this is no longer possible. Is there such a thing as a 'rodding point' which could be inserted into the downpipe at ground level? A garden hose or spiral wire could then be used to safely clear the blockage from below.**

A Blocked gutters and downpipes are a perennial problem and, if left blocked, can result in serious dampness problems and wood rot where the overflowing water soaks the walls below. There are various wire and plastic guards that can be fitted over the gutters, although in some cases these can clog up themselves and even make matters worse. Both Terrain and Polypipe make a small section of pipe incorporating an access door, which can be fitted to an existing downpipe, and used for rodding.

PLASTERING

The term plastering refers to spreading any wet material onto a wall. 'Plaster' can be lime, clay, chalk, cement or gypsum, used on their own, mixed with each other and/or with sand, earth, straw or lightweight aggregates.

Unfortunately, mention plaster to any modern builder in Britain and he will know only one type – pink gypsum, or calcium sulphate. This is a wonderful material which sets hard in ninety minutes and gives a smooth trowelled finish on plasterboard or dry internal cement-rendered brickwork. But expose it to any degree of long-term moisture and it starts to dissolve. Many of the so-called 'rising damp' problems in ground-floor flats in old Victorian properties are actually gypsum plaster efflorescence, caused by the combined influence of internal condensation, raised external ground levels and leaking window sills. The original lime-and-sand plaster coped with all this without a problem, but the gypsum can't cope with it.

To be fair to the gypsum plaster industry, they make a large variety of products for use in different circumstances. British Gypsum, for example, make and market thirteen types of plaster for the British building trade, including special formulations for application to plasterboard, brick-work and lightweight blockwork. But the average builders' merchants only stocks two – bonding backing coat and multi-finish skim coat – so these are the materials that jobbing builders use, to the exclusion of the more specialized products. British Gypsum have an excellent technical advice department and can arrange next-day deliveries to most parts of the UK, but most builders carry on regardless.

It is also a shame that British builders are afraid of using lime plaster. It is easy to use, and hydrated lime is available in bags at most builders' merchants. Mix it one-to-four with washed sharp sand, cover it with polythene sheeting and leave it to 'sweat' overnight, and it will match the lime plaster used on most Victorian houses. Any left over can be kept in buckets, with an inch of water on top, and it will stay usable for ever. Animal hair reinforcement is also easily available from specialist suppliers, and 'Fibrin' polypropylene fibres are a useful modern equivalent.

Builders have been persuaded that lime plaster 'won't work', probably by the propaganda of the cement industry. But its cause is not helped either by the 'lime loonies' – a group of mostly middle-class conservation enthusiasts who have discovered the joys of working with lime, but who insist that the only way to do it is to use traditional lime putty, preferably slaked in oak vats from quicklime fired in medieval kilns. This dotty purist approach makes real working builders very suspicious, and hardens their belief that the hydrated lime in bags from the builders' merchants is a 'different material', which will only work if mixed with cement. But I have been using hydrated lime and sand for ten years for bricklaying, pointing and plastering. It works fine.

STAINED PLASTERBOARD CEILINGS

Q Recent storms caused rainwater to come through my plasterboard ceiling. A builder has said that this will cause the plaster to crumble and the ceiling will have to be replaced. Is there a less expensive way of dealing with this, as the ceiling appears to be intact?

A Modern plasterboard with a gypsum plaster skim finish is not the best at coping with a soaking, but as long as the ceiling is still intact, and shows no signs of sagging, then it should dry out, and not need replacing. Even when there is serious water damage, it is usually possible to cut out and replace small damaged areas, and it is rarely necessary to replace a whole ceiling.

RESTORING AN OLD CROFT

Q I am bringing a derelict croft house back into use. All the internal cladding of the stone walls has fallen off and only traces of laths remain. My options seem to be rendering in cement, rendering in plaster or lining with heavy plasterboard on a wooden framework. Are there other options and have you an opinion on the best way forward?

A All these three suggestions would seem to me to be unwise. Applying modern materials to old buildings can often cause problems. You need to find out what type of internal plastering system was used originally, and try to replicate it as closely as possible. I suggest you contact the Society for the Protection of Ancient Buildings (SPAB) for advice [CONSERVATION].

LIME RENDER

Q We are renovating part of an old house which has walls of thick slate and lime mortar. If we were to render the inner walls should we use a lime render and would this allow a plaster finish?

A Lime render, lime plaster. The only difference is the grade of sand. If you mean should you use gypsum plaster, then the answer is no.

DURABILITY OF LIME RENDER

Q You often mention the advantage of using lime to repair render and brickwork on old houses. I have mixed and made sample patches of both lime render and cement render, and the lime render, whilst looking good, never appears to be particularly robust (i.e. when knocked by kids' bikes, etc.) Am I doing something wrong or is lime render a 'look but don't touch' finish?

A Lime mortar and render hardens by carbonation (reacting with carbon dioxide from the atmosphere). So it takes many months, or even years, to reach the same hardness as cement render. This is why it is able to accommodate movement and moisture so well, and why it even retains the ability to 'self-heal' cracking for many years. If you want to speed up the hardening process then keep it moist with a light spray of water from a garden sprayer, especially in hot weather. In the winter, fresh lime render needs protecting from frost.

FINDING A LIME PLASTERER

Q I have tried to follow your advice about plastering (on my 1904 house), but I cannot get any plasterer to carry out lime plastering. They all wanted to skim it with 'Universal one-coat' or 'Thistle finish'. I mentioned possible damp problems, etc., but they all told me there wouldn't be a problem. I have since succumbed to pressure from the wife to finish the job, and have had it plastered with Thistle finish. Will this be OK in the future or should I persevere and try to find a lime plasterer for the other rooms?

A The problem with gypsum plasters is that they dissolve when they get wet, which is why they are unsuitable for the insides of solid exterior walls on old houses. Lime plastering is not difficult, but the current generation of plasterers have never been exposed to it, and so are afraid of the unknown. You could compromise by asking your plasterer to use Tarmac's 'Limelite' lightweight renovating plaster, which contains lime but also some cement [PLASTERING].

MATCHING OLD PLASTER

Q Our 1934 house was architect-designed and traditionally built, using lime plaster. We have cracks in some internal walls, due to cracked and leaking drains, which have been replaced or lined. The insurance company now want to have the cracks repaired and replastered using modern gypsum plaster. When I told them I thought they should use lime plaster, they replied that lime plaster 'was only used in the past because today's modern materials weren't available'. I maintain that it should be renovated to match the original. Do I have a case?

A Yes. You should always use plaster to match the original, otherwise cracks could open up between the old and new. Your insurers' statement about lime plaster reveals a worrying ignorance. It's a bit like saying you shouldn't go on holiday to Bournemouth, and that people only went there in the past because aeroplanes hadn't been invented! In any case, gypsum plaster is not a 'modern' material; it was known to the ancient Greeks and Romans. But lime plaster is better.

SAVING AN OLD CEILING

Q Our Victorian house has ornate plaster coving and ceiling roses in two downstairs rooms. Unfortunately the ceilings are not in good repair and we have been warned that they may fall down. Is there a way of repairing them without removing the plaster, or having the decorative elements removed and replaced? We are loath to just rip them down and lose the features.

A Old lath-and-plaster ceilings can usually be repaired, and they are well worth keeping, as the dense lime plaster has much better sound-insulation qualities than modern plasterboard. The usual problem is that the plaster has lost its key with the laths. If the floorboards in the room above can be lifted, then the ceiling can be propped up from below, and a fresh coat of plaster spread on top, which will bond it back together. If the floor above is inaccessible, then the ceiling can be screwed up to the joists from below, using expanded metal lathing to reinforce any weak areas.

It is usually easier to repair a lath-and-plaster ceiling than to replace it.

REPAIRING PEBBLE-DASH

Q Our external walls are part pebble-dashed, and I have noticed that there appears to be a blister in one area. I am concerned that it may split and fall off. Is there some way we could repair this area before it becomes a major job?

A If the house was pebble-dashed from new, then the blistered area is probably due to poor adhesion in that one spot, and it is not a fault that is likely to spread across the wall. If the house was originally built with face brickwork, however (check by looking at similar properties in the street), then the pebble-dash may have been applied later, to hide cracks or weathered bricks, and it is possible that other areas will delaminate in time. You could check by tapping gently with a hammer and listening for a hollow sound. Small isolated areas can be repaired, but if the damage is widespread then it would make more sense to hack it all off, fix expanded metal lathing to the wall, and re-render. Any experienced plasterer should be able to do pebble-dashing. It is basically two-coat render work, with the 'pebbles' (pea shingle) flicked into the top coat.

PAINTING
AND DECORATING

Most people who opt for so-called 'maintenance-free' PVC-U windows and roof-line products do so because they don't want the hassle of painting the existing woodwork. So, instead of paying someone else to do it – say £500 to £750 every five years to rub down and gloss an average terraced house – they would rather give £5,000 to some cowboy trader to rip out all the existing windows and external woodwork and replace them with plastic of no known origin or specification, and uncertain longevity. The economics just don't add up. If these people made similar decisions at work, they'd have to justify themselves with cost–benefit analyses, and they'd realize it wasn't worth it. But because it's their home, they go into a blind panic, and believe what they read in the adverts. And because almost everybody else down the street has gone for plastic windows, they think they'd better get them as well. The replacement window and roof-line industry gets rich on this lemming-like behaviour.

This dislike of routine maintenance accounts also for the sale of so-called 'breathable' textured external wall coatings – they aren't breathable and they cost five times the price of getting the wall painted properly – and 'one coat' paints, which a professional decorator described to me as a 'pudding-like' paint which never dries.

Given a modicum of care and attention, timber doors and windows will last for ever. This means a light sanding down, and touching up or recoating on an occasional basis with proper spirit-based primer (on bare wood), undercoat and gloss. If you are not prepared to do it, or pay someone else to do it, then maybe you shouldn't have bought a house in the first place. If you've never tried it then give it a go – it could change your life. Do bear in mind the toxicity of lead paint, though (see HAZARDS). This is one of the most toxic of building materials, is present in huge quantities in homes (it was used in Britain up to 1992) and is a known danger to children. The lack of public awareness, and government publicity, about this problem is worrying.

External brickwork should not be painted – it traps the moisture. The only sympathetic coating on old houses is traditional limewash. Again, if you try it yourself you may get hooked – it's better value than watching the telly.

CONFLICTING OPINIONS

Q We have asked for quotes from two builders to redecorate woodwork and masonry on our 1960 terraced house. One of the builders suggests scraping off all loose, flaking paintwork, and painting with two coats of masonry paint. He also thinks the windows are not worth keeping, and should be replaced with double-glazed windows. The second builder also suggests scraping the loose paintwork and then 'stabilizing' and using two coats of masonry paint. He thinks the windows can be rubbed down, repaired where necessary and coated with two coats of timber stain preservative. We haven't the slightest idea which method is best.

A It sounds as though you need a professional painter and decorator, rather than a builder [PAINTING AND DECORATING].

PEELING WINDOW SILLS

Q I live in a large Victorian house. Every two or three years I have to have my window ledges repainted white since the paint seems to peel off and crack. The current painter says this is normal, particularly at the back where there is more sun. However, another friend told me that if the painter strips off all the paint back to the bare stonework, the paint should last for seven to ten years. The current painter says this is not so and it's not worth the extra effort.

A External stone sills are subject to the extremes of the weather, but I would say that five years should be a reasonable life expectancy for a modern masonry paint. The peeling could be due to water penetration at the joint between the sill and the bottom rail of the timber window. But if it occurs over a wide area, then it is more likely due to poor surface preparation or cheap paint. It is probably not necessary to strip the paint right off, but it should certainly be sanded back hard to remove all loose or flaking areas, and then the whole surface should be given two coats of masonry stabilizing solution – this is a proprietary resin-based product, not to be confused with PVA adhesive. Then two coats of a quality smooth masonry paint, and application of an external-grade silicone sealant at the joint between sill and bottom rail.

If the paintwork is neglected, timber windows will soon decay.

95

PAINTING PUTTY

Q We still have all the original windows (complete with 'ripply' glass) in our ninety-year-old house. However, I am fed up with linseed-oil putty. The back of the house, facing north, is not so much of a problem, but the windows in the front, which get the full hot/cold, wet/dry treatment, have to be resealed almost annually, when the putty inevitably shrinks and cracks. Is there no end to this interminable chore? I have tried 'frame sealants' and, while they do not harden to the ceramic-like brittleness of old putty, I find their adhesion and consequent protection value questionable.

A It sounds as though you are not protecting the putty with paint. Linseed-oil putty should remain moist and flexible for many years, but it does need to be protected – it's the paint that keeps it from drying out and cracking. The glazing rebate in the window should be primed first, to stop the wood drawing the oil out of the putty. And as soon as the putty has become firm (after a few days), it should be painted with an oil-based paint – undercoat and two gloss coats. Try to let the paint flow slightly onto the glass, to seal the join between glass and putty.

SEALING SANDY WALL SURFACES

Q We are about to re-wallpaper our interior walls but notice the plaster is very sandy and gritty. We have been advised to prime the walls with either a water-based stabilizing solution or an oil-based alkaline-resistant primer. From your experience do these actually work, or could you suggest an alternative?

A Resin-based stabilizing solutions are generally used on exterior work. For inside walls, water-based PVA should be sufficient. Make up a weak solution in water and brush it on. When dry give it a light sanding, and if there are still any crumbly areas give them a further coating. Traditionally, decorators used rabbit-skin glue size for this purpose.

OILY DEPOSITS

Q The previous owners of our flat burnt incense sticks and oils in the living room, staining the walls and ceiling with a soot-like deposit. Both walls and ceiling are wallpapered, painted with matt emulsion. How can we clean the surfaces before freshening them up with more emulsion? We don't want to repaper if possible.

A It is an interesting fact that condensation does not occur only with water vapour, but also with oils and fats. For example, the walls and ceilings of restaurant kitchens and fish-and-chip shops can become saturated right through with condensed oils, and will never take a water-based paint. With luck, your walls will not be that bad, and you may get away with washing them down with detergent and painting with vinyl emulsion. But if the paint won't take then you will have to strip off the paper, taking the oils with it. Any obviously stained areas of plaster should be sealed with Ratcliffe's Styptic or Polycell Stain Block before repapering.

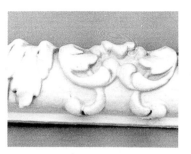

Chemical paint stripper can work well on mouldings and cornices.

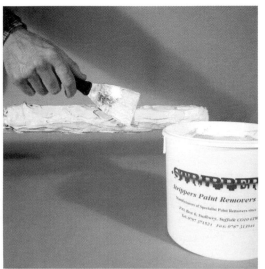

PAINT STRIPPING

Q In my 1930s house we have panelled wooden doors which originally had a dark varnish finish. They have been overpainted several times and are in generally good condition although the paint build-up is excessive on some mouldings. We would like to strip back to the wood before redecorating and have considered sending the doors to a company that uses a caustic soda bath. They have advised us that the doors should be left for a week before repainting. How do you rate caustic soda stripping against Nitromors or a hot-air gun?

A Dipping in caustic soda is quick and easy, but it is not very good for old doors. It can make them shrink and warp, and some carpenters say that it damages the glued joints, causing them to fall apart. Blow lamps or hot-air guns are the traditional method, but unfortunately this exposes you to lead poisoning from the paint fumes. If you use this method wear a respirator, and do not allow children or pregnant women in the house. Chemical paint strippers are often the quickest and safest way of removing paint [PAINTING AND DECORATING].

EXTERNAL PAINT REMOVAL

Q Our Edwardian house has been vandalized by a previous owner. The lovely old brickwork has been painted cream. Is there a way to remove the paint and restore the bricks to their original state?

A It can be done, but the method depends very much upon the type of paint and the state of the bricks. Some firms employ a basic sandblasting technique, and this is almost always disastrous, since it removes the surface 'fire skin' from clay bricks and leaves them prone to water absorption and weathering. High-pressure steam is a gentler method, and there is also a patented water/air vortex technique for stubborn coatings. Chemical paint strippers may also be successful.

EXTERNAL WALL COATINGS

 Q I was given a demonstration by a company's sales manager of the way in which their coating keeps out moisture but still permits the wall to breathe. The demo consisted of a transparent cylindrical container. Halfway down was a segment of porous building block that had been covered by the wall-coating material. I was asked to fill the top of the container with water. There was no evidence of water passing through the block – it remained dry. Then air was pumped into the bottom of the cylinder. Bubbles of air were seen to be emerging from the block of building material and coating. Pump air – bubbles. Cease pumping, no bubbles – no water passed from top to bottom. The work is also independently insured.

A This is a demonstration that air under pressure passes through the coating, not that moisture vapour not under pressure would do so. So it does not mimic real conditions, and sounds like a clever sales trick. The problem with these coatings is that if you get condensation forming within the depth of the wall – i.e. the wall becomes damp from within, with liquid moisture – then it will be unable to escape. As the demonstration shows, liquid moisture will be trapped within the wall.

REMOVING TEXTURED COATINGS

 Q We have a seventeenth-century farmhouse which the previous owners had spray coated with one of the 'textured wall coatings' that you warn against. I do believe it is creating a damp problem as it is cracking and water is now seeping into the structure. And, as you have also warned, we found that the 'guarantee' was worthless as the company was no more! Anyway, what hope for the house? Can this stuff be removed, and at what sort of cost?

A These textured coatings sound like a good idea, as they offer the promise of long-term waterproofing of the walls. What the salesmen do not point out, however, is that many dampness problems are caused by water vapour produced inside the house, and that the coating will have the effect of trapping this moisture in the walls. Also, as you have found, if the coating cracks, then rainwater will be able to get in, and will then be trapped behind it.

The good news is that the coatings can be removed using chemical methods. There are two different types of coating, which respond to different strippers. Both are painted on with a brush, and washed off with water. Strippers Paint Removers will provide you with a trial pack of both types for £12. When you have found which one works best, it will cost around £2 per square metre to treat the house [PAINTING AND DECORATING].

REMOVING ARTEX

Q What is the most efficient way to remove Artex from my walls and ceilings?

A Artex and other textured paint finishes may contain asbestos fibres, and should be treated with care. Any potential danger comes from inhaling the dust, so it is best removed wet. The easiest method is to use a steam wallpaper stripper (about £30 from builders' merchants or DIY stores) and a scraper, and to seal the scrapings in plastic bin liner bags before they dry. The bags should be labelled 'asbestos', and disposed of specially by the local authority refuse department.

STAINING ABOVE HEATERS

Q The walls above each of my night-storage radiators have become grey/black from the heat. If I put washable wallpaper on the walls will I be able to wash the marks off – or can you suggest anything else?

A Staining on walls above heaters is usually just grime from the air. The flow of hot air creates static on the wall surface and this causes the dirt to stick. Yes, you can wash it off, and shelves fitted above the radiators will help divert the heat around the room and minimize the problem.

SURFACE PREPARATION

Q I've bought the paint for the front room of my Victorian basement flat, stripped the wallpaper and found that the plaster underneath is uneven and cracked. I really don't want to put wallpaper back up, but if I just put paint on the walls they will look terrible. Is there anything I can do to make the surface any better?

A Yes. Wallpaper it. This kind of property was originally finished internally with lime-and-sand plaster. Lime plaster is a wonderful material, as it moves with the walls, and any severe movement is usually accommodated by a series of small cracks spread across the whole wall, rather than – as with hard modern materials – one big crack down the middle. But the Victorians would not have dreamed of painting straight onto the plaster. They always lined the walls with thick lining paper, and this helps to iron out the cracks and absorb movement.

The correct way to deal with cracked lime plaster on old walls and ceilings is to rake out and fill any particularly wide cracks, and sandpaper when dry. Then apply two layers of heavy-grade (1,000-gauge) lining paper. The first layer should go horizontally ('cross-lining'), and the second layer vertically. When dry, the newly papered surface will take emulsion paint and give a nice soft finish.

PAINTING TILES

Q Our bathroom tiles are over forty years old, very dingy white, and we would like advice on suitable treatment/paint for them. I understand that this painting may be a specialist job, following my viewing of a TV programme.

A I am not a big fan of painting ceramic tiles, as the effect can often look amateurish. But it can be done, as long as you are sure the tiles are still firmly fixed to the wall (check for loose ones by tapping and listening for a hollow noise). Use a special tile paint, and follow the manufacturer's instructions to the letter. For the best effect, rake out the old grout first using a proprietary raking-out tool, apply the paint finish and then re-grout using a colour to contrast with the painted tile colour.

REMOVING GRAFFITI

Q Our front boundary brick wall has been covered with black spray-paint graffiti. We have approached the local authority, who boast that they are carrying out a campaign against graffiti and have a team to remove it, but they have quoted us a price of £15 per foot for removal. We have asked them if we can buy the gel they apparently use, to carry out the work ourselves, but they won't help us. Have you any advice on what to use and where to buy it?

A Removing graffiti is the same as removing paint from any other surface. Success depends upon identifying the type of paint, and using a chemical stripper that will not damage the surface or result in permanent staining. For specialist advice call Strippers Paint Removers [PAINTING AND DECORATING].

BLEEDING KNOTS

Q We have been renovating an old cottage. A number of the doors and windows had blisters caused by oozing from knots that had not been sealed. We have stripped off the paint down to bare wood and treated the knots with proprietary knotting sealer prior to repainting. Sadly, a few months later the knots are oozing once more. I deduce that while knotting compound works well on new wood, it will not properly seal old wood that has been painted. What is the secret?

A Knotting does not always work on new wood either. Some knots are very resinous, and will always bleed through. The staining is usually worse through water-based acrylic paint, but even with gloss the resin can dissolve the undercoat and form a blister. Next time try two coats of aluminium-oxide primer.

REMOVING BLACK MOULD

Q The house we're buying has been empty for twelve months, with no heating or ventilation. Consequently, the walls have black mould on large areas. Have you any suggestions for removing it? I know we need to get it heated and the windows open, but we need also to decorate. Or do you think we should leave the decorating alone until we get the house dried out and then remove the mould?

A Wash it off with clean water containing a splash of bleach. Much cheaper and safer than proprietary fungicide solutions.

DAMPNESS

Questions about dampness constitute by far the largest proportion of my weekly postbag. Some of these concern genuine stories of water penetration – through roofs, walls and chimneys – which builders have been unable to stop. Many more describe black mould growth on walls, green mildew in wardrobes and water running down the insides of windowpanes, which are all symptoms of condensation (see CONDENSATION).

Condensation is the result of water vapour produced within the home which, as a result of inadequate heating and ventilation, is allowed to condense out as liquid water on and within the building structure. Condensation is easy to cure, but some people just refuse to open the windows.

But by far the largest number of queries concern a dampness problem that does not actually exist. This is the notorious 'rising damp', which surveyors and damp-proofing salesmen say they can detect using electrical meters. Selling damp-proofing on the basis of electrical meter readings must go down as one of the most successful confidence tricks in history. There is no independent scientific evidence to support the claim that British homes suffer from endemic rising dampness, and in every case that I have investigated the property was either bone dry, or else had obvious defects such as leaking gutters, raised outside ground levels or condensation problems. But surveyors, estate agents and mortgage lenders all go along with the 'rising damp' myth, and so homeowners continue to fork out £200 million every year for this unnecessary and often damaging work.

Electrical moisture meters are calibrated for use on timber, not wallpaper or plaster. They will always give high readings on walls at low level in old houses because of condensation (warm air rises, cool air sinks, walls are colder at the bottom and so that's where the condensation is concentrated).

But if rising damp is a myth, people ask, then why are damp-proof courses built into new buildings? The history of the damp-proof course is an interesting one, and dates from the 1877 Building by-laws – themselves following the Public Health Act (1875), which was concerned mostly with drainage and sewage disposal. So the original idea seems to have been to stop sewage – which in those days was often still running down the streets – from soaking into walls. Water will not rise by capillary action in brickwork built with cement or strong lime mortars. Suffice it to say that in Holland, much of which is below sea level, DPCs are not used. Whatever, most British houses built post-1877 have DPCs built-in – usually two courses of slate – and there is no evidence that they 'fail', or become porous over time, although most surveyors seem to accept these old wives' tales without question.

In any case, clay soils will always absorb water preferentially over brick walls (because the soil expands as it gets wet, creating a 'suction' effect), so there will only be free water available to soak into the wall once the soil has become saturated – in other words, in swamp conditions. And if your house is standing in a swamp, then you need land drainage anyway.

Oh, and by the way, if anyone tells you that your dampness problem is due to an 'underground stream', then that's part of the myth as well.

DAMP WALLS
RISING DAMP?

Q I am in the process of selling my house. The buyers' mortgage lender insisted on a survey for rising damp, and the surveyor's report says that there is extensive damp in all walls. There is no evidence of damp, such as wallpaper lifting, and a recent TV programme concluded that treatment for rising damp is seldom justified. What is your advice about current practice?

A Rising damp is a myth. The 'surveyor', who says there is extensive dampness in all the walls, is actually just a salesman for chemical damp-proofing products. Tell your buyers that they need an independent dampness survey carried out to the standards described in Building Research Establishment Digest 245 [CONSTRUCTION LITERATURE/DAMPNESS AND TIMBER SURVEYORS], and under no circumstances allow them to deduct the cost of damp-proofing works from the asking price.

DAMP PATCHES ABOVE SKIRTINGS

Q My detached 1926 house is built with Accrington brick. There is a damp patch above the skirting board in one of the rooms, which a local builder, using a moisture meter, 'diagnosed' as rising damp. You have expressed doubts about this kind of diagnosis on several occasions, but I have seen advertisements for the 'Schrijver' damp-proofing system, which they claim is new to this country. What is your opinion of this system?

A Electrical moisture meters on their own cannot be used to diagnose the existence of rising damp, and the date of your house indicates that it will have been built with a damp-proof course, and so should not require any further form of damp-proofing. Unless you have had a proper moisture analysis using the method described in Building Research Establishment Digest 245, then any form of damp-proofing is likely to be a waste of money [CONSTRUCTION LITERATURE]. The damp patch in the plaster must have some other source, such as a leaking gutter, cracked window sill or raised ground level. If your builder cannot locate the problem then you need an independent expert [DAMPNESS AND TIMBER SURVEYORS]. The Schrijver system appears to be a version of the old – and discredited – Knapen tube (or 'atmospheric syphon') system, which has been independently tested in Germany and France, and as far as I am aware has never been shown to cure rising damp.

(Further investigation of this problem – by Abbey Independent Surveys – revealed that the house was built with cavity walls, and builders' debris had blocked the cavity, allowing ground water from outside to track across and produce a stain on the plaster. Removing a couple of bricks and cleaning the debris out of the cavity solved the problem.)

CONFLICTING DIAGNOSES

Q I am buying a basement flat. Under 'essential repairs' the valuation survey report stated: 'You are advised to obtain a specialist rising damp report from a member of the British Wood Preserving and Damp-proofing Association, and carry out their recommendations in

Atmospheric syphon-type systems have never been independently proved to cure rising damp.

full. Any treatment undertaken should form part of a long-term insurance-bonded guarantee.' On the strength of this the mortgage lender withheld some money and we have now had four quotes from BWPDA firms. All of them indicated different damp spots in different parts of the house, and their estimates ranged from £600 to £3,750. Is there any reputable contractor you can recommend who provides an independent report on damp, preferably one whose views are respected by mortgage lenders?

A Yes. Not a contractor but an independent surveyor [DAMPNESS AND TIMBER SURVEYORS]. In my experience, there's no such thing as a reputable 'contractor'. Almost all damp-proofing/timber-treatment contractors make their money by offering free surveys and then saying you need work done. The unreliability of their diagnoses is underlined by the fact that, as in your case, different 'specialist' firms usually come up with different proposals.

DO I NEED A DPC?

Q I am rebuilding an old house next door to my own in order to make the two into one. With the walls stripped of plaster, etc., I am now not sure what to do about a DPC. The bricks are very old, rock hard in the centre but soft on the outside so if I drill them and try to inject damp-proof fluid it won't go anywhere. I have read your comments with great interest and would like to believe I don't need a DPC, but it is a lot of work if it all goes wrong. There are no obvious signs of dampness apart from one wall where the ground level outside is very high.

A I think you should relax and stop worrying about something that hasn't happened yet. If the bricks are 'rock hard', then they won't allow moisture to pass through them, so there is no point damaging them by drilling, and then trying to inject a fluid that is not needed. If the ground level is high outside one wall, then you should lower it if at all possible.

DAMP WALLS CAUSED BY RAISED PATIO

Q The damp-proof course of our 1917 house has been bridged by the patio laid against the external walls, in some areas up to 9in (225mm). The under-floor air vents are also below the patio level and fill with water in heavy rain. This has caused problems to decorations internally. Three solutions have been suggested: (1) Lift and relay the entire patio below the DPC (a large and expensive job); (2) Lift the patio stones adjacent to the wall, dig a trench out to below the DPC, bitumen paint the walls and relay the patio stones; (3) Take an angle grinder and remove 4in (100mm) of stone around the walls, dig the trench out, bitumen paint the walls and fill the trench with pea shingle. Your recommendation, please?

A No. 1 is the only option worth doing. The others will be throwing good money after bad. If your sub-floor vents are channelling surface water then you could soon have a rotten floor to cope with as well. The finished patio needs to be at least 150mm below DPC level, and sloping away from the walls. And definitely no bitumen paint anywhere, as it will simply trap moisture behind it.

DAMP WALLS CAUSED BY
SOLID FLOORS AND CHEMICAL DPCs

Q A few years ago a damp-proofing firm replaced my timber floor with a concrete one, and chemically treated the walls against damp. This has been unsuccessful, and there is damp visible in the walls which they treated. They say that chemically retreating the walls would be the best solution. With the concrete floor and associated membrane, your previous comments would suggest this isn't a solution.

A Chemical damp-proofing is very rarely successful, and if it hasn't worked once, then there is very little point in repeating the process. It sounds as though removing the suspended timber floor with its sub-floor ventilation has upset the moisture equilibrium in the house, and forced moisture up into the walls. No amount of chemical injection or replastering will deal with this; the only long-term solution would be to remove the concrete and reinstate the timber floor.

DAMP METER READINGS

Q I am buying a three-hundred-year-old stone/flint cottage in Somerset. The property is very sound, but the surveyor says his damp meter 'went off the scale' and has advised we install a chemical damp-proof course. The ground floor is concrete laid – presumably – over some sort of membrane, but one room is original flags on bare earth. There are no visible signs of damp in the house – no patches of mould or peeling plaster; the property doesn't smell damp or musty and feels warm and dry – and we've heard that installing DPCs in properties of this type can result in more problems than it solves. Any advice?

Chemical damp-proofing is usually unnecessary and rarely successful.

A This sounds like another case where an old house is in an acceptably dry condition, but an ignorant surveyor has misused an electrical moisture meter to invent a problem that does not exist. And you are right – trying to 'damp-proof' a historic building like this can create problems. The most serious damage is usually caused by hacking off old lime plaster and replastering with a strong sand-and-cement mix. This should be avoided at all costs.

PENETRATING DAMPNESS: CAVITY WALLS AND CONSERVATORIES

Q Our conservatory abuts the south-south-west-facing wall of our house, and during wet weather the bricks become saturated and water drips through above the opening between conservatory and house. I have been advised that repointing or a tile/slate hanging over the wet wall might be the answer.

A When cavity walls are saturated, water tends to run down the inside of the outer leaf until it meets an obstruction. In your case this is the lintel above the entrance to the conservatory. When an extension or conservatory abuts a cavity wall it requires the insertion of a cavity tray above the roof line of the new addition, to throw water clear to the outside. This can be done from the outside by cutting out short sections of brickwork.

INSERTING CAVITY TRAYS

Q You have described the need for cavity trays, which is exactly the problem with my 1920s house. It has had two bay windows extended, with much larger roofs. During south-westerly gales the ceiling leaks in the ground-floor rooms where the bays cut through the outside wall. But how do you retro-fit damp-proof trays in the cavity? Local builders don't know how!

A Cavity trays are needed wherever a bay, or extension, or conservatory, butts up to an external cavity wall. The fitting instructions are simple: (1) Remove two or three bricks; (2) Insert section of cavity tray; (3) Replace bricks; (4) Move along a bit and repeat steps 1 to 3. Where the extension has a pitched roof, the cavity tray has to be installed in stepped sections to follow the pitch. Anyone who does not know how to perform this basic construction operation should not be describing themselves as a builder. Retro-fit cavity trays are available from several manufacturers [DAMPNESS].

DAMPNESS IN OLD FARM BUILDINGS

Q We live in an old farmhouse which was extended by the architect-owner by converting some single-storey farm buildings. Several areas of dampness have appeared on the walls; some cover many square feet whilst others appear as random isolated patches roughly circular in shape. We have sought advice from the local council, local builders and a reputable damp-proofing company. The latter advised us it was not rising damp, and that the wall is dry in depth. The external pointing is in good condition, and the roof and gutters are sound. Nobody can explain why the dampness has appeared or how to stop it.

A The damp patches could be due to salt contamination in the walls from animal urine, which is a common problem in converted farm buildings. The salts are hygroscopic, i.e. they attract moisture from the atmosphere. This can be easily tested for using the method described in Building Research Establishment Digest 245 [CONSTRUCTION LITERATURE]. If this proves to be the cause of the problem, then the salts can be drawn out by repeated application of a chalk poultice. Or, if you replaster using a breathable lime plaster, then they may crystallize out on the surface as efflorescence, and you can wash them off. Alternatively, you can line the walls with a drained, ventilated membrane system.

UNNECESSARY DAMP-PROOFING

Q **We've just moved house, and it was recommended that we have damp-proofing done, which involved hacking off the plaster and replastering, etc. Our house was built in the 1930s and does have some wallpaper peeling off in corners near the floor on the external walls only, and not in every room. The only places it is happening is where the front doorstep joins the house, and at the back where the ground level has been raised by a layer of concrete. The problem is, it is written into our mortgage agreement that we have the damp-proofing work done.**

A I would be surprised if your mortgage offer states that you 'have to have damp-proofing done'. It is more usual that you are asked to have further investigation of possible dampness undertaken. Your 1930s house cannot possibly need a new DPC as it was built with one in place. It may have minor condensation, leaking gutters and the raised ground levels that you mention, but it does not need chemical damp-coursing or replastering. You should write to your mortgage lender saying that there is no evidence of rising damp (electrical meter readings are not evidence). If they insist then pay for an independent survey and report, which will stop you having to repeat the process when you come to sell.

ELECTRICAL DAMP-PROOFING

Q **I have an old property – fifteenth century in parts. The floor level in one of the rooms is 2ft (600mm) below the ground outside. At some time in its history somebody has put in a 'reverse osmosis' electrical damp course. Was this a con, or could it really work? There is a plug behind one of the doors permanently switched on with a sign on it saying 'under no circumstances to be switched off'!**

A Several versions of these electrical damp-proofing systems have been produced over the years, all of which consist of wires inserted into holes or buried under the plaster. The 'reverse osmosis' type did not use electrical power, but was claimed to work by 'short-ciruiting' electrical forces in the wall. Other systems claim to pass electrical currents through the wall. They have been independently tested, and found to have no effect on the moisture content of walls, even though some of them were installed with thirty-year 'guarantees'.

DAMP FLOORS
LEAKING PIPES UNDER FLOOR

Q I have a twenty-five-year-old detached house and the central-heating pipes and water-supply pipes are all embedded in the concrete flooring. I am confident that the damp-proof course is OK. However, there is very serious 'rising damp', which I assume must be from a leaking underground water pipe. Is there an easy way of determining this, or will it be necessary to dig up the floor to try to ascertain what is causing the problem?

A Concrete corrodes copper pipes. These days they have to be sheathed if they are buried, but many houses of your vintage had them just screeded over. Instead of digging them up, the easiest thing would be to cut them off, and replace with new pipe runs in skirting ducts (floor ducts where they cross doorways).

Q I have recently bought an old cottage. The ground-floor living room has damp, and it is proposed to have a concrete floor with a membrane for damp-proofing, with wooden sleepers and boards on top. There is no provision for airbricks, which I thought were necessary to preserve the timber. The contractors state that airbricks aren't needed. They propose to leave the concrete for ten weeks to dry out before putting in the flooring. Can you tell me if this is satisfactory?

A This sounds like a typical case of an old cottage being threatened by inexperienced builders using modern materials. If you want a wooden floor, then why not construct a proper suspended timber ground floor, ventilated underneath (with airbricks, as you suggest)? This will ensure that any moisture coming up out of the ground will be vented away, keeping both the floor and the walls dry. The contractors' plan for a damp-proof membrane covered with concrete will only trap moisture below it, and probably result in water being forced up into the walls.

DRYING OUT AFTER FLOOD

Q Our bath overflow pipe leaked and has caused every wall in our ground-floor flat to absorb water to about 1m high. There is no central heating. From what you've written, it would seem that anti-damp paint would just trap the moisture in the walls.

A Heating and ventilation are the accepted ways of drying things out. If you want to speed up the process then use a dehumidifier. These can be bought for around £200 or hired from a tool-hire shop.

DAMPNESS FOLLOWING FLOODING

Q I am pretty convinced that my father's house does actually suffer from rising damp. He lives in a cottage that was built over two hundred years ago and was recently flooded. After three weeks of drying time the house was redecorated, but the damp is now causing the paint to flake off the walls. Are there any DIY rising-damp treatments that we can do?

A Flooding can take months to dry out. The place doesn't need damp-proofing, it needs drying. Try a dehumidifier.

COB HOUSE 1

Q We have just moved into a damp Devon farmhouse built of stone and cob. Broken gutters and downpipes and built-up ground levels are obvious culprits for the damp, but the local conservation officer says that the modern cement render is exacerbating the problem. Three damp-proofing firms all say that cement render is fine, and they're also unanimous about injecting silicone damp-proof courses as part of the remedy. Who is right about the render? And is silicone damp-proofing suitable for thick cob walls?

A Your local authority building conservation officer is absolutely right. Cob, which is a mixture of local earth and straw, must be allowed to breathe. Plastering it internally with sand-and-cement render will cut down evaporation, and will actually make it wetter, rather than drier. It should be plastered with a traditional lime mix, and any external decoration should be with limewash. Silicone injection damp-proofing is ineffective at the best of times, and it would be plain stupid to try to inject it into an earth building.

COB HOUSE 2

Q We have recently bought a cottage in Dorset which is part-thatched and constructed with cob walls. Obviously it has no damp course, and is believed to be situated over or very near to underground springs, which can well up in winter when the underlying chalk becomes saturated! The floor is brick, probably laid straight onto earth. The Society for the Protection of Ancient Buildings, in its leaflets, advocates leaving things alone, and that cob walls can disintegrate if dried out, and that plenty of ventilation and airflow should control the damp. We are thinking of digging out and laying a waterproof membrane over the whole floor area, and hoping that this will be sufficient to stop rising damp and to leave the walls alone. Do you think that this is an advisable course of action, and do you have any alternative suggestions?

A I would think that SPAB have got it right. Who told you about the 'underground springs' – a damp-proofing salesman? It is quite true that cob walls need a certain moisture content to maintain their integrity. I cannot think of any reason to dig up a sound brick floor, and a membrane would be wholly inappropriate for a building of this type – it would upset the moisture equilibrium and possibly damage the walls by making them too wet. The floor needs to be allowed to breathe, and should not be covered with carpet or any other floor covering apart from loose sisal matting or similar. It sounds to me as though you may have bought this historic building without quite understanding the implications.

CONDENSATION

Condensation is one of the great banes of modern living. Energy-saving propaganda – much of it government sponsored – entreats us to insulate everywhere, draught-proof our doors and windows, fit double glazing and turn the heating down. All these measures increase the likelihood of condensation, which, when it occurs within the fabric of walls, floors and ceilings, lowers their insulation value and, paradoxically, allows more heat to escape than before.

All the moisture that condenses out on windows and within walls is produced by the occupants. People may refer to their homes as being 'damp', but usually the property was dry until they came to live in it.

The most obvious symptom of condensation is misting on the windows, but if it is happening on the windows, then it is happening within the depth of the walls as well.

An example: 55 per cent relative humidity at a room temperature of 20°C is a perfectly normal, average sort of state in an occupied house. If you look up the tables, they will tell you that the dew-point temperature in these conditions is about 10.5°C. In other words, if any surface falls to 10.5°C or lower, then condensation will form on it. So if you take a cold can of beer out of the fridge, then it will soon be wet with condensation.

Now, if the outside temperature should fall to, say, 5°C, then there will be a temperature gradient through the wall, and where it falls to 10.5°C or below – just over halfway through the wall –

Black mould is a sympton of condensation.

the warm air passing through it from the room will be cooled enough to condense. If this condensed moisture is trapped in the wall by, for example, external paint or render, then it will not be able to evaporate, and will stay in the wall and feed the black mould that grows on the wallpaper.

Black mould is a prime symptom of condensation. Another is green mildew on leather goods in the wardrobe. The solution is to keep the bathroom and kitchen doors closed – to stop the moisture produced in these wet rooms from spreading through the rest of the house – and to open a few windows.

It is also important to keep the windows and walls above dew-point temperature, which means keeping the heating on in cold weather. The British habit of having the central heating on for two hours in the morning and four hours in the evening may sound sensible, but scientific analysis shows that it is not energy efficient. The condensation that occurs within the walls lowers their thermal insulation value, and allows valuable heat to escape. In cold weather it is better to keep the heating on permanently, but to turn down the water-temperature dial on the boiler, to provide a constant gentle heat.

CONDENSATION OR RISING DAMP?

Q Is there any way of distinguishing between condensation and a problem with the damp-proof course? When I bought my bungalow four years ago I paid £40 to take over a Certificate of Guarantee for a full damp course and woodworm treatment – valid for thirty years from 1995. I then discovered damp marks in the bedroom, so I called out the damp-proofing company. The man who came dismissed it as 'condensation'.

A Condensation occurs when warm, moist air from within the house meets cold surfaces – usually cold outside walls and windowpanes – and turns into liquid water. Rising dampness is very rare, and so-called 'damp proofing' usually consists of little more than internal replastering. Unless your bungalow was built before 1877, it will have a damp-proof course built in, so it is unlikely to have needed damp-proofing in the first place, and the 'guarantee' will be meaningless. The definitive way to distinguish between condensation and rising dampness is described in Building Research Establishment Digest 245 [CONSTRUCTION LITERATURE].

PASSIVE STACK VENTILATION

Q I am a council tenant, and I have been told that we are to have a 'stack' ventilation system fitted in the building. What does this mean, and do you think it is a good idea?

A Passive stack ventilation is basically a reinvention of the chimney. Victorian houses were often built with extra flues in the chimney breasts – some flues were to take smoke from the fireplaces, and others were to ventilate the rooms. The idea of the modern passive stack is that it will ventilate rooms without the need for electric power and so, with luck, there will be less resistance from council tenants to using it to keep their homes free from condensation.

The principles of passive stack ventilation, and details of how to construct a system using 100mm PVC-U waste pipe or flexible ducting, are described in the Building Research Establishment Information Paper IP 13/94 [CONSTRUCTION LITERATURE].

MILDEW IN WARDROBE

Q We have lived in a detached bungalow for just over twelve months and have become concerned about dampness, particularly in the main bedroom. The bungalow is double-glazed and centrally heated. Over the winter months there have been signs of mildew on some of our shoes kept on shoe racks at low level in the wardrobes.

A The minimum relative humidity for mildew to grow on leather is 72 per cent, so this is the level of moisture in your wardrobes. You need to provide extra heating and ventilation in the bedroom, and to stop water vapour entering from the kitchen and bathroom by keeping the doors closed.

BLACK MOULD IN THE WARDROBE

Q My daughter's house, which is over a hundred years old, has severe problems with black mould creeping up the walls from skirting-board level, wherever the wall is enclosed by cupboards or wardrobes. The house has a modern central-heating system and double glazing. The walls are solid brick. I am assured that there is a damp-proof course, and there is no evidence of damp on the outer wall. What is the prime cause of this and how can it be remedied?

A The black mould is caused by condensation. This occurs when moisture produced by cooking, showering, drying clothes, etc., meets the cold, unventilated surfaces at the back of the cupboards. The double glazing will not be helping, by cutting down on the natural ventilation, but the main problem is probably due to leaving the bathroom and kitchen doors open, and thus allowing moist air to find its way into the other rooms.

CONDENSATION IN ROOF SPACE

Q We had our roof retiled two years ago. The builder used a lightweight plastic type of felt under the tiles, which was different from the original heavy tarred hessian felt. In cold weather we now have condensation running down the inside of the felt and dripping onto the ceiling insulation. The builder suggested increasing the insulation from 4in to 8in (200mm) depth. We did this, but it didn't make any difference. The builder has now fitted some mushroom tile vents in the roof, but the problem continues. We have lived in the house for nearly forty years, always used the loft for storage and have never experienced condensation before.

A The condensation problem has been caused by the new plastic sarking felt, which has cut off all the natural ventilation to the roof space. The manufacturers claim that this stuff is 'breathable', but experience suggests otherwise. Warm, moist air from the house is finding its way up into the cold loft, is unable to be ventilated away and condenses out on the cold, impermeable surface of the plastic sarking felt. Your builder's suggestion to increase the thickness of loft insulation will have made matters worse, because, by keeping more heat in the rooms below, it will have made the roof space even colder. There is one simple, permanent solution to this problem, which is to go up into the loft with a Stanley knife and cut the sarking felt out from between the rafters. If this sounds too drastic for you, then some readers have suggested various Heath Robinson methods for holding the overlapping layers of felt apart, to allow a greater draught.

CONDENSATION IN BATHROOM

Q We have a big problem with condensation in the window area of our bathroom. It has rusted a venetian blind; it runs off the tiled window sill and wets the wall below, causing the paint to peel off; and there is black mould growing in the window recess. The window is already double-glazed, and I wonder whether fitting secondary glazing would solve our problem – in effect creating a triple-glazed window. There is a fan vented to the outside but it seems quite ineffective.

A Adding an extra layer of glass is unlikely to solve a serious condensation problem. What is needed is better ventilation, to get rid of moist air before it has a chance to condense out on the cold surfaces. The double-glazed window should have a permanent trickle vent at the top, and after bathing or showering you should leave the fan running, or the window open, until the surfaces are dry. Most bathrooms also need permanent heating, to keep the surfaces above dew-point temperature. An electric towel rail or tubular electric heater below the window may be all that is needed. A 120W heater uses only as much electricity as a couple of light bulbs, and will pay for itself in saving money spent on repairs and redecorating.

CONDENSATION CAUSED BY CAVITY INSULATION

Q Some six or seven years ago the cavity walls of our house were insulated. Since then, in colder weather, condensation on the windows has got progressively worse. We do not have or want double glazing. Is there any remedy?

A The cavity-wall insulation will be keeping your home warmer, so the air is capable of holding more water vapour than before. But at the same time, it will be keeping the inner surfaces of your walls warmer as well, so that condensation does not occur on them. The result is to concentrate the condensation effect on the remaining cold surfaces, the windowpanes. The solution is better ventilation, so that the moist air is removed to the outside of the house before it has a chance to condense on the windows. It is especially important to keep your kitchen and bathroom doors closed, and use the cooker hood and extractor fans whenever these rooms are in use. You should also open a few windows and give the house a good airing at least once every day.

CONDENSATION ON WC CISTERN

Q I get condensation running down my toilet cistern all winter. I have tried lots of things to prevent it. The latest is to put in an airbrick. This did not work, so now my wife is fed up with me not solving the problem. Can you help?

A The first thing is to make sure the cistern is fed from the cold-water tank in the loft, rather than direct from the mains. The tank water will be slightly warmer, and so will allow a higher relative humidity before attracting condensation. The second is to fit an electric extractor fan in place of the airbrick, and to use it whenever the bathroom is used. Most bathrooms would also benefit from permanent heating – such as a 120W tubular electric heater. Readers have also suggested drip trays clipped to the flush pipe (although these are no longer made commercially) and lining the inside of the cistern with 10mm polystyrene (such as ceiling tiles) to keep the surface above

113

Condensation occurs when warm, moist air meets a cold surface.

dew-point temperature. One exasperated reader has even plumbed his cistern to fill from the hot-water system. If all else fails, then install a dehumidifier.

USE OF DEHUMIDIFIERS/HUMIDISTAT FANS

Q Following a roof leak I borrowed a neighbour's dehumidifier, and was amazed at how much water it collected from the air. But how useful do you think a permanent dehumidifier would be, compared to, say, a humidistat-operated extractor fan?

A Extractor fans work by expelling warm moist air, which is then replaced by drier, colder air from the outside. Every bathroom and kitchen should have one – in the kitchen in the form of a cooker hood. Unfortunately during wet weather the air being drawn in will also be moist, meaning the fan has to work longer to achieve a result.

Humidistat-switched fans are supposed to switch themselves on whenever the relative humidity reaches a certain level – usually 65 per cent. The trouble is that many of them contain very cheap humidity sensors, and simply do not function as they are supposed to. I have tried several of these fans, and none of them has functioned satisfactorily for more than a few months.

Dehumidifiers are a much more efficient way of controlling moisture levels, regardless of the weather conditions, and are especially useful in homes where the windows are kept closed for security purposes, or where washing is regularly dried indoors. They work by passing air over a cooled element, where it condenses and drips into a container. The container must be emptied when it gets full, but most models can also be permanently piped to the existing drainage system.

WHAT HUMIDITY?

Q What is the optimum level of humidity for a house – I cannot find the information in the book accompanying my dehumidifier. Obviously 100 per cent is rain and 0 per cent a bit drastic – what should I aim for?

A Opinions vary about this. Owners of antique furniture and musical instruments are often critical of dehumidifiers, as too dry an atmosphere can cause shrinkage and splitting, especially in thin timbers. A 'normal' relative humidity on a dry summer day in Britain will be around 55 per cent – most people will find this comfortable, and it is too low for moulds and mildew to grow. Humidistat-switched bathroom extractor fans are usually set to come on at 65 per cent. So the optimum level is probably

CONDENSATION

114

between 55 and 65 per cent. The difficulty comes when you try to measure this, as the humidistats on dehumidifiers and extractor fans are notoriously unreliable, as are the dial-type hygrometers which some people have on their walls, and the 'sling hygrometers' used by some surveyors. A truly accurate electronic hygrometer will cost upwards of £200, and need annual recalibration.

CONDENSATION REDUCED BY PERMANENT HEATING

Q For forty years I have had our boiler on for four hours in the morning and six hours or so in the evening. You now advise leaving the boiler on continuously (though reducing the boiler stat at night). Would this not increase the fuel bill to a great extent?

A The idea is to keep the walls above dew-point temperature, and so stop condensation forming either on them or inside them. The problem with the typical British 'morning and evening' heating practice is that between times the walls cool down and condensation occurs. Then when the heating is switched on again half the energy is used to evaporate the condensed moisture (known scientifically as the 'latent heat of vaporization'). If the room thermostat is left on 15°C and the boiler thermostat is turned down to '1' or 'min', rather than turning the heating off completely, then this problem should be avoided. Readers who have followed this advice usually report that their fuel bills go down, not up.

Q In order to follow your advice on permanent low-level heating, in my case this would mean turning the boiler thermostat well down from its usual setting. Would this not mean that the boiler would switch on and off far more often in an attempt to achieve the temperature required by the room thermostat? I would have thought this would mean uneconomic use of the boiler.

A No. The boiler does not run continuously anyway, whatever the water temperature. Once the water has reached the temperature set by the boiler thermostat, then the boiler modulates, firing up and running for a few minutes at a time to keep the temperature at that level. Running it at a lower temperature will not alter this pattern.

HEATING ON OR OFF?

Q My system has thermostatic valves on every radiator instead of a central room thermostat. If I turn the boiler down at night and leave the pump on, surely as the temperature drops in a room the thermostatic valve will call for more heat from the radiator, which means more hot water from the boiler, and it will simply remain fired up all the time to meet the demand. It is impractical to turn every valve (some twenty) down individually and so twenty-four-hour gas usage must be more expensive than say eight hours' usage.

A The idea is to keep a flow of warm water going round the whole system in very cold weather, so as to prevent the wall temperature falling below dew point. To this end, your TRVs should be kept open, not closed down. You should turn down the water temperature on the boiler. I should add that TRVs should not be seen as a substitute for a room thermostat, and you should consider having one of these fitted. Preventing condensation and keeping the walls dry should improve the thermal insulation of your home and so save energy.

WOODWORM AND WOOD ROT

Regular news reports about the health problems suffered by Gulf War and Balkans War veterans are timely reminders of the dangers posed by exposure to toxic chemicals. Years after the events, there is disagreement over the causes of ill health suffered by returning troops, but the finger of suspicion points at the many chemicals encountered in the course of modern warfare. Unfortunately, some of those chemicals are used by the building trade as well.

Worryingly, chemicals in the house can pose risks even greater than when they are encountered on the battlefield. For one thing, their effects can be longer-lasting because they are trapped within the building, and for another, occupants can be exposed to them for longer periods. Young children and retired older people especially can be at high risk, as they often spend eighteen hours or more per day indoors.

But perhaps the most significant finding of the research into so-called Gulf War syndrome is the fact that combinations of two or more chemicals can be more damaging to health than the sum of each individual substance. For example, one researcher fed chickens with 'safe' doses of the insecticide permethrin (used to de-louse Iraqi prisoners) and the common insect repellent DEET (diethyl toluamide), and found that they became ill and died. Each chemical on its own had no significant impact; it was the cocktail effect that did the damage.

These old woodworm holes are only in the sap-wood at one corner of the joist.
They have not weakened the timber and do not need any treatment.

These findings deserve wider publicity, because permethrin has been sprayed in millions of British homes as a woodworm treatment, and it is also present in new clothes, carpets and soft furnishings, to prevent moth damage. Meanwhile, DEET is the active ingredient in insect repellents sold over the counter in pharmacists. So anyone using an insect repellent and living in a house sprayed with permethrin timber treatment could be exposing themselves to the same chemical combination as the Gulf War veterans. Not to mention those unfortunate chickens.

The timber-treatment industry has put much effort into persuading the public that its products are risk-free. It defended its use of the deadly organochlorines DDT and dieldrin until they were finally banned in the 1980s, and then continued to spray homes with the organochlorine lindane until it, too, was withdrawn from use. It then put its weight behind permethrin, and I was even told on an industry training course in 1994 that it was quite safe to drink a pint glass of this stuff. Strange, then, if it is so safe, that the industry is now moving away from permethrin and switching to boron, the latest 'safe' pesticide.

But like its predecessors, boron is a poison. If it wasn't, then it wouldn't be used to kill insects and fungi. And, like its predecessors, boron has never been tested for the effects it has on health when it is combined with other chemicals. So if you buy a house which has been previously sprayed with permethrin, and your surveyor advises you to have the empty woodworm holes sprayed again with boron, what effect will this chemical combination have on your health? Nobody knows, because the research has never been done.

In any case, most woodworm holes are the harmless relics of insects that departed many years ago, and spraying them is unnecessary. And when scientific research has suggested that Parkinson's disease may be linked to a cocktail of two readily available gardening pesticides, isn't it time for some serious research on the combination effects of all these common chemicals?

HEALTH DANGERS

Q Can you suggest any safe woodworm fluid for an attic which has worm holes? We would be concerned for our children's health particularly. We have installed modern Velux windows and need to protect these from any live woodworm. What would you suggest?

A I cannot recommend any woodworm fluids. They are all nerve poisons (see HAZARDS). Your worm holes are probably many years old. They are actually 'flight holes' of the adult beetles leaving the wood. There is no justification for using insecticides unless you have definitive evidence that there is a continuing active infestation, and that this cannot be dealt with by normal construction methods, i.e. central heating and ventilation. Your new Velux windows are unlikely to be affected by wood-boring insects – the timber in them is kiln-dried and sealed with a water-based varnish.

Q I have discovered old woodworm holes in my bathroom floorboards after removing old lino tiles. Since the boards have been exposed to air this last week, new holes have appeared, with fresh sawdust around them. How can I get rid of these myself without the deadly sprays the companies use?

A You don't have to do anything to get rid of them, because they have already gone. Your lifting of the lino has coincided with the spring flight season. It is quite likely that the lino tiles were trapping moisture and keeping the floorboards damp. Now that they have been lifted, and as long as your house is properly heated and ventilated, then the timber will probably dry down to below the 11 per cent moisture needed to support wood-boring insects. If you are really worried, then boiled linseed oil is a safe natural insecticide.

DEATH-WATCH BEETLE?

Q I have found that my hundred-year-old Victorian terraced house has death-watch beetle, judging from the ticking coming from different locations in its pitch-pine timberwork. I'd greatly value your advice.

A Death-watch beetles prefer hardwoods, especially oak, so it would be unusual to find them in pitch pine. Are you sure it couldn't be expansion/contraction noises you are hearing?

TIMBER TREATMENT – SAFE IN KITCHEN?

Q I need woodworm treatment for a kitchen. Can you suggest a treatment that is safe to use in a kitchen environment? I have been told that certain products are not allowed where there is food preparation.

A In my opinion no chemical insecticide could be regarded as 'safe'. If you really have active woodworm in your kitchen (and not just old flight holes in the floorboards), then the way to get rid of it is by normal heating and ventilation. If wood is dry then nothing can live in it. An additional measure is to use an ultraviolet 'Insect-o-cutor' to kill any adult beetles which emerge in the spring. This is a useful device to have in a kitchen anyway.

WOODWORM IN OLD FURNITURE

Q An antique beechwood chair which I bought a few years ago has active woodworm – i.e. sawdust coming out of new-looking holes. I treated it with an anti-woodworm fluid. Now I am wondering whether I need to treat the house timber (house built in 1880s) and the other furniture (mainly oak). I would hate to do that, partly because of the pollution and partly because I am asthmatic and just doing the one chair affected my breathing for a few days. On the other hand, everyone tells me that eventually the worms will eat half my house! I take comfort from what you say about the worms preferring sapwood, but wonder why they invaded the chair in the first place – it is definitely not a new chair. I live in an area where there are lots of garden trees, and the window is often open, so any beetle wanting sapwood would have no trouble finding it.

A Woodworm is not infectious, and there is no reason why it would spread from one piece of furniture to another or to house timbers. Each infestation results from the female adult beetle laying eggs in an environment that she thinks will be suitable for her offspring – i.e. moist nutritious wood. If you have moist nutritious wood anywhere in your house then adult female beetles – which are flying around everywhere between April and July – will lay eggs in it. If the wood is dry, as it will be if you live in a normal heated ventilated house, then they won't. The infestation in the beech chair probably happened five years ago when it was stored in damp conditions. Three to five years is the life cycle of the insects. Once this generation has hatched out and flown then that will probably be the end of it – regardless of how many chemicals you spray around the place.

Dry rot only lives on wet wood. Removing the source of the moisture, and increasing the ventilation, will get rid of it.

DRY-ROT DIAGNOSIS

Q I have recently discovered that I have dry rot in my house, and I am ready to invite some-one into my house to give me a quote for sorting out this problem – but who? Where do I start – carpenter, plasterer, general builder, dry-rot specialist – who would you suggest as the best starting place?

A The first step is to ensure that the diagnosis of dry rot is accurate. There is nothing 'dry' about dry rot. This is a fungus which will only live on very wet wood, and in very humid conditions. If you have come across some decayed timber which is now dry, then it was probably left by a previ-ous case of wet rot, caused by a water leak that has now been repaired. If you really have dry rot in the house, then it must be caused by a rainwater or plumbing leak, and the correct course of action is to locate the leak and have it repaired, by a builder or plumber as appropriate. A 'dry-rot specialist' will usually be a commission-paid salesman from a company that sells chemical timber treatments – and he will therefore specify chemical treatment. For independent, non-chemical, advice see DAMPNESS AND TIMBER SURVEYORS on page 170.

DRY ROT AND WOODWORM

Q We have dry rot in one room of our Victorian house, and there is evidence of woodworm throughout the floor, which I do not believe is active. I have been advised that the walls and floors need treating, and I am reluctant to do this because a ninety-year-old lady lives on the ground floor. Are there any chemicals that are safe to use with her living in the building, or is there another remedy that would stop the spread of infestation, so that treatment could be carried out at a later date?

A I follow the advice given by the Health and Safety Executive and the Building Research Establishment, that timber infestation should be dealt with by correct building practices – i.e. repairing sources of moisture ingress and drying timber out by normal heating and ventilation.

Fungi and insects only attack damp wood. My personal view is that there is no such thing as a 'safe' chemical pesticide, especially in cases involving the very young or the very old (see also HAZARDS, Timber-treatment chemicals).

DRY ROT IN BRICKWORK?

Q **I have what a few builders call 'a serious problem, mate'. The problem is I have dry rot on one of my walls (outside wall with a gully). The rot has eaten away my stairs and strands appear to be coming from between the brickwork (I hacked off all the old plaster and mortar) over a certain area. I have taken away all the damaged wood and believe that I have found where the damp is coming from. My problem now is what to do with the wall; should I plasterboard it up or get it rendered and plastered?**

A The key things are to stop the source of moisture ingress – which you appear to have done – and allow the affected area to dry out and 'breathe'. To this end cement-and-sand renders are usually a bad idea, especially if the house is old and the original plaster was lime-and-sand. Similarly, plasterboarding the area would be a bad idea, as any future problems would be hidden from view. The ideal would be lime plaster to match the original, but if you can't find anyone to do traditional lime-and-sand plastering then something like Tarmac's Limelite is a good second choice. Avoid gypsum finishing plasters as they do not perform well in damp conditions.

DRY-ROT TREATMENT

Q **My local wood-treatment company have told me that even though my windows are to be replaced with a set of PVC-U French doors, and the house has a concrete floor, it will still be necessary to treat and replaster the surrounding walls as the dry-rot fungus can live in them and spread throughout my house. (The walls are cavity brickwork construction.) Can dry rot live in mortar?**

A Dry rot is a fungus that lives on wet wood. If you remove the source of any moisture, and if – as in your case – you have very little wood in the house, then there will be nothing for it to live on. Irrigating brickwork with fungicidal chemicals is an expensive process that involves removal of the existing plaster, and subsequent replastering. It is a trick that timber-treatment companies have been using for years to extract the maximum amount of money from their customers, but it has no scientific basis, and is a complete waste of money and effort.

REPAIRING ROT IN ROOF

Q **Can you advise me on how to treat dry rot in the roof of an old house, without using 'specialists'. The roof has been repaired and there is no more ingress of water.**

A It would be unusual to find dry rot in a roof space, since it needs a large amount of water and high humidity in unventilated conditions. Roof spaces are usually too warm and draughty for it. The damage was probably wet rot, caused by the leaks. If these have been fixed, and there is good ventilation, then nothing further should need to be done.

INSULATION

Insulation is a good way of cutting heating costs and energy waste. Houses constructed before 1945 often had minimal insulation, and thus took a lot of energy to heat. As fuel costs rose in the 1960s, householders were encouraged to put 50mm of fluffy quilt in their lofts, and after the oil crisis of 1973 this was raised to 100mm. We are now encouraged to have at least 200mm (8in) of insulation above our bedroom ceilings. The 1970s also saw cavity-wall insulation introduced for new buildings: first 25mm, then 50mm, and now 75mm.

The trouble with this approach is that successive thickening of insulation does not necessarily result in corresponding savings in energy. The law of diminishing returns applies. So if your uninsulated home costs £1,000 per year to heat, then wrapping it in the latest specified thickness of fluffy stuff may well reduce that outlay to £500, but doubling the thickness will not reduce the heating costs to zero. Homes in northern Europe will always need a source of internal heat, although the current government obsession with insulation encourages people to believe otherwise, and this can have unfortunate consequences.

The chief problem with a spartan fuel regime is an increased risk of condensation. Some pensioners and other low-income families have annual fuel bills of less than £150, and they achieve this by keeping their windows permanently closed, taking the fuses out of mechanical extractor fans and blocking up air vents. The inevitable result is black mould growth on ceilings and walls, and green mildew on shoes and clothes in the wardrobe. Local authority tenants on income support are especially likely to live in such conditions, and there is usually a friendly local damp-proofing company on hand to persuade them that they are victims of 'damp', and to encourage them to sue their landlords to have their homes 'damp-proofed'. Many cash-strapped local authorities waste millions of pounds of council taxpayers' money every year on this sort of nonsense.

The 2002 version of the Building Regulations produced yet another increase in the thickness of wall insulation. New homes are also to be subject to airtightness tests, which will ensure that ventilation is kept to a minimum.

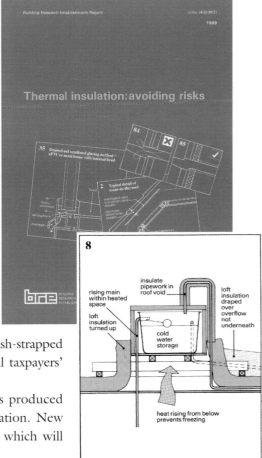

This all means that new houses are set to become hermetically sealed boxes, full of chemical timber preservatives, mineral wool fibres and formaldehyde emissions from plastics and adhesives. Condensation will be a major problem, but will probably be dwarfed by the epidemic of asthma and other allergic reactions which will affect the children brought up in these ghastly buildings.

If you are thinking of improving your home's insulation, then before you do anything you should get hold of a copy of the BRE booklet 'Thermal Insulation – avoiding risks' [CONSTRUCTION LITERATURE].

CAVITY-WALL INSULATION 1

Q **I am contemplating installing cavity-wall insulation and looking at the materials available I feel that foam would be the best on the basis that polystyrene beads would restrict any further maintenance on the wall, i.e. window-frame replacement, and mineral wool could be detrimental to my health, as I suffer from emphysema. We have all heard of the advantages of cavity-wall insulation, but are there any disadvantages? I have heard of damp spots appearing on the inside of walls, for example.**

A Cavity walls were first built in exposed coastal areas, in order to keep out wind-driven rain. Filling the cavity with insulation will always hold the risk that moisture will be able to find its way across to the inside, whatever the insulation material. There is also the possibility that the installation will be less than perfect, leaving unfilled air pockets – these will leave 'cold spots' on the inside walls which attract condensation. Another problem concerns wall-tie corrosion; cavity insulation makes the outer brick leaf colder, and therefore wetter, which can accelerate rusting of the wall ties. And if the ties then have to be replaced, there is no satisfactory way of refilling the holes in the insulation, whatever the material. The cavity-insulation industry denies the existence of these problems, but in my experience they are quite common. I do not think cavity-wall insulation is a good idea.

Thermal image of a house with cavity wall insulation. The red 'hot spots' show where it has not been properly installed.

CAVITY-WALL INSULATION 2

Q I have had my cavity walls insulated with mineral wool, and now damp patches have appeared on the inside walls. Is it possible to have the insulation removed? It was blown in, so could it possibly be sucked out?

A Several readers have reported problems with penetrating dampness since having cavity-wall insulation installed. The British Board of Agrément approval for these products clearly states that they are unsuitable for areas of high exposure to wind-driven rain, and that a thorough inspection of the walls should be undertaken first, to check for watertightness. Needless to say, these requirements are often ignored. All cavity insulation can be removed. Mineral fibres and polystyrene granules can be vacuumed out, whilst solid foam insulation must be manually broken up and scraped out.

EXTERNAL WALL INSULATION

Q I am having the 1950s extension of my eighteenth-century stone cottage reroofed. At the same time, I would like to improve the insulation in the walls. To avoid disturbing the interior fittings, an architect friend has suggested using insulating panels on the outside of the walls. I gather these are quite new, and they certainly seem to be new to the builders who are quoting. Also, I am slightly worried that adding a layer on the outside could trap moisture and so cause damp, or perhaps just not work.

A External insulation is almost always a good idea, as it keeps the walls warm and thus helps prevent condensation. It can be applied to most types of houses, apart from those with face brickwork. There are two main systems: one consists of fixing insulation boards to the walls and rendering over them; the other uses a lightweight insulating aggregate in the render. The insulation is stopped above DPC level, and window sills may have to be extended to cope with the extra wall thickness. For details of specialist companies call the Insulated Render and Cladding Association [PLASTERING].

ROOFS

Q We have a problem with a well-insulated slate roof. In the winter it keeps the house wonderfully warm but in summer it becomes unbearably hot upstairs as the hot air in the roof has nowhere to go. We have no vertical walls up there to put a vent and local builders have suggested air conditioning. We cannot believe this is the most efficient way of dealing with the problem.

A Insulation is great for keeping heat in, but it always needs to be combined with ventilation, in order to allow moisture and excess heat to escape. I presume you mean your roof is insulated between the rafters, as opposed to insulation of the top-floor ceilings between the ceiling joists. And when you say there are no vertical walls, I guess you have a hipped roof, with four pitched sides, rather than a gable roof with two. You could either install grilles at high level and connect them to ridge vents, in place of two or three existing ridge tiles, or fit one or more small skylights which can be opened in warm weather. Avoid large roof windows, which can make the situation worse by allowing excessive solar heat gain – just like a greenhouse. A range of roof windows and ventilation accessories is available from The Loft Shop [LOFT CONVERSIONS].

LOFT SPACES

Q My loft has electrical cables clipped to the sides of the joists. I have roll insulation at various thicknesses between one and three inches at present but would like to increase this to 8in (200mm) as recommended. It seems inevitable that I will cover the cables. Is this acceptable or a fire hazard?

A Cables carrying electric current always generate heat, and burying them under insulation can allow this heat to build up. In practice, this is only a serious problem for 13A power cables, and those in your loft are likely to be only for the 5A upstairs lighting circuit. But to be on the safe side it should be a simple matter to unclip them from the joists and pass the new insulation quilt underneath.

Ceiling insulation should always be draped across the joists, rather than in between them, but there should be no insulation beneath water tanks – these need warmth from the rooms below to prevent freezing, and should be securely lagged around the sides and over the top. And don't forget to lag any exposed water pipes.

INSULATION GRANULES

Q My loft floor is insulated with granules – I do not know what they are made of. Now an insulation firm has told me that polystyrene granules rot electricity cables. This is alarming, but is it true? And how can I tell whether my granules are polystyrene?

A Most loose-fill loft insulation is expanded vermiculite, made by heating a naturally occurring mineral. It has a grey, flaky, slightly reflective appearance. Slightly less common is expanded perlite, also made by heating a mineral, which has the form of small white beads. Perlite looks similar to expanded polystyrene, but it is hard when pressed between finger and thumb.

Expanded polystyrene beads are a familiar material, used in a bonded form to make the packaging for electrical goods, etc. If you can squash the individual beads in your fingers then they could well be polystyrene. It is true that polystyrene reacts with the PVC sheathing of electrical cables to make a sticky mess on the surface. The cable manufacturers say that this should not represent a fire risk, but should be avoided nevertheless. In loft spaces insulated with loose polystyrene fill, the lighting cables should be protected with conduit.

If you suspect you have loose polystyrene fill in contact with your cables then the simplest way to check is to inspect the cables themselves, and see if any of the granules have stuck to the cable sheathing. For safety, you should turn off the electricity at the consumer unit before handling the cables.

EFFICIENT INSULATION MATERIAL

Q I have just bought a house with a large uninsulated room in the roof space. It is too hot to use in summer, and too cold in winter. To be practical, any insulation will have to be applied to the inside of the walls and ceiling, and I am prepared to forgo a few inches of space. What is the most efficient insulation material to use, both thermally and economically? I wish to finish with a surface which can be papered or painted in the normal way.

A With insulation, the thermal and financial efficiencies are inextricably bound. If you save money by using cheap insulation, then you will pay for it in the long term by using more energy for heating (or for cooling, in the summer). The most efficient insulation material is rigid polyurethane foam boards, and these are available with plasterboard bonded to one face. You can glue these to existing surfaces, tape and fill the gaps between the boards and decorate on top. The cheaper alternative is glassfibre or mineral wool, but this is less thermally efficient, and will require a timber framework to hold it, and a separate plasterboard finish to cover it. It may still work out slightly cheaper, but only in the short term.

BELOW GROUND FLOOR

Q **My house has wooden floors and copious amounts of airbricks. While I am aware of the importance of the airbricks, there is a definite chill around the ankles in icy and windy weather so I wonder whether it would be practical to install baffles, around 2in (50mm) larger than the airbricks, to stop the wind blowing directly into them. Does that sound like a good or bad idea to you?**

A Bad idea. Any sort of obstruction will impede the air flow below the floor and could lead to a build-up of moisture. If you are troubled by draughts into the ground-floor rooms, then draught-proof the gap between floor and skirting. But the best thing would be to insulate the ground floor by lifting the floorboards, draping an insulating membrane across the joists and fitting insulation slabs between the joists, before re-fixing the boards. That way, you will have a warm floor, but preserve the ventilating effects of the air flow below it.

DRAUGHT-PROOFING

Q **I live and work in what was a derelict Georgian building now restored almost to its former glory, with original very beautiful sash windows which are a bit draughty, particularly in the bathroom! Is there a method of reducing the draught?**

A There are several types of draught excluder for sliding sash windows. The best ones are routed into a groove up the sides. Cheaper ones are like rows of brushes tacked to the frames.

HAZARDOUS POLYSTYRENE

Q **Our Homebuyer Survey advised we remove the potential fire hazard of polystyrene covering on one wall of the bedroom of our bungalow, which is in a very exposed rural location. Assuming the polystyrene was to reduce the cold effect of the outside wall, would it be practical to batten, plasterboard and skim this one wall to reduce its coldness?**

A Polystyrene ceiling tiles and wall coverings are not a 'fire hazard' as such, and there is no requirement to remove it. But the fire service hates it because when there is a fire, the polystyrene can melt, catch fire and drip like burning napalm. And it gives off horrible carcinogenic fumes. So it would be just as well to get rid of it. You could easily insulate your bungalow from the inside as described, although you should incorporate a vapour barrier on the warm side of the insulation, to stop condensation occurring within the insulated wall. Better still to insulate it on the outside, using external cladding or an insulated render.

SOUND-PROOFING

According to a report from the World Health Organization, noise is the most widespread pollutant on the planet, presenting a significant threat to health, well-being and quality of life. And figures from the UK's Chartered Institute of Environmental Health show a consistent year-on-year rise in noise complaints to local authorities.

With noisy neighbours, the Institute recommends communicating with them as the most effective way of dealing with the problem. This is often easier said than done. As I write this I am trying to ignore my neighbour's dog, which barks from eight in the morning till ten at night. When I first politely drew this to the neighbour's attention she told me that it was natural for dogs to bark. On the second occasion she accused me of harassment and said she would call the police if I complained again. The local environmental health department say that barking dogs do not constitute a 'statutory nuisance' under the Environmental Protection Act (1990), and that they are unable to take action.

So, since we now live with so much noise – traffic, dogs, television, amplified music – and since the legislation is so useless, it may be easier to soundproof our homes than to deal with the noise at source.

Noise from outside, such as traffic and barking dogs, should first be approached by draught-proofing around doors and windows and fitting secondary glazing. Secondary glazing is not to be confused with double glazing, which has a small sealed gap – around 15mm – between the two sheets of glass, and is good for thermal insulation. Secondary glazing creates a bigger air gap between itself and existing windows – 100mm to 200mm – and this is better for reducing noise. Fitting secondary glazing is cheaper than complete replacement double glazing, and offers the advantage of retaining the original fenestration pattern in older houses.

Secondary glazing cuts down road noise and preserves the original windows.

Noise from immediate neighbours – whether through walls or floors – enters in two ways: impact sound and airborne sound. Impact sound is most likely to be the footsteps of the people in the flat above, and becomes worse when they follow the latest trend for taking up the carpets and having bare wooden floors. The solution involves physically separating the floor and ceiling, so breaking the path of the vibrations. The best way to do this is to construct a new floor above, with joists between, but not touching, the original ceiling joists below. This will raise the floor level slightly, and doors will have to be trimmed to fit. Alternative, but less effective, solutions are to relay the existing floor so that it 'floats' on acoustic rubber strips, or to construct an insulated false ceiling in the downstairs flat.

Older houses converted into flats during the last ten years should have a fair measure of soundproof-

BRE   *Improving sound insulation in homes*

Many people are bothered by neighbour noise. The problem can occur in any type of attached house, flat or bungalow but most commonly in flats that have been converted from large houses. You may be bothered by your neighbour's noise because:

- you are unusually sensitive to noise
- your neighbour behaves unreasonably
- the sound insulation between your homes is poor

While everybody sometimes hears some noise such as raised voices, laughter or occasional loud music, you should not be able to hear your neighbour's normal conversation or television. You can look for a legal or DIY solution to the problem. This document outlines some of the DIY measures possible.

First of all you have to decide how the sound is travelling into your home. It may be coming directly through the party wall or floor or it may be coming along another route called a flanking path. The most common such path is the inner leaf of an external cavity wall. Some examples of flanking paths are shown in Figure 1.

the case, upgrading the floor is almost certain to be effective.

Remedial Treatment: Walls
The following steps for construction are suggested, see Figure 2:
- build a studwork frame, attached to the ceiling and floor but not fixed to the original wall
- hang mineral wool inside the cavity, and tack between the studs or to a batten on the wall
- line the studwork with two layers of plasterboard, making sure the joints between the sheets in the first and second layer do not coincide
- seal perimeter and all other sound paths with flexible sealant

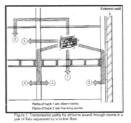

Figure 1. Transmission paths for airborne sound through rooms in a pair of flats separated by a timber floor

It is essential to determine the path of the sound so that the remedial treatment can be chosen correctly. *Some information on how to diagnose the sound path is contained in leaflet XL4'.*

The unwanted noise travelling along direct and flanking paths makes the structure vibrate and this causes the sound to radiate into your room. A solution is to build another wall or ceiling beside the original, but not connected to it. In flats converted before June 1992 there may have been little or no sound insulation improvement undertaken on the floor. If this is

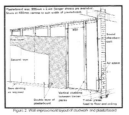

Figure 2. Wall improvement layout of studwork and plasterboard

ing, supervised by the local authority building-control officer, but earlier conversions may have escaped their attentions, as might buildings where planning relaxations were granted – to preserve ornate Victorian ceilings, for example.

Airborne sound, if loud enough, can make the walls and windows vibrate as well, but its usual entry route is via gaps. If you can smell your neighbours' cooking or cigarette smoke, then you will probably also be able to hear their noises, travelling along the same paths. In terraced houses, a common route is through the cracks which open up between front walls and party walls; locating these gaps, and sealing them with a flexible filler, can sometimes achieve good results. Chimney breasts in party walls are also a route for sounds and smells, when the internal brick lining of the flues may have broken down.

More serious soundproofing of a party wall involves constructing a new timber stud wall close to, but not touching, the original brickwork, filling the space with sound insulation quilt and finishing with high-density plasterboard or plaster on metal lathing. Proprietary plasterboard sheets with soundproofing quilt already attached, such as British Gypsum's Triline system, can be fixed straight on to the existing wall with dabs of adhesive [PLASTERING].

Readers can obtain a free leaflet, 'Improving sound insulation in homes', from the Building Research Establishment website [SOUNDPROOFING].

NOISE THROUGH PLASTERBOARD WALLS

Q My house is built to 'modern standards', and the walls of the bedrooms surrounding the bathroom transmit all sounds with embarrassing clarity. I am erecting fitted wardrobes down the bedroom walls and I wondered if there is a soundproofing sheet which I could fit to reduce noise transmission?

A You can fit a special plasterboard sheet with soundproofing quilt attached, such as British Gypsum's Triline system. Better still, construct a separate stud wall with 50mm x 50mm timber, with a 50mm gap between this and the original wall. Fill between the studs with 100mm soundproofing quilt and finish with two layers of 12.5mm plasterboard with staggered joints.

NOISE THROUGH FLOORS 1

Q My problem is with airborne sound – television, music, loud conversation (occasional bedroom noise!) – from the flat below. While not deafening, it is irritating. I live in a top-floor conversion flat of a large Edwardian terrace (conversion pre-building regulations of the early nineties). An architect friend has suggested laying a product called Fermacell (a sandwich of dense fibreboard and insulation material) on the floorboards. This, however, will raise the floor level 30mm and will involve lifting skirting boards and, possibly, the fireplace. It is also expensive – £1,500 for just one room – plus costs of redecorating and relaying carpets. As my problem is not severe, merely irritating, can you suggest cheaper solutions?

A Airborne sound travels through gaps, so you could try sealing the gaps between your floorboards by lining the floor with hardboard, which would be a lot cheaper than the Fermacell and is only 3mm thick. Before you fix the hardboard – with serrated 20mm hardboard nails every 150mm – you might as well lift a few floorboards and put some glassfibre or mineral wool quilt between the joists. Be careful not to bury any power cables under the quilt, but let them sit on top of it, otherwise they may overheat. After the hardboard is fitted (rough side up), seal the junction between the floor and skirting board with decorator's flexible filler applied with a mastic gun.

But before you do anything, why not see if you can get your neighbours to contribute to any proposed works. After all, I'm sure they can hear you too, and it is in both your interests to upgrade the soundproofing of your properties.

NOISE THROUGH FLOORS 2

Q I have recently bought a rather nice flat, rebuilt from a burnt-out hotel c. 1947. The problem is that I can hear my neighbours above change their minds. They are aware of the problem (noise goes both ways) and have had two layers of rock wool 800mm put between the joists underneath their floorboards and above our main bedroom ceiling. This has made a big difference and now all we can hear is their boards creaking (a bit) and their loo flushing.

Now we would like to do our bit. What can we do to insulate our ceilings without spoiling the decor? We don't mind losing a bit of height (say 200mm) and re-coving. If we are shown to be doing our bit then I think we could persuade them to do the rock-wool treatment over the remaining rooms.

SOUNDPROOFING

Another potential problem is that they are talking of putting down a hardwood floor. That would seem to nullify all the insulation efforts. We will have to try and persuade them otherwise. Local builders don't seem to have much of a clue.

A If your upstairs neighbours are going to spend money on a new floor then this would seem like an ideal opportunity to effect a complete acoustic break, so that they put in new floor joists between your ceiling joists. You could offer to contribute to the cost, and keep your existing ceiling intact. Alternatively, they could lift their existing floorboards and lay the new ones on acoustic rubber damping strips on top of the existing joists – not as effective, though. Details in the BRE leaflet [SOUNDPROOFING].

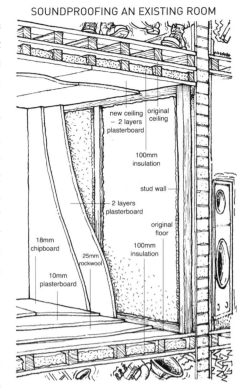

SOUNDPROOFING AN EXISTING ROOM

new ceiling – 2 layers plasterboard

original ceiling

100mm insulation

stud wall

2 layers plasterboard

original floor

18mm chipboard

25mm rockwool

100mm insulation

10mm plasterboard

FALSE CEILING

Q My builder has just attempted to improve sound-proofing in my bedroom (because of noise from the flat above). He was going to rip down the ceiling and start again with fibreglass insulation followed by a double thickness of plasterboard hung from metal strips. However, when he started to pull down the old ceiling he found, to his surprise, that it was already stuffed with fibreglass insulation. So he left the ceiling as it was and simply hung more plasterboard from metal strips, then plastered it. It hasn't made that much difference.

A The trouble with suspended ceilings is that they are hanging from the joists above, and so can act as a sounding board for transmitted sound. They only really work with new joists spanning the whole room. And whilst false ceilings can help in stopping airborne sound from the bottom flat going upwards, they are less useful the other way round. There is a lot of ignorance in the building trade about this. Extra insulation on top of the new plasterboard might have helped, but it sounds as if it's too late now.

POLISHED FLOORBOARDS

Q I have bought a two-bed top-floor flat in a Victorian conversion, and I want to strip the floors, polish them and put rugs down. However, the lease states 'to cover and keep covered with carpet and underlay all floors except kitchens and bathrooms'.

Has anyone come up with a system of insulation that has an effect equal to carpet and underlay? As this is apparently a standard clause, do people either ignore the clause completely and just strip the floors, or respect it totally and stick to carpet? The sanding hire people say most people ignore it, but I do not want to upset the people downstairs.

A You are right to consider the result of your actions on your downstairs neighbours, as stripped wooden floors are a major source of irritation, and can lead to serious disputes. In your case, your lease clearly states that the floor must be carpeted, and this provision may have been imposed by the local authority when they gave planning consent and Building Regulations approval for the conversion of the property into separate flats. If you ignore this then you could find yourself on the wrong end of legal action from the neighbours and the freeholder.

There are various ways of installing soundproofing divisions between flats, but they are a lot more complicated than the scheme you describe, and are not guaranteed to be 100 per cent effective. The effect of heels on a polished timber floor can be like drumsticks on a drum, and it might be heard not just downstairs, but next door too. My advice is to accept that your flat is not suitable for bare floors, and to stick with the carpet. Console yourself with the thought that polished wood floors are a fad, and they will not always be as fashionable as they are now.

NOISE FROM BARE FLOORS

Q We bought and remodelled an older home. My husband tore out layers of carpet and padding. We got the floor back to the original hardwood floor, but now we can hear everything that goes on in the house from outside. Is there a product or something that can go under the house to solve the problem? We have a crawl space basement. Also is there anything else that can solve this problem without destroying what we have already finished?

A Maybe you have discovered just why the previous occupants had all that carpet! I don't see why you couldn't fix glassfibre insulation between the floor joists, and finish off with moisture-resistant chipboard screwed to the undersides of the joists. Ideally you should have a layer of polyethylene sheet on top of the insulation (i.e. on the warm side) as a vapour barrier, to stop warm moist air from the living rooms causing condensation in the basement.

BRICK WALL

Q My neighbour proposes to have built a 6ft (1,800mm) high brick wall to cut down the traffic noise. Her house is only some 20ft (6m) from her boundary with a pavement and busy road. She would ideally like to sit in her garden in the lee of the wall in some peace, but I am not sure the wall will give her the relief she expects from such a large outlay. Also, would she need permission for the wall?

A Boundary walls under 2m high (1m if within 1m of highway) do not need planning consent unless you are in a conservation area. Solid brickwork is a good direct sound blocker, although there will still be airborne sound refracted around the sides and over the top. But in general, if the wall blocks the view of the traffic then it will also block its noise. It may be possible to construct a quiet corner by returning the wall down one or both sides of the garden, as well as just along the front. Brickwork is expensive, but if built to a high standard, with an attractive facing brick, then a garden wall of this nature will also add to the value of the property.

CONSERVATORIES

Adding a conservatory is one of the most popular home improvements, and the off-the-shelf-conservatory industry is experiencing an unprecedented boom. But, although the idea of a glass-walled 'room in the garden' is a seductive one, many readers have discovered that things can go wrong, and conservatories can often be either too hot or too cold to use.

The main drawback is that of overheating – or 'solar gain' – caused by too much sun shining on too big an area of glass. The extent of this problem can be gauged by the fact that the number of adverts for conservatories in the glossy magazines is almost equalled by those for conservatory sun blinds and air-conditioning systems. I must say that building a conservatory as a suntrap, and then paying money and using energy to cool it, has always struck me as one of the greater absurdities of the home-improvement game, but this is what many people end up with.

The 'too much sun' part of the equation comes about through building a conservatory in the wrong place. For most houses, there is little choice about this, and the conservatory is plonked down outside the back door, whichever direction it faces. When there is a choice, many people assume that a south-facing aspect will be the favourite. But researchers at Cranfield University have found that over the course of a year, a southerly orientation actually provides fewer hours of comfortable occupation than one facing north. They also found that the higher the thermal value of the glazing, the lower the number of comfortable hours. In other words, single glazing is better than double glazing.

The 'too big an area of glass' is partly a design problem, and partly due to the Building Regulations. Conservatories get hot because of the greenhouse effect, where the sun's heat is able

Fully glazed conservatories are often too hot or too cold.

to pass in through the glass but, after being reflected off internal objects, it has a different wave-length, and is unable to get out again. Only a small area of glass roof is required for this build-up of heat to become excessive, but in order to stop a conservatory being classed as an extension, and thus becoming liable to building control, at least 75 per cent of the roof must be glazed. So most conservatory firms, to avoid the hassle of applying for Building Regulations approval, and of having their work inspected by the building-control officer, do not offer any alternative to the completely glazed roof.

Another situation where the building-control officer should be involved, but often is not, is when a conservatory is connected to the house by means of a permanent opening, rather than a closable door. This effectively makes the conservatory part of the habitable space, and therefore, for energy-conservation reasons, imposes restrictions on the area of glass, which is limited to around one-quarter of the floor area of the whole house.

The best way to keep a conservatory from overheating is ventilation. This requires vents at both low and high level, to allow a through convection current to flow. Many owners are persuaded to buy internal sun blinds, but are not told that these are ineffective without through ventilation, and in fact can sometimes make things worse, by exacerbating the greenhouse effect described above.

Anything else? Oh yes, it is rumoured that only 30 per cent of the price of a PVC-U conservatory covers the cost of the thing – the rest is profit and salesman's commission. You see, the sun always shines for someone.

MISTING IN POLYCARBONATE ROOF

Q **I have condensation within the layers of my five-layer polycarbonate conservatory roof. The roofer has carried out resealing, but the problem persists.**

A This type of sheeting does not include a desiccant material, so it must be allowed to breathe. Sealing the edges will only trap moisture between the layers. All the interstices must be drained and ventilated at both ends.

ROOF LEAKING

Q **I have a largish conservatory, well constructed with sealed double-glazed units set in wooden frames, but the roof leaks. The glass roof panels have been put in traditional glazing bars on a putty bed and then fastened in with wooden strips also bedded in putty and then painted. I have in mind to fix some sort of a covering strip spanning the wooden glazing bar and lapping the glass on each side, but can't find anything suitable.**

A I am afraid your conservatory has been completely wrongly glazed. Whatever you cover the joints with, water will still find its way down the sides of the sealed glazed units (SGUs) and, worse, will be trapped there, leading to premature internal misting. The only worthwhile solution would be to take the glass out, scrape away the old putty and re-bed the glass on load-bearing glazing tape, leaving drainage channels between the edges of the glass and the glazing bars. The timber beading should also be fixed to the glazing bars using the tape (which is sticky on both sides). That way, air will be able to circulate all round the edges of the SGUs, and any water that does get in will be able to drain out without attacking the seals.

Conservatory sun blinds stop glare, but will not prevent overheating.

OVERHEATING

Q We have a south-facing conservatory which gets much too hot to use in summer despite having roof blinds and front blinds inside the glass. We can open the door, windows and rooflights but these really need to be closed if we go out. Would air conditioning be a solution?

A Conservatories are often too hot for comfort. Internal sun blinds are ineffective without through ventilation. The problem is that once the sun's rays have passed through the glass, then the heat is inside, and it makes no difference to the internal temperature whether this is absorbed and re-emitted by the blinds, or by the floor and furniture.

I suggest you try to get permanent low-level vents fitted in the walls and/or doors, and investigate the possibility of locking the rooflights in an open position, so that you can leave them open when you go out. Of course, the advisability of this would depend on whether you have a lockable door between the conservatory and the house – otherwise you could compromise your insurance cover.

The idea of building a conservatory as a sun trap and then installing air conditioning to cool it has always struck me as slightly crazy.

CONSERVATORY HARD TO HEAT

Q Heating our new conservatory during the winter months seems difficult beyond belief. It's 4 metres square, has a glass roof, and is north facing. A radiator has been fitted running off the main central-heating system, but that does no more than take the chill off. Do you have any suggestions? We want to be able to use the conservatory all year round.

A A conservatory is basically a glass box, which is largely transparent to transmitted heat. So it will warm up rapidly when the sun shines, and cool down just as rapidly when it doesn't. The insulation value of glass is very low, and if you want to heat your conservatory during the winter months, then you will waste a lot of heat and money. In the British climate, a conservatory is unlikely to provide more than two hours of comfortable temperature per day, and using it as a habitable space will require a large expenditure on either air cooling or heating.

DRIVES, PATIOS AND OUTSIDE JOBS

Having a drive in front of your house can be a great boon, and most motorists who live in terraced town houses would love to have the private off-street parking that a drive provides. However, a drive is like a small private road, and like a road it needs a certain amount of maintenance – cleaning and occasional resurfacing. All drive surfaces need diligent below-ground preparation if they are to last, and cracking, crumbling concrete or tarmac is often a symptom of shoddy construction.

Of the various choices of surface, gravel is the most luxurious, but also the most expensive, and it requires annual raking and weed-killing. Concrete is probably the hardest wearing and lowest maintenance. A good professionally laid concrete drive could easily last for fifty years. Shame it looks so ugly.

Pattern-imprinted concrete needs cleaning and resealing every few years. Tarmac is the most likely to be installed by cowboys and anyway, like tarmac roads, after a few years it breaks up and has to be resurfaced. Brick and concrete-block paving looks nice, and it is easy to dig up and relay damaged areas, but it can be slippery when wet, and weeds grow in the joints.

Mosses and lichens will grow on all surfaces, especially badly drained ones (i.e. those with an insufficient slope for surface water to run off) and in shaded locations. If they bother you, then scrub them off with a stiff yard broom, or commit yourself to a lifetime of applying proprietary path and patio cleaner-type herbicidal chemicals. I don't fancy them myself.

New homes are now having to be built with smaller areas of hard paving, to limit the surface water run-off going into the main drains, and grass-block paving (where grass grows in gaps in plastic or concrete pavers) looks set to be a big seller. Maintenance is as easy as mowing the lawn.

So you pay your money and take your choice. But if you're getting a new drive installed, then the most important things to look out for are proper subsurface preparation, and attention to drainage. Rather than answer a newspaper advert by a nationwide drive company (which will only pass your details on to a regional franchisee), you would be better contacting local groundwork contractors through the Yellow Pages. Get them to give you a detailed written specification of what they propose to do.

Drives are like icebergs. The most important part is below the surface.

WHICH DRIVE SURFACE?

Q I have been given conflicting advice regarding my drive, which has quite a steep slope down to the garage. One contractor (who does either tarmac or blocked paving) recommended the tarmac, as it would give better grip during icy weather, but the second contractor (who only does block paving) disagreed, saying he thought the opposite was the case.

A And if you asked a contractor who did gravel drives, no doubt he would recommend his product as being better. Actually, he might have a case, although from the sound of it, you might have to keep sweeping the gravel out of your garage. A fourth possibility is perforated plastic grass blocks, which you back-fill with soil and plant with grass seed. But otherwise, I think you should decide which surface you prefer, in terms of appearance and cost, and keep a bag of road salt in the garage for those few days every winter when it might be needed.

PATTERN-IMPRINTED CONCRETE

Q Our front garden is covered with compressed smooth concrete, indented to resemble cobbles. Alas, the colour (black) was not incorporated in the concrete but sprayed on afterwards. This peeled off and subsequent repainting with aggregated exterior floor paint is wearing off under traffic. As it is pointless to repaint flaky paint, could the very smooth concrete be roughened to hold paint, or is there any other suitable treatment?

A This type of patterned driveway is made from fibre-reinforced aerated concrete, with an impression of bricks or cobbles being rolled into the top as it hardens. The surface colouring is usually trowelled into the top, so that two-tone effects can be achieved, but also because colouring the concrete right through would be expensive. Once the top wearing surface has been worn away, there is really nothing that can be done to patch it up. As you have discovered, paint or any other surface coating will simply wear away or flake off. Thousands of people have had these drives installed, often under the impression that they would be 'maintenance free', and were not told that they would need to have the surface resealed every three to five years (at a cost of £600 to £800) to prevent the colour wearing off. Your options are to have the damaged areas repaired by a specialist contractor, or to cut your losses and have it dug up and replaced with a more permanent surface, such as block paving.

RAISING GROUND LEVEL WITH DRIVE

Q We are planning on having our crumbling driveway and soggy front lawn replaced with imprinted concrete to make a much larger drive and parking area. We live in a 1930s bungalow with a double row of blue bricks as the damp-proof course. The upper row was drilled and injected to improve damp-proofing on the recommendation of the building society's surveyor before we moved in. The salesman suggested that the slope on the lawn, which is towards the bungalow, could be reduced a little if the surface of the concrete was raised. This would bring it up to the level of our porch and to the lower edge of the double blue bricks of the damp-proof course. Drainage would still be needed and this is proposed to be along the front wall (and around the bay windows). At the moment all paths, garden, etc., are 6in below the blue bricks. Is having the concrete this high a good idea?

A On no account should you allow anyone to raise your external ground levels. This will result in nothing but problems (see DAMPNESS). You have already been ripped off once by paying for an unnecessary DPC injection – there is no way that a double course of Staffordshire Blue engineering bricks could allow dampness to rise and, equally, they could not possibly be 'improved' by chemical injection.

Raising ground levels with a drive or patio can lead to dampness problems inside.

GRAVEL DRIVES

Q Have you any advice on creating a gravel drive? Gravel is all the rage round us, but my neighbours' drives seem to be just piles of shingle tipped out over their existing driveways. Every time they move their cars pebbles spill out over the road, creating a hazard to the windscreens of passing vehicles. How should one lay a gravel drive to avoid this?

A A properly constructed gravel drive is like an iceberg, in that 90 per cent of it is out of sight below the surface. The top layer should be only two layers of gravel thick, stuck into bitumen, and none of it should be finding its way onto the public highway. The preparatory work should be the same as for any drive – excavate 250mm of soil, line with a geotextile, roll in 150mm of Type 1 roadstone and 75mm of Type 2 hoggin, each of which has to be carefully compacted with a vibrating roller. Then comes the hot bitumen and the final gravel surfacing.

Unfortunately, as you say, many people's idea of making a gravel drive is to order a truckload of pea shingle and spread it over an existing drive. This might look good for a few weeks, but will quickly disintegrate as the stones are either pushed down into the soil or scattered around the garden by spinning car wheels. Like many other construction operations, finished appearances can be deceptive, and mask a lot of preparation work. A gravel drive is not a DIY job, and specifications and quotes should be obtained from experienced groundwork contractors. The cost, for a straight single drive, will be in the region of £50 per m², so a simple straight run up to the house, twice the length of your car, could set you back around £1,000.

GEOTEXTILES

Q **You have referred to the use of a geotextile (e.g. for lining drives and soakaways). Is this a heavy-duty plastic membrane which is porous to water transfer, such as those sold in garden centres which suppress weeds and roots? I would like to know a little more about this product and who manufactures or supplies it.**

A 'Geotextile' is a fairly loose term which covers a number of different products. The ones I have referred to are used to line excavations for drives or other below-ground installations, with the purpose of allowing water to escape downwards, but preventing soil and silt from percolating upwards. Geotextiles can also be used to strengthen weak soils, and stabilize steep slopes, such as those at the sides of road embankments. And yes, there are also versions used to suppress weed growth and allow young hedge plants to get a head start [DRIVES & PAVING].

TARMAC

Q **Some time ago, together with several neighbours, I had my drive surfaced with tarmac by a company no longer in business. At the time we were all happy with the result. However, the surface of the tarmac now appears to be crumbling where the edge meets the pavement. Is there a product available on the market that can be applied to seal the surface, or have we all been caught out and bought an inferior product?**

A 'Tarmac' is a name that is somewhat loosely applied to a number of bituminous surfacing materials. The quality and grade vary hugely, as do the skill and diligence with which they are applied. The preparatory work should be the same as for any drive, and the tarmac finish should comprise two layers with a total thickness of at least 50mm, applied hot, and rolled in with a heavy roller.

Cowboy firms often just spread a thin layer over hardcore, or on top of the existing surface, and don't roll it hard enough. Then it can start to break up after the first winter's frosts. There is not much point trying to stick it back down with anything if the foundation is inadequate, although some readers have recommended sealing crumbling tarmac with resin, a process which is apparently used in tennis-court construction.

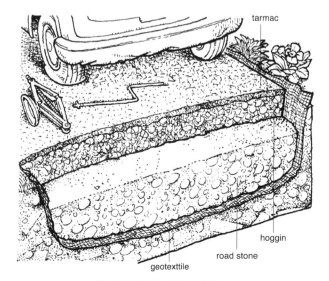

SECTION THROUGH A DRIVE

137

GRASS PAVING BLOCKS

Q I have been trying to trace a supply of perforated blocks which have grass growing out of the holes, but which allow cars to be driven across them. The local garden centres and builders' merchants have not heard of them despite the local council using something similar on road verges. Where can I find these elusive blocks please?

A There are several types of grass-paving system, which allow cars to be driven across or parked on grassy areas without sinking. Councils often use perforated concrete blocks, but the new plastic versions are lighter, easier to lay and accommodate a larger area of grass. Grass-paving systems are likely to become more widely used as regulations require new homes to have more car parking spaces, and the environmental rules on surface drainage are tightened up. Two suppliers are Hoofmark Ltd and Hauraton [PAVING].

Note, however, that none of these systems produces a really satisfactory grass surface. The perforated concrete blocks seem to dry the ground out, so that the grass turns brown quickly in dry weather, and the plastic paving systems hold the water, leading to moss growth.

CONVERTING FRONT GARDEN

Q I am thinking about using my front garden as a car-parking space. What are the legal requirements for doing this?

A You will have to consult your local authority highways department. On minor roads there is usually no problem, as long as traffic will not be emerging onto the road in an area of restricted visibility. However, on a 'classified' road – a principal road or bus route – planning permission may be needed. You will then have to pay the local authority to drop the kerb and rebuild the footpath as a ramp, and you will be liable for any costs incurred by the utilities companies for rerouting or ducting service pipes or cables. The total cost could reach several hundred pounds, although some local authorities offer special deals, usually when they are resurfacing the road.

WASHED-OUT GROUT

Q I have used a power washer to remove the accumulated grime from our patio paving slabs, and this has flushed out some of the mortar from between the slabs as well. Is there an easy way of replacing this – can a suitable mix be brushed dry into the gaps and then wetted with a watering can, or must I go back to a more tiring premixing of the mortar and subsequent hands-and-knees job with a small trowel? And what is the best mix to use?

A Power washers are useful tools, but care is needed when using them on building materials, as the destructive effect of the water jet can be surprisingly large. They can easily blast mortar away, take the faces off soft red bricks and even damage PVC-U door and window frames. If you want to make a mortar that will withstand future pressure washing, you will need to use a strong (3:1) sand:cement mix, applied wet, and compacted firmly into the joints. A brushed-in dry mix will never set as hard. But the easiest solution would be simply to brush in dry sand, and to go easy on the pressure washing.

CONCRETE PATIO BREAKING UP

Q Last spring we laid a new patio which was constructed in two sections, laid on hardcore and finished with ready-mixed concrete. Our problem now is that one half is perfect but the other has completely broken up and appears to have reverted to ballast. The weather conditions were dry at the time and the sections were laid within a few days of each other. The builder considers that the concrete supplied by the ready-mix supplier was at fault. I would be most grateful for your comments.

A I am interested in your observation that the weather conditions were dry at the time the concrete was laid, and that it was poured on top of hardcore. Fresh concrete needs to be kept wet for at least a week (and preferably for twenty-eight days) in order to achieve full strength, which results from a chemical reaction between the cement and the water. The correct procedure is to cover the hardcore base with a 50mm layer of sand blinding, and spread a polyethylene sheet membrane on top of this. The concrete is placed on top of the polyethylene, and in dry weather it should be covered with hessian and sprayed with water. Sandwiched between the membrane and the damp hessian, the concrete will be able to cure properly. Without either, it will probably have dried out before curing could occur. If your builder still thinks the ready-mix concrete suppliers are at fault, then there is a British Standard test that can be used to determine the mix proportions.

RUST MARKS ON PATIO

Q My cast-iron patio furniture has stained the paving slabs. I've cured the source of the problem by painting the feet of the table and chairs with a bitumen-based product but the rust marks have defied all attempts to remove them.

A You could try brick-cleaning acid if it really bothers you, but it seems a bit drastic and you may end up with clean patches that stand out as much as the rust stains!

CAST-IRON RAILINGS

Q I have bought some old Victorian railings to fix on top of my front garden wall, to restore it to its original style. I note that the original railings (presumably removed during the Second World War metal-salvage campaign) appear to have been bedded in some sort of lead or metal compound. My builder seems to think this is old-fashioned and unnecessary, and that he can fix the railings into drilled holes and fill the holes with cement. Other people say this will lead to corrosion. What is the correct method, and who can I engage to do the work properly?

A Old cast-iron (or modern steel) railings should be set in lead, for two reasons. One is that the lead helps stops the iron from rusting. The other is that the lead is soft, and helps to absorb thermal-expansion movement, which might otherwise crack the wall which the railings are set into. Melting and pouring lead is not difficult, and you – or your builder – should be able to find a local roofer or metalworker who has the necessary gas burner and crucible.

TREES
AND PLANTS

Ivy can cause serious damage to buildings.

Buildings and trees have an interesting relationship. On the one hand, most people like seeing mature trees, as they have a softening impact on the urban landscape, and are homes for insects and bird-life. On the other, trees have recently become demonized by insurance societies following a series of expensive subsidence claims. As a result, surveyors are now very quick to recommend 'further investigation' of trees near houses, and some arboriculturists (tree surgeons) are quick to recommend felling. The surveyors' and insurers' main fear is that as a tree grows, its roots will extract increasing quantities of water from the soil, causing drying shrinkage and subsidence. In reality, subsidence and cracking that can be directly attributed to the presence of a tree is extremely rare. There is always seasonal drying and shrinkage in soils anyway, but trees seem to get the blame for this whether they are guilty or not. And there are many cases where trees have stood for a century or more within touching distance of a house without causing any damage at all.

Decisions on whether mature trees should be removed or left standing should be taken only after joint consultation between an arboriculturist and a structural engineer – the one to access the condition of the tree and its roots, and the other to look at how these factors are likely to affect the building. If a mature tree has historic or landscape value, then there are simple steps that can be taken to prevent its roots from damaging a building, and keeping the tree may actually add more to the value of the property than removing it. For further advice call The Tree Care Company [TREES].

SURVEYOR SAYS CUT IT DOWN

Q **The surveyor's report on my London house drew attention to a sycamore tree in the garden, and recommended that it should be felled. But there are no signs of cracking in the property and I am reluctant to cut down a beautiful mature tree, which also shades the garden from the southern sun. Is there any evidence that trees actually damage buildings?**

A The idea that trees and buildings don't go together is largely myth, but surveyors are paranoid about being sued for negligence, so they prefer to recommend their removal. The fear comes from the idea that tree roots extract water from the subsoil, and where this is shrinkable clay – i.e. in London and most of southern England – then it can result in shrinkage, foundation movement and subsidence. In reality, more subsidence is caused by leaking drains making the subsoil wet and plastic, but since this is happening out of sight below ground it generally gets overlooked. Trees are a more obvious target. The Building Research Station published some research in 1949 suggesting that in certain circumstances fast-growing trees such as poplar, elm and willow close to houses might cause problems, and this has been misinterpreted and thought to apply to all trees and all houses. Local authorities often prune or pollard trees because of their supposed threat to buildings, but some experts say that this is pointless, and just makes the tree grow faster, and extract more ground water, in order to recover.

Ironically, cutting down a mature tree on a shrinkable clay subsoil can sometimes cause cracking where none existed before. This is because the tree, the soil and the house are existing in equilibrium, but when the tree is removed, the excess water causes the subsoil to expand, pushing the foundations upwards.

Trees and buildings can co-exist happily together.

DAMAGE FROM ROOTS

Q Surface roots from a neighbour's tree are damaging the surface of my drive. Is the neighbour liable for this damage? Would I need their permission to root prune?

A You are free to prune whatever grows on your side of the fence – as is the case with overhanging foliage – as long as the tree is not protected by a tree-preservation order. But it would be a shame if your pruning damaged the tree or made it fall over. Younger trees have more chance of recovery following root pruning than mature ones. If the roots are really causing damage to a particular structure, then the best bet would be to dig a narrow trench next to the building, cutting through the roots, as deep as you can manage, and drop a sheet of thick polythene down it. Tree roots grow towards moisture, so they'll turn back when they hit an impermeable barrier.

VIRGINIA CREEPER

Q Our 1958 house has a large Virginia creeper covering the front and side walls up to roof level. I am concerned that this plant may cause damage to the mortar between the bricks, although I have seen no evidence of this so far. In general, is it a good idea to have such a plant attaching itself to the walls or would I be better advised to remove it?

A I believe the term Virginia creeper can apply to more than one species. But in general this type of plant does not damage masonry, unlike ivy, which roots in the mortar joints.

NEW TREES AND NEW HOUSE

Q I have bought a house on a new development that has a small paved and planted front garden containing three wild cherry trees, each about 3–4m tall, some 1.5–3m from the house front wall. As the trees develop will they pose a threat to the house foundations?

A Modern houses are built with deep concrete foundations, which are often supported by piles, and are most unlikely to be affected by trees. Count yourself lucky to have a new home with established trees already in place.

THREAT FROM NEW TREES

Q Roots from a neighbour's willow tree have travelled about 50ft under my garage floor and into my main drain, causing damage and expense. I am now having trouble convincing my local council that the twenty willow trees they have planted 15ft from my front door are likely to cause similar trouble. The council assures me I have nothing to worry about. I would like to confront them with written evidence from an expert, but my problem is where to find one.

A There is a high level of ignorance about the relationship between trees and buildings. On the one hand, many homeowners and surveyors wrongly believe that all trees cause soil shrinkage and subsidence damage; on the other, genuine problems caused by fast-growing species such as willow and poplar are often ignored in the belief that all trees are beneficial. The fact is that every situation needs to be assessed individually by a trained arboriculturist, acting, where necessary, in tandem with a structural engineer. For advice contact The Tree Care Company [TREES].

TREES AND PLANTS

MODERN HOUSES AND SELF-BUILD

We are accustomed to the fact that as the years go by things get better. Health care, transport, communications – all these have improved ten-fold over the last hundred years. So it is only natural to expect that the homes built today will, similarly, be superior to those built in the Victorian and Edwardian eras. Sadly, this is not the case. The reasons for this are complex, but the underlying problem is that whilst a particular model of car, say, undergoes a constant process of year-on-year refinement, each individual car is only expected to last for five to seven years. So the manufacturer knows that if he is to achieve brand loyalty, and persuade satisfied customers to come back for more of the same, then he had better provide good after-sales care, and make sure that next year's model is better than last year's. Homes are not like that. They are expected to last for at least forty years, or a lifetime, whichever is the longer. And nobody buys a house because of the name of the builder – they buy it because of its location.

So the builder knows that no matter how well he builds a property, he is never going to achieve brand loyalty or get customers coming back for another one in a few years' time. So he might as well build it as cheaply as possible and maximize his profits.

This philosophy is reinforced by the Building Regulations, which govern new construction work. The Building Regulations lay down a set of minimum standards, but since modern speculative house-builders build to the minimum anyway, they build to the requirements of the Building Regulations and not a jot more. Which is why

Most modern houses are built to the minimum possible standards.

most modern houses are flimsy, noisy and hard to heat. This often comes as a shock to people whose lifetime dream has been to buy a wonderful new house, which needs no repairs and minimal maintenance. What they often get is cracking plasterboard walls and ceilings, creaking floors and second-rate plumbing. And a builder or developer who has no interest in coming back to repair faults.

Many new homeowners are provided with a ten-year warranty from the National House-Building Council (NHBC), and are disappointed when they discover that it only covers structural defects, and not internal cracks, binding doors or constantly blocking waste pipes. The NHBC warranty is somewhat unusual in that it is an insurance policy taken out by the builder, but paid for by the customer as part of the house price. If owners had to take out the policy themselves, then they might take more care to read the small print first, but then that's probably why it is done that way.

On the other hand, for those prepared to build their own homes, and who will not be trying to cut corners, modern techniques and materials mean that a very high quality product can be built for the same cost or less than an off-the-shelf house from a speculative builder. The self-build home market in Britain is growing every year, and it has never been easier for ordinary people to build a real dream home.

LEAKY WALLS

Q My house is two years old and very well constructed to the latest standards (I assume!) except that where the plasterboard dry lining is punctured, e.g. by pipes coming through the wall under the bath, there is a tremendous draught. Surely this is not correct. On the outside wall there are narrow vertical plastic vents at first-floor level; my neighbour believes these are vents into the void between the inner wall and the liner, but if that is correct then any wind will penetrate into the house via areas like the bathroom?

A The extent of the problem depends upon whether it is a timber-framed house, or just plasterboard stuck onto the inner block leaf of a conventional cavity wall. The vents are weep holes, situated along the top of the cavity-tray lintels. They are not there to ventilate the cavity. The draught is clearly due to some very poor construction quality, and the first thing you should do is give the builder the opportunity to rectify it. You need to engage an independent professional to make sure the work is done properly, though. You don't just want a dollop of foam gunned in to fill the gaps.

NHBC PROBLEMS

Q In my nine-year-old house the connection from a washbasin has been plumbed in downstream of a WC and protrudes about 70mm into the 100mm soil pipe. This causes frequent blockages and build-up of sewage. The builders and the National House-Building Council have declined to take any action to correct the faulty plumbing. Can you suggest any way in which I can get some action from the builders or the NHBC?

A The NHBC ten-year warranty covers only structural faults. And new houses are not even covered by the normal legal protection of the Sale of Goods Acts. If you buy a car or a stereo system then you are protected by statutory rights, but, unbelievably, property – the biggest single investment most of us ever make – is not covered by the Act. The NHBC trumpets its warranty as being some kind of wonderful consumer protection but it is in fact a simple insurance policy, taken out by the builder but passed on to – and paid for by – the customer. And, like all insurance policies, the decision on what to pay out for in claims is determined solely by the insurer. Your problem is not untypical.

A big problem is that chartered surveyors often advise purchasers that the existence of an NHBC warranty means that a full building survey will not be needed. This is a big mistake.

SELF-BUILD

Q I'd like to build my own house (or more accurately contract a builder to do it) but have no real idea where to start. Can you offer any advice?

A Building your own house is a great idea. It is the norm in European countries, unlike in Britain where the market is dominated by volume-speculative house-builders. You can engage an architect to design it and run the operation for you, or, if you want to save some money and have a more hands-on experience, there are a number of good self-build books available. I recommend *The Housebuilder's Bible* [CONSTRUCTION LITERATURE].

SELF-BUILD: TIMBER FRAME

Q I am considering buying a piece of land to build my own house on. Whilst staying with friends over in the States I have been very impressed with their timber-framed houses. A big plus is they seem to be relatively easy to erect. What are the downsides and are there any reputable UK suppliers, or do I have to import direct from USA?

A There are lots of 'kit' houses available from British and European suppliers for self-builders. Most of them are timber-framed, which is OK as long as they are assembled to a very high standard, but remember, a timber-framed house that performs well in Scandinavia, Germany or North America may not do as well in the damp, temperate British climate. Cold climates are dry climates; the UK's climate is moderate and very wet. Other self-build systems include hay bales, rammed earth and pouring concrete into pre-formed polystyrene formwork. There are three monthly self-build magazines, *SelfBuild*, *Build It* and *Home Building & Renovating*, and an annual show, and a host of self-help books.

TIMBER-FRAMED HOUSES

Q We are constantly being told that timber-framed houses are superior to (i.e. better insulated than) brick houses. If this is the case, why do we not see them being built everywhere?

A A significant proportion of new houses being built are timber-framed, but developers do not like to advertise the fact, because of problems that have been associated with this method of construction in the past. They are clad on the outside with brickwork, and many owners are under the impression that they have bought a brick house.

The insulation is right on the inside, next to the living space. This allows them to warm up quicker and makes them appear better insulated than masonry construction. Unfortunately, the part of the frame on the cold side of the insulation stays cold, and is therefore prone to condensation. It is therefore vital that there is a perfectly installed vapour barrier on the warm side of the insulation, to stop water vapour produced by the occupants from crossing to the cold side and condensing, where it could cause the frame to rot. Very often the vapour barrier is inexpertly installed, or punctured by electricians and plumbers who do not understand its importance. It is essential that the building contractor understands these principles and supervises the work accordingly.

The thermal-insulation quality of timber-framed houses is not so much a product of the frame itself, as of the thickness of insulation built into it. New brick-and-block houses conform to exactly the same thermal-insulation standards, and they are likely to have better structural and sound insulation qualities as well.

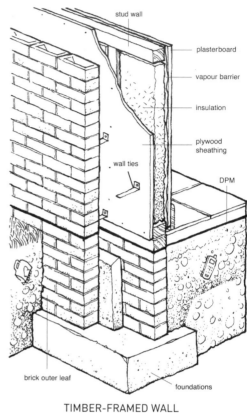

TIMBER-FRAMED WALL

Labels: stud wall · plasterboard · vapour barrier · insulation · plywood sheathing · wall ties · DPM · brick outer leaf · foundations

HOW TO IDENTIFY TIMBER-FRAMED HOUSES

Q If I was looking around a house with a view to buying it, is there any easy way to determine if the property is in fact timber-framed? I could of course ask the vendor, but they might not wish to tell me.

A All internal wall surfaces in timber-framed houses are lined with plasterboard, and sound hollow when tapped. Some brick-and-block houses are also lined with plasterboard ('dry lining') but this doesn't sound quite so hollow, and is sometimes only done on visible surfaces, not in the backs of airing cupboards, behind kitchen units, etc. The sure-fire way is to look in the roof space – in brick-and-block houses the gable walls will be bare blockwork; in timber frame they will be plasterboard.

OUTSIDE TAP IN TIMBER-FRAMED HOUSE

Q I wish to install an outside tap – teed off from an internal pipe – in a timber-framed house. I have been told that this is not recommended, as it will perforate the membrane.

A Modern timber-framed houses should not be confused with traditional oak-framed English vernacular buildings (such as the famous 'black-and-white' Herefordshire cottages). Modern houses often have a brick outer leaf built in front of a 100mm x 50mm timber stud wall, lined internally with plasterboard. In order to stop condensation occurring in the cold space between the brick wall and the timber, and causing wood rot in the frame, it is important that there is a continuous, uninterrupted vapour barrier below the surface of the plasterboard. This is usually a sheet of polyethylene, and it has to be carefully sealed around the edges of anything that punctures it, such as electrical wiring or plumbing pipes.

STEEL-FRAMED HOUSE

Q My parents are buying a 1960s bungalow which we have been informed is steel-framed – i.e. no breeze-block support walls. I have never come across this in a domestic house. Are you aware of any problems with these sorts of houses? We have only been told that the internal layout is very easy to change.

A In general, steel-framed houses have performed well over the years. Surveyors and mortgage lenders are suspicious of them, as they are with any 'non-traditional' construction. See if you can find a suitably interested local structural engineer to do a survey.

NEW SWITCH AND SOCKET POSITION

Q The power sockets on the walls of our new house are quite high up – about 450mm from the floor – and the light switches are approximately in the middle of the door height. We were told that there is now a European law which says this is the requirement, in case the occupant is disabled. Is this true?

A There is no 'European law' about this, but the latest Building Regulations require all new homes to be accessible for wheelchair users and other disabled people (and remember that most of us experience a disability or immobility problems at some time in our lives). If you really don't like the position of the switches and sockets, then you can get them relocated after you have bought the house, or add additional switches and sockets at your preferred height.

BUILDERS

Probably the most-asked readers' question is, How can I find a good builder? The answer is that there is no foolproof way. There is one professional body – the Chartered Institute of Building (CIOB) – that represents degree-level construction professionals who, mostly, work for reputable contractors. Unfortunately for the readers of this book, these contractors work mostly on large commercial and industrial developments, and are not interested in small domestic repair and maintenance work – even though this accounts for around 50 per cent of the total market. However, the CIOB does operate a scheme called the Chartered Building Company Scheme, to put householders in touch with small- to medium-sized construction companies, and there have been recent moves to expand and promote this [BUILDING ORGANIZATIONS].

From there on down we are talking about trade associations. These generally claim to check members' financial standing and professional repute, but this is often perfunctory and does not confer any legal protection upon verbal agreements entered into with its members. The best way to protect yourself against shoddy workmanship is to have a signed contract with your builder, and then you are both covered by civil law. There is a simple Joint Contracts Tribunal (JCT) document called 'Building contract for a homeowner/occupier', which can be bought from the Construction Confederation for £10.99 (and is also promoted by the National Federation of Builders – see below). But in my experience, most homeowners are too timid to suggest it to their builders, and most builders are too scared to sign it. Both sides need educating. If both client and builder became more accustomed to contractual agreements then the work would get done better, a lot faster, and builders would get paid on time.

The most influential trade association, which covers medium-sized construction companies, is the National Federation of Builders. They are keen to present their members as the reputable side of the domestic sector and they are probably right. Members offer customers a building insurance guarantee scheme (Benchmark Plan), for an extra payment, which means that most customers refuse it.

Successive governments have refused to implement a compulsory registration scheme for builders, and the latest attempt at voluntary registration, the Quality Mark, seems doomed to failure, since it asks reputable builders – who already have far more work than they can handle – to pay to join the scheme, whilst it does nothing to legislate against the cowboy operators.

HOW TO FIND A BUILDER

Q We need a few simple repairs doing to our flat – moving a radiator, putting up some shelves, plastering a ceiling, etc. We have called seven separate builders, of whom only two came round to look at the work, and neither of them has ever called us back. How on earth can we find a decent builder to do this work?

Some builders prefer big sites to domestic repair and maintenance work.

A There are no easy answers to this one. There are plenty of good builders around, but they are usually booked up for months, if not years, in advance, and can afford to be choosy about which jobs they take on.

Builders who do work in the domestic sector are there for a variety of reasons: they may prefer the relative peace and quiet away from the big sites, and the ability to choose their own hours, or they may really like the conservation aspect of restoring old houses; or it may be because they are complete cowboys who wouldn't last five minutes on a proper site, and only work for cash because they are signing on the dole, avoiding paying tax or have been made bankrupt.

The usual advice is to use a builder recommended by friends or relatives. This may or may not work. It is likely to put you in touch with someone who is polite, turns up on time and feeds the cat when you're away, but is no guarantee of their construction skills or knowledge.

Another suggestion is to use a builder who is a member of a trade association. This is no guarantee at all, as trade associations exist largely to protect their members from the public. (The Federation of Master Builders, for example, whilst it claims to check applicants' accounts and credit worthiness, does not require any evidence of construction training or qualifications.) Two exceptions to this are CORGI (Council for Registered Gas Installers) and the NICEIC (National Inspection Council for Electrical Installation Contracting), which have rigorous checking and monitoring procedures and can initiate legal action against interlopers.

At present the best advice is to direct all your building work via a registered architect or surveyor. There is a common misconception that architects' and surveyors' fees are an expensive addition to the costs of repairing or altering a building. But if you are not in a position to specify and supervise building works yourself, then you may well end up paying builders for unnecessary or substandard work. A good local architect or surveyor will specify building works, employ contractors and supervise the whole operation, and should be able to save you a sum well in excess of his fees, whatever the value of the property.

HOW TO ENGAGE A BUILDER

Q We have found a local builder through recommendations. He came round twice, once to see what we wanted and another time to measure up. He's provided a single page of typed estimate saying not much more than the external size of the proposed extension, that the price includes supply of plans and seeking planning approval, and allows for external rendering to match existing. No painting included in estimate. That's all it says. Estimate is £31,200 plus VAT.

Is this usual? I am very uneasy about commissioning work on such a flimsy estimate, but everybody speaks highly of the man and his work seems to be of a high standard. How

should I take things forward? Is there a standard form of contract that should be drawn up when employing builders?

A I would say that for a project of this size it would be unwise to engage a builder whom you know only by word of mouth on an imprecise design-and-build contract (which is what you have described). Your builder may well be totally trustworthy, trained and experienced – but it would still be as well to have an independent construction professional supervising operations and acting as your middleman [ARCHITECTS, SURVEYORS AND ENGINEERS].

CASH JOB

Q I've recently had a lot of different building jobs done. Each time the materials were needed, the builder asked me to make out a cheque for the suppliers. When all the jobs were done, he asked if I would pay his bill (the labour) in cash. This is obviously to avoid tax, or he may even be bankrupt and can't put any money in his bank account. It doesn't bother me how I pay him, but could I be considered to be a party to him avoiding tax?

A The Inland Revenue has recently tightened up the rules with regard to construction-site work, and trade employers have to be careful to make due deductions or to collect exemption certificates from subcontractors. But as a private householder this is not your concern. Whether you pay by cash or cheque, it is up to your builder to declare his profits to the taxman, and nothing to do with you. However, you would be wise to get an invoice or receipt for work done, in case problems arise later. And the best thing is always to have a written contract with a builder before work starts, such as the JCT Building contract for a homeowner/occupier [CONSTRUCTION LITERATURE].

TRADE ASSOCIATIONS

Q We have had three quotes for damp-proofing our 1920s terraced house, one for £550, one for £2,300 and one for £7,875. The last is from a member of the British Wood Preserving and Damp-proofing Association, and my husband thinks that they must know what they are talking about. But how can there be such a difference in the three prices?

A In the first place, it is highly unlikely that your 1920s house needs damp-proofing, since it will have been built with an integral damp-proof course, which will still be doing its job (see DAMPNESS).

The British Wood Preserving and Damp-proofing Association is a trade association, not an officially sanctioned professional body. Its members like to boast that they are more highly trained than non-members, and use this to justify higher prices and more extensive works. But in my experience members of this association are just as likely as non-members to misdiagnose problems, and specify unnecessary treatment.

INSURANCE

Q I am about to have an extension built by a small-sized local building company. Should I tell my buildings insurer, and is there any insurance I should take out during the work for damage against the main house? Also is there an insurance that gives me legal protection should I encounter any difficulties?

A   You should give full details to your insurers. This is because the finished work will increase the rebuilding costs of the property, and you may find yourself under-insured in the event of making a claim. There is also the question of increased security risks while the building work is taking place (scaffolding, temporary window and door openings, etc.) – your insurers are unlikely to raise your premiums for this, but again, there could be a problem if you make a claim and you haven't told them. Damage to the main house whilst the extension is being built should be covered by your builder's public liability insurance, so make sure that he is adequately covered.

Regarding your relationship with your builder, you will be legally covered during the course of the work providing you have signed a suitable contract, and you can cover yourself against possible future defects by entering into a warranty scheme, which is usually available for around 1 per cent of the contract price.

STANDARDS OF WORKMANSHIP

Q   **We are having a kitchen fitted by a national company. In one place where the worktops have to join, there is a gap and they are not at the same height. The carpenter says this will be solved with a joining strip. The worktop also stops short of the wall, but the carpenter tells me not to worry as the tiling will cover this up. But the gap is big enough for a tile to slip through. Are these acceptable degrees of error, or a bad job which I should ask to be rectified?**

A   It's entirely up to you. There are no British Standards for fitting kitchen worktops, but I would have thought you could reasonably expect them to be level all round, and fitted to a tolerance of 5mm. So, if you are not happy with the standard of work, then complain. But to whom? The carpenter is probably not employed directly by the 'national company' but is a jobbing builder doing the job for a fixed price. His margins are tight, and he doesn't have time to do things twice. The salesman who sold you the kitchen is the one making the big money, so stop the cheque and get him round to explain himself.

LATE BUILDERS

Q   **Why aren't house-builders subject to 'penalty clauses' for delays, in the same way that road-builders are? Our new house is now ten weeks late.**

A   If the builders were working directly for you, then you could have incorporated a penalty clause for late completion into the contract. But if you are buying your new house from a developer, no such contract will apply. In fact, you will find that you have very little legal protection at all, as property is not even covered by the Sale of Goods Act. You actually have more consumer rights when you buy a tin of baked beans than when you buy a new house.

SURVEYORS

If you have bought a home that is older than you are, then your mortgage valuation survey may well have recommended further investigation by 'specialists' for timber and dampness defects, drains, cracks, heating system and electrics. Even if you thought to avoid these nasty-sounding problems by buying a recently built property, there may still have been some bad news in the surveyor's report, such as a recommendation for further investigation of the state of your cavity-wall ties.

For many people, especially first-time buyers, this turn of events can be confusing, because, having commissioned a survey and report from a chartered surveyor, they thought they had already paid for an authoritative investigation. The last thing they expected was a list of other people they should consult because the chartered surveyor did not wish to express an opinion.

For, sadly, when you engage a chartered surveyor, you are not necessarily employing an experienced construction professional. More often than not you are getting someone who got an A level in geography, spent three years in the classroom at a 'new university' and then got a job in a surveying practice. There they will have been taken under the wing of a slightly older surveyor, who probably advised them to 'forget everything you learned at college' (no big problem), and took them out to do a couple of mortgage valuation surveys. These entail filling in the blank spaces on a printed form, such as, 'State whether main water, drainage, electricity and gas are connected', an acceptable reply to which will be, 'All mains services appear to be connected but have not been tested.' You could do better yourself.

A clue to the limited nature of surveyors' investigations can be had from the clothes they wear to work. Most surveyors turn up in their best

Surveyors can only look: they can't touch.

153

suits, hardly well equipped for climbing up into the loft or having a poke round in the gutters. They won't even want to get down on one knee for fear of dirtying their trousers, which rules out looking at the drains or even lifting the edge of a carpet. In fact, the standard Homebuyer Valuation includes the stock phrase, 'Furniture, wall hangings, floor coverings, insulation material and stored goods have not been moved.' So if you are selling a house and you don't want the buyer's surveyor to notice some particularly dodgy detail, just hide it with a few tea chests or a bit of carpet. I once looked at a place where a huge crack between the main house and the kitchen addition was covered with a calendar of pastoral scenes. The surveyor had missed it completely.

Even when they do try to 'investigate' a bit deeper, most surveyors manage to give the impression of being totally ignorant. In one study, 93 per cent of surveyors questioned did not know how to use an electrical moisture meter correctly to diagnose dampness problems in walls. The result is that rather than risk making mistakes and laying themselves open to future compensation claims for negligence, surveyors always recommend 'further investigation' by others of tricky subjects like dampness. So their reports give carte blanche to cowboys to come in with estimates for thousands of pounds' worth of unnecessary work, all sanctioned by the surveyors and, therefore, by the mortgage lenders.

But why get a survey done at all if it is likely to be so inadequate? The answer lies in the Building Societies Act (1986), which requires a written valuation report to be obtained on the occasion of each advance. Since demutualization, most of the building societies are now actually banks, and are not governed by this rule. But old habits die hard. As Adam Smith pointed out, all professions are a conspiracy against the public.

TYPES OF SURVEYS

Q **We are always told that we should not rely on the mortgage valuation, but should pay extra for a more detailed survey. But having done just this during the recent purchase of my terraced house, I feel that it didn't tell me any more than I could see for myself. Should I have paid even more for a full survey? What exactly are the advantages and disadvantages of the different types of survey?**

A Good question. The basic valuation (£250 to £350) is carried out on behalf of the mortgage lender, for them to judge whether the property has sufficient collateral for them to lend money against it. Even though the buyer pays for the valuation, in law the documentation belongs to the lender. So if the surveyor fails to spot a costly defect, then you might find it difficult to sue them afterwards.

With the Homebuyer Survey and Valuation (£500 to £600) you are engaging the surveyor to work for you directly, so if he fails to spot a defect then you may be able to sue him. But obviously surveyors are aware of this, which is why they hedge the wording of their reports so carefully. Hence the prevalence of phrases such as '. . . xyz appears to be in good order', and '. . . floor coverings and furniture have not been moved', because surveyors know that in order to be found guilty of negligence in court, it is not enough to prove that they missed something – it must be shown that the defect was clearly visible or that they should have been able to infer its presence from symptoms visible to them at the time of the inspection. This accounts for surveyors' use of electrical moisture meters on walls, even though they know that the readings are meaningless. A judge in a noted court case ruled that a surveyor would have been able to spot some hidden dry rot if he had used a moisture meter on the wall nearby, so ever since surveyors have always recommended that clients should have further investigation by damp-proofing and timber-treatment companies.

The wording on the Homebuyer Survey and Valuation report form is set by the Royal Institution of Chartered Surveyors (RICS), although some firms of surveyors amend the wording in their own versions of the form. Also, the quality of the survey varies according to the type of surveyor. Most Homebuyer Surveys are carried out by General Practice (or GP) members of the RICS, who are often little more than estate agents or valuers. A more specialized surveyor will belong to the Building Surveying division of the RICS, and may also have engineering experience or qualifications, in which case he may be more knowledgeable about building construction, and more confident about making judgements about the state of a house.

The more expensive Building Survey (£800 upwards) should be a much more thorough investigation, carried out by a Building Surveying RICS member, or a structural engineer. You would expect anyone undertaking a Building Survey to wear overalls, and to bring a set of ladders so that they can access the roof space (although they are still unlikely to go up onto the roof, and will state in their report that they have not done so). They should lift manhole covers to inspect the drains, and may use tools to lift carpets and floorboards (although this may not be done if the sellers are still in occupation, and do not give their permission).

TYPES OF SURVEYOR

Q When we moved house four years ago I was very disappointed by the performance of the surveyor, who I felt did very little for his fee, landed us with a huge bill for damp-proofing (which turned out to be unnecessary) and failed to point out the things that we really should have spent our money on, like the leaking roof. We are planning to move again in the next couple of years, and would like a better service. Can we get a survey from a different kind of professional (an engineer, perhaps) and would this be acceptable to the building society?

A The RICS has a near monopoly on simple mortgage valuations, because of the 'panel' system operated by the major chains of estate agents. But Homebuyer Surveys and Building Surveys (which can include valuations) are carried out by professionals who belong to other organizations as well, including the Chartered Institute of Building (CIOB), the Association of Building Engineers (ABE) and the Institution of Civil Engineers (ICE). Finding someone who is going to provide you with the quality of survey that you expect is a matter of contacting members of these bodies, finding out if they do domestic survey work and quizzing them with regard to their experience and attitude. Valuations from members of these professional bodies should all be acceptable to mortgage lenders.

HOMEBUYER SURVEYS

Q I am hoping to move house but the survey has concerned me. I have had the 'expert' builders' quotations – on the advice of the surveyor – and the roof is apparently 'shot to pieces'. I also need a damp course to the ground floor, etc., etc., etc. I really don't know whether to go

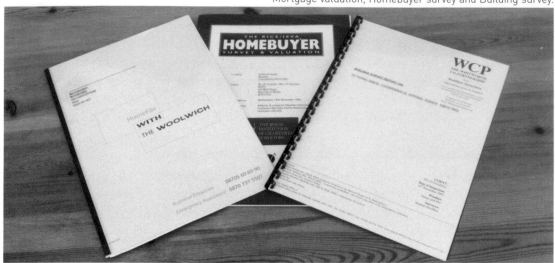

ahead with the purchase now or not. One quote yesterday came to £14,000! Apparently I need a whole new set of PVC-U windows, as well as fascias, soffits, etc., which are rotten. I made the mistake of asking the various builders to quote for points marked in the survey and they really have gone to town. Where can I obtain honest advice? My mortgage lender (on the basis of the survey) is withholding money until the damp/timber treatment is carried out to the surveyor's satisfaction – so I need to make up the shortfall *and* pay for the work.

I don't really trust any of the opinions given. The surveyors are so careful about protecting themselves that apparently nearly everything 'probably' needs replacing.

A In general I advise against damp-proofing, timber treatment, PVC-U windows and PVC-U fascias, as these items are usually (a) unnecessary, (b) damaging to the house and (c) damaging to the environment. The roof may or may not need repairing, depending upon age, type, etc. 'Shot to pieces' seems to imply some kind of war damage which, as far as I am aware, is uncommon in present-day mainland Britain. It sounds to me as though you need independent advice, rather than asking contractors to quote for specific items. When builders are called in to quote for work on newly purchased homes they tend to smell mortgage money and worried new owners, and react accordingly [ARCHITECTS, SURVEYORS AND ENGINEERS].

PARTY-WALL PROBLEMS

Q We have recently had plans drawn up to add a single-storey extension across the whole of the back of the house, and these have been passed by the council. I have read in a book that cognizance has to be taken of the Party Wall Act (1966). The architect is very sanguine and says just go and chat to the neighbours, but my understanding is that we need written permission from the neighbours on both sides. Both are elderly and I cannot find a speci-men consent letter not written in intimidatory legalese. Do I really need written consent?

A You should seek expert advice from a surveyor experienced in party-wall legislation. You will have to pay a professional fee for this, but it could save you a lot of trouble in the future [ARCHITECTS, SURVEYORS AND ENGINEERS].

DODGY SURVEYOR

Q I bought an Edwardian ground-floor flat a year ago and was ordered by the surveyor to have a new damp-proof course injected into the external walls. I got this done and thought that damp would never be a problem. Then I read your article stating that 'rising damp' is a myth, and also found that in two rooms that were treated there is a serious damp problem caused by condensation. I've paid £300 plus VAT for completely pointless work. Do I have any comeback?

A It depends what you mean by 'ordered by the surveyor', and the wording of his report. You could try suing for negligence and damages, but your costs may come to more than the £352.50. The Royal Institution of Chartered Surveyors (RICS) has an arbitration system for disputes with their members, and this may be the best first step. In any event, you should contact the surveyor in writing and make your feelings known, and see what the response is.

SURVEYORS: WHAT ARE THEY FOR?

Q Why do I have to pay for a survey before I can buy a house? The things that the surveyor comes up with are laughable. What I want to know are the things I can't see for myself, i.e. structural deficiencies, etc., but I have to seek further professional advice on such matters because 'fixed floor coverings have not been lifted', etc. However, it is very helpful to be told that 'the interior decoration requires some attention' and 'the kitchen units would benefit from some updating'. Having average eyesight I can spot that for myself!

A It's all to do with the Building Societies Acts. Building societies – unlike banks – were bound by these acts to commission independent valuation surveys before lending money against a property. Now that most building societies have been demutualized – i.e. they are effectively the same as banks – there is no legal reason why this charade should continue. But the whole property industry is hamstrung by inertia and complacency, and it is difficult to see the surveying profession changing practices that it has been doing for years. It's a bit like the First World War soldiers' lament – 'We're here because we're here, because we're here because we're here . . .'

HOUSE LOG BOOK

Q We have heard a lot about a proposed 'house log book'. I have made enquiries in various bookshops but to no avail. I am wondering if you can give me any guidance as to how I might obtain such a book in which to record bills, location of taps and other useful information for a prospective purchaser.

A I think the house log was just somebody's bright idea, and doesn't exist in the real world. In my view it would be totally impractical, and lead to pre-emptive disinformation, much like the government's proposed Home Information Packs.

HAZARDS

The history of construction is littered with materials which in their day were thought to be the answer to every problem, and which later turned out to be damaging to health. The most notorious of these is asbestos, which was widely used as a fireproof lagging material and is now known to cause cancer and respiratory illness. But hot on its heels comes lead, used for water pipes and in paint, which is associated with nervous disorders, reduced intelligence, hyperactivity and behavioural problems, especially in children. Although it was banned in Australia in 1906 and the USA in 1978, lead paint continued to be used in Britain until 1992.

Formaldehyde adhesives, used to bind together the particles in many types of building board, are a known respiratory hazard, and their use is strictly controlled in a number of American states. But they remain in widespread general use in the UK.

The most toxic substances in construction are pesticides. Concerns have been expressed about the safety of these chemicals for more than thirty years, but in the UK many of them continue to be licensed as 'safe' by the Health and Safety Executive (HSE), and they are routinely sprayed in thousands of homes every week – usually as a precaution against imaginary problems. Among the letters in this section are some from readers whose health has been ruined by exposure to these supposedly safe treatments.

ASBESTOS WATER TANK

Q We bought our thirty-year-old council flat a few years ago and had central heating fitted. The council are now installing heating in the remaining tenant-occupied flats and replacing their asbestos water tanks with plastic. Our tank is tucked away on top of the airing cupboard and seems perfectly sound. In view of the asbestos scare do you think the tank is a health hazard?

A The main dangers come from the brown and blue varieties of asbestos, which were used mainly for insulation and pipe lagging, and these should always be removed by specialist contractors when found. Water tanks, wall panels and corrugated roofing sheets were usually made from the less dangerous white asbestos, mixed with cement. Asbestos is only dangerous when the fibres get into the air and are inhaled, so if your asbestos-cement tank is in good condition, then it should not represent any problem, and the safest option is to leave it undisturbed.

ASBESTOLUX GARAGE CEILING

Q I am concerned about the ceiling of my garage. The house was built in 1974 and has an attached garage which backs on to the kitchen. The ceiling is covered in 'asbestolux' boarding and is there, I understand, for fire-safety reasons. Is it asbestos? Is it dangerous? It is attached by nails and there is a broken piece at one end. Are we likely to find surveyors insisting the broken sheet, or the whole lot, should be removed or replaced if we came to sell the property?

A Asbestolux does contain white asbestos. It is safe as long as you don't disturb it and inhale the fibres, so the best thing is probably to leave it alone for now. If you decide to remove it, then you should contact your local authority environmental health department for advice about disposal, or for details of local approved removal contractors.

ARTEX

Q My lounge has an Artex ceiling with the characteristic scalloped finish. What can I do to achieve a plain surface?

A Artex is a brand of textured paint used to make decorative patterns on plasterboard, or to cover up cracks in old ceilings (although this is rarely successful). Other brands are Wondertex, Suretex and Newtex, but they all tend to get referred to as 'Artex'. The big problem with these textured finishes is that they may contain asbestos. The Artex brand was still being manufactured with asbestos as recently as 1984. So textured finishes should not be drilled or dry-sanded, as the asbestos fibres could be released into the air and inhaled.

It is possible to remove Artex wet, using a steam wallpaper stripper, and taking care to bag up the scrapings securely while still damp. The bags should be labelled 'asbestos', and disposed of specially by the local authority refuse department.

Textured finishes can also be covered over with plaster, so long as the surface is first primed with diluted PVA adhesive. A specialized product called Artex Ceiling Finish is also available. The dilemma is that the newly plastered surfaces should really be labelled, to warn future generations that asbestos lurks beneath.

Artex ceilings may contain asbestos.

LIGHTNING PROTECTION

Q My house has a large area of flat roof comprising copper panelling on plywood decking. I am concerned about its vulnerability in a thunderstorm, since the house is high in the Pennines. Is this type of roof more prone to being struck by lightning, and should it be 'earthed' in some way or another?

A Any building can be struck by lightning, regardless of the nature of the roofing material. But most damage comes not from direct lightning hits, but from electrical discharges being conducted in via overhead telephone cables and television aerials. Protection against lightning therefore involves two processes – first, a traditional lightning conductor on the highest point of the building, to prevent lightning strikes and fire damage; and second, electronic anti-surge protectors on TV, telephone and mains electrical supplies. For details contact the National Federation of Master Steeplejacks and Lightning Conductor Engineers [HAZARDS].

RADON GAS

Q I am hoping to buy a retirement cottage in Herefordshire, but the surveyor's report states that it is in an area affected by radon gas. Is this a big problem, and how can it be dealt with? My wife is now very worried about possible harmful effects on our health, and for our visiting grandchildren.

A Radon is a natural radioactive gas that seeps out of the ground in certain areas, chiefly those with underlying granite. The radioactivity is low, and usually harmless, but if it is allowed to enter a house it can build up to higher levels. The main health fear is an increased risk of lung cancer from breathing the gas over long periods. Surveyors are obliged to mention the risk in a given area, but this does not mean that a particular house will have a radon problem. You should be able to get a more detailed assessment from the local authority environmental health department. In any case, preventative measures are easy. For a house with a suspended timber ground floor, the usual method is to fit an impermeable membrane below the floorboards, and ensure that the existing subfloor ventilation is adequate. With a solid floor, a membrane is also applied, sometimes with the addition of a hollow polyethylene radon sump below floor level. This is attached to a vent pipe that disperses the radon gas above roof level. For more details contact Proctor Group Ltd [HAZARDS].

MDF

Q As a lifelong DIYer I am a relative newcomer to the use of MDF board. It cuts and routs well and cleanly. But when visiting B&Q to purchase and have a large board reduced to a manageable size I am regaled with reports of how MDF is banned in the USA as a hazard. There is also a warning on each board to wear a protective mask when using powered machinery, which is not always practicable for small operations. What are the true hazards associated with MDF?

A The hazards of MDF (medium-density fibreboard) come from the fine nature of the dust, which can cause respiratory problems, and from the 'out-gassing' of the formaldehyde-based adhesive. It is not true that MDF has been banned, in the USA or anywhere else. There are regulations over its use in confined spaces such as woodworking shops where prolonged daily exposure is a factor, but occasional DIY use probably represents a threat no greater than that of, say, white spirit; i.e. take all reasonable precautions, and remember that some people will be more sensitive than others. When MDF has been stored for over three months, the adhesive is reckoned to have all 'out-gassed', and there are alternative but more expensive types, using safer adhesives, which are used in hospitals and nurseries.

LEAD PAINT

Q **I stripped a window in my 1930s flat using a heatgun and then saw an article about lead content in pre-1950 paintwork, and felt faint at what I read, especially with a fourteen-month-old son who gets everywhere. I'm now awaiting a blood test for lead content! Why are we not made aware of the danger of this from paint retailers/DIY programmes, etc.?**

A Lead paint is not confined to pre-1950s decor; it was used in the UK up until 1992. I think it is fairly obvious why the paint manufacturers and DIY retailers would not want to shout about this from the rooftops, and TV makeover shows are interested only in 'entertainment', not public education. A better question would be why does our government not make more effort to warn people about this danger, and a cynical answer would be that it might expose them to huge compensation claims.

There are thousands of tonnes of lead paint on woodwork in British homes, and its removal by burning or dry-sanding represents a serious risk to young children and foetuses. Lead test kits are available from McDougall Rose decorators' suppliers and from B&Q. But the British Coatings Federation, who produce advice leaflets [PAINTING AND DECORATING], do not generally encourage removal of lead paint at all. They recommend that where the paint surface is in sound condition it should be sealed in by overpainting, although they stress that the householder then has a responsibility to maintain the painted surface in good order.

I feel that this is fudging the issue. If old lead paint is sealed in by overpainting, then surely labels should be posted to warn future generations that a dangerous neurotoxin lurks beneath the surface of their skirting boards. Homes in some US states already carry such legal disclosure notices.

LEAD WATER PIPES

Q **My house is over a hundred years old and the mains water supply comes into the house through the original lead pipes. All the pipes inside the house have been replaced. Is this water safe to drink, or should the lead pipes be replaced?**

A The amount of lead that finds its way into the drinking water depends upon several factors, including the hardness or softness of the supply. The only way to find out if your supply is safe is by asking your water supplier to test a sample taken from your kitchen tap, which they should do free of charge. Regarding replacement pipes, the service pipe which leads from the company stop valve (under the pavement) into the house is your responsibility; the 'tail' which leads from the main to the stop valve is the water company's, and you may have trouble persuading them to replace this. The European Drinking Water Directive requires lead levels to be halved by 2003, and reduced to a fifth of their current levels by 2013, but it is likely that this will be achieved mostly by phosphate dosing rather than wholesale pipe replacement. Further information is available from British Water [PLUMBING, HEATING AND DRAINAGE].

GAS FUMES

Q Could you explain why it is that while there are strict regulations covering flues for gas heaters and boilers, it is acceptable to have four top burners, grill and oven all in use at the same time on a gas cooker in an enclosed kitchen?

A The answer to this is that gas cookers are not expected to be in constant use, nor to be left burning unattended. Also, the regulations require that a kitchen with a gas cooker must have an openable window – so if you have all the burners lit as you describe, the room would be so hot that you would be forced to open the window anyway. In addition, kitchens smaller than 10m³ must have permanent ventilation. My own view is that all kitchens should also have cooker hoods, extracting direct to the outside, rather than recirculating the fumes through the filter.

MOULD GROWTH

Q A few months ago, water penetrated the outside wall of our front bedroom. We have cured the leak but we now have mould growing on the inside wall. My wife has read that it is dangerous for your health to allow the mould to continue to grow. Is this true? If so, what is the best way of getting rid of the mould (without further endangering your health)?

A Some people are sensitive to high concentrations of certain mould spores, and this can contribute to health problems such as asthma and other allergic reactions. But in most cases mould spores are harmless. Wherever you go, there are millions of mould spores in every cubic metre of air, and a patch of mould on the wall is unlikely to harm you.

As long as you are sure the leak is fixed, then things should clear up of their own accord, but if you want to hasten things along then wipe with a dilute solution of bleach in water. This is also good for black mould growth on bathroom windows, and usually keeps it away for a couple of months. Safer and considerably cheaper than proprietary mould-removing chemicals.

TIMBER-TREATMENT CHEMICALS
MULTIPLE TREATMENTS

Q We have bought a barn-conversion property. Our surveyor noted evidence of slight wood-boring beetle activity, and also commented that the timber had been treated before, although there is no documentation or guarantee from this treatment. We engaged a timber-treatment firm, who agreed with the surveyor that infestation was not serious, confirmed that there had been prior treatment, but could not determine what with. They suggest further treatment with an inorganic boron compound in order to issue us with a guarantee. Is this a good idea?

A I am in favour of the Building Research Establishment and Health and Safety Executive advice that if timber is dry then it will not be attacked by insects or fungi. So in a normally heated and ventilated building it is not necessary to use chemical preservatives. Old flight holes are not evidence of continuing active infestation, and will generally only be in the sapwood at the surface of the timber, so they will not necessarily have weakened timbers below their design strength.

Many people claim to have become ill following chemical timber treatment in their homes.

Previous treatment can be easily identified by gas chromatography. But if the property has previously been treated then you should be asking (a) how can there be continuing infestation (i.e. is there a continuing moisture problem allowing infestation to continue)? and (b) what would be the health effects of introducing an additional chemical, effectively creating a chemical cocktail?

PERMETHRIN

Q I have been renovating my Victorian house myself. Where there has been evidence of wood-worm I have treated the floor with a product with permethrin in it. However, I am faced with a living-room floor with holes from woodworm. Would you repair, replace or treat? I have installed central heating. Will this help? I'm concerned for the health of my kids.

A The central heating means that the timber will dry down to a level unable to support insect activity. Obviously any boards that have been damaged very badly should be replaced, but woodworm holes in floorboards generally only occur in the sapwood at the corners or edges of the boards, and do not affect the strength sufficiently to justify their replacement. Beyond that, the holes are only a cosmetic problem. Many people claim to have been made seriously ill by permethrin, and children are usually more susceptible, since the effects are inversely proportional to body weight.

ILLNESS CAUSED BY PERMETHRIN

Q In July 1985 we moved into a Victorian house, and had the timbers sprayed with permethrin. We moved in the day after it was done but many floorboards were still up. Shortly after our move, both my young daughter (then two and a half) and I developed myalgic encephalomyelitis (ME). I am convinced that the woodworm spraying was the cause of our illness.

We have been ill for fourteen years and do not now have any hope of a full recovery for either of us. The medical profession offers little or no help. I have written to you to raise awareness of this possible result of spraying with toxins.

A There are many thousands of people in your position, who have become ill following exposure to permethrin. But since it is licensed as 'safe' by the Health and Safety Executive (HSE), physicians will refuse to acknowledge that it might have injured you and your daughter. They are more likely to prescribe antibiotics, steroids and tranquillizers, before deciding that your condition is a mental problem. Pesticides victim support is currently being organized by the Pesticide Action Network [PESTICIDES].

CHEMICAL DANGERS

Q I have ME and have not been able to work for five years. I ran my own damp-proofing and timber-treatment business for sixteen years, and during the early years I was actually carrying out the treatments myself. I strictly followed all health and safety procedures as detailed on the product literature and later as required by COSHH (Control of Substances Hazardous to Health Acts). The blood tests I have had show high levels of dieldrin, DDT, DDE, HCB (hexachlorobenzene), pentachlorophenol and carbaryl. I presume all of these, being persistent chemicals, will stay where they are in my blood for many years to come. During the period that I was using these products the chemical company assured me that their products were safe. But then they are forced into changing their formulations and moving on to different products, permethrin being a good example. This they advertised as a safe, natural product, but now they have all moved on to using boron.

A As you will probably have found out by now, the industry and the Health and Safety Executive (HSE) will never believe that you followed the instructions properly. They define the chemicals as 'safe' – so they could not possibly accept that, even when used as directed, they can cause illness.

TREATED TIMBER DECKING

Q I am considering having timber decking installed in our back garden, but all the companies I have contacted want to use timber which has been pretreated with preservatives. They say it is not possible to use untreated timber outdoors. But I am concerned about the possible dangers these chemicals may pose to our young grandchildren, who will doubtless be crawling around on the boards when they come to visit. How safe are the preservatives used on decking, and is there any alternative to chemical treatment?

A The manufacturers claim that the vacuum process used to impregnate timber with insecticides and fungicides locks the chemicals into the wood, and that there is no risk of them leaching out or posing a health risk. However, I share your concerns. The chemical formulations used are generally CCA (copper/chrome/arsenic) salts, and I would not recommend allowing children to come into contact with them. You could use untreated softwood and apply an annual coat of boiled linseed oil, which is a safe and natural preservative, but the best solution would probably be to use a rot-resistant timber such as yellow cedar, which weathers naturally to a silver-grey finish, and will last for twenty years or more without the need for chemical treatment.

PESTS

Wherever you live, you will be competing for living space with some kind of animals or insects. Physical exclusion is always preferable to – and usually more effective than – trapping or poisoning. And people who are worried about sharing their homes with birds or bats should be aware that these creatures are responsible for keeping the insect population in check. Get rid of them and you could find your life being made intolerable by flies!

BIRDS

Q We have just acquired a bungalow with the highest roof of the adjoining properties, and seagulls seem happy to sit and sun themselves (sometimes as many as fifteen). Could you please advise what can be done to deter them? We get a lot of mess from their droppings.

A Birds like to sit in places where they can keep an eye out for food, and you are probably quite right that they choose your roof because it is the highest. You may therefore have problems evicting them. And note that under the Wildlife and Countryside Act (1981), you are not allowed to do anything that might injure wild birds. But there are humane physical deterrents, such as anti-perching spikes. These are rows of thin stainless-steel pins sticking out from a polycarbonate backing strip. They are glued in place, and cost from around £5 per linear metre. Builders and roofers can order them from builders' merchants, or they can be bought direct from Woodland Properties [PESTS/ANIMALS].

BIRDS IN ROOF

Q I had my wooden fascia boards replaced with PVC-U recently. This was partly to reduce the maintenance aspect, but mainly to prevent birds getting in as they have been damaging the roofing felt. I was assured that the birds wouldn't get in but I now have more than ever. There are gaps between the straight edge of the board and my curved pantiles. Is there something that I can fit myself to prevent this happening, and are birds in the roof a big problem?

A I am personally not bothered about birds in the roof, unless their squawking youngsters wake me up early. Roofs in older houses would not have been built with sarking felt anyway, so damage to it should not be a problem. Obviously you want to make sure your water tanks have secure lids, so they don't contaminate them or drown themselves in them. But there are a number of proprietary products which seal the spaces between fascias and pantiles, but still allow ventilation through to the roof space. They are plastic strips with flexible comblike fingers on the top edge, which mould to the profile of the tiles. It sounds as though this is what you really needed all along, rather than the PVC-U fascias. Try a specialist roofing supplies merchants.

ULTRASONIC REPELLERS

Q Do you know if ultrasonic deterrents for mice actually work? We have a pitched roof adjoining a flat roof which in turn is accessible from a bankside, and we think that the mice are using this route to get into our loft through the eaves. We wonder if an electronic device in the loft space would work.

A These devices are claimed to use various combinations of electromagnetic fields and ultrasonic sound to repel rats, mice and insects and yet, curiously, to have no adverse effects on household pets. Several companies advertise these products, and claim to have independent scientific research supporting their efficacy, but when investigated by the Advertising Standards Authority, this has been found to be bogus. Some readers have claimed they are sure the repellers have kept mice out of their homes, but there are several factors that affect the presence of mice, and it could be that installing the device has coincided with other changes affecting their behaviour. In my opinion the main effect of these devices is to remove money from gullible punters' pockets.

MASONRY BEES

Q Every summer I notice dozens of bees emerging from gaps in the brickwork of my cottage (soft red bricks, lime mortar, built 1880), and I am worried that they are burrowing into the mortar to make nests. How can I get rid of this pest?

A Some homeowners get worried when they see bees emerging from holes in their brickwork, but so-called masonry bees, *Osmia rufa*, have simply adapted from their natural home in soft sandstone rocks, and it is rare for them to cause serious damage to brickwork. They do not sting, and they are solitary creatures that do not live in colonies or build nests, as such, but lay their eggs in holes and crevices that they find. If you have a lot of them, then it may be a sign that your brickwork has unfilled perpend joints (vertical joints), and it may be an idea to think about raking out and repointing with lime mortar.

BATS

Q My house was converted from an old timber barn, by building lightweight block walls on the inside of the timber frame. In the two summers that I have lived here, pipistrelle bats have made my life intolerable. They are creating a colony within the cavity walls, their points of entry and exit being the gaps between the wooden cladding under the eaves.

I know that the bats are a protected species and I have no desire to harm them. However, the noise they create within the cavities, particularly in the small hours, is sufficient to ruin a good night's sleep – night after night, all summer long.

A Bats, which are suffering a dramatic decline in numbers, are voracious insectivores, and perform a valuable service in keeping insect numbers down. They are being deprived of

Bats are harmless and eat a lot of insects.

roosting sites in houses by the ubiquitous plastic ventilation grilles, and by the current trend for filling cavity walls with insulation. The spraying of timber-treatment chemicals in loft spaces has also taken its toll on the bat population, although the Wildlife and Countryside Act (1981) achieved a notable success in clamping down on this practice. British bats are completely harmless; they do not use nesting materials and, unlike mice, they never nibble cables or wires. There is no known health risk associated with British bats or their droppings.

Most bats roost in roofs between April and June. *Pipistrellus* like to nest in cavity walls, and can be noisy for a few weeks during the breeding season. You may be able to lessen the noise nuisance by building an insulated soundproofing stud wall on the inside. But if you are determined to evict them then English Nature should put you in touch with your local bat worker. Further information from The Bat Conservation Trust [PESTS/ANIMALS]

CLUSTER FLIES

Q We have been building a house surrounded by fields and dairy farms. Every autumn we have been inundated with flies nestling in enormous 'clumps' in the frames of the windows. It is no exaggeration to say that when a window is opened a hundred flies are disturbed. They are fairly dozy and will eventually die on the floor or fly out through the open window. But however much fly killer I use, they keep accumulating. Neighbours have a similar experience. Do you have any solution to this problem?

A These flies are either *Pollenia rudis* or *Dasyphora cyanella*, both known as cluster flies, or *Musca autumnalis*, known as the autumn fly. They breed outside in decaying matter in farmland, and are attracted to warm, south-facing walls. They get in through gaps, and once inside they are then attracted to the light at the windows. Most of them die of dehydration but some hibernate over winter. They seem to prefer some houses to others, and people whose houses have been invaded by cluster flies can find it very difficult to keep them out. You can cut down the numbers entering by sealing all the gaps around the windows, and draught-proofing the opening casements, but some will always find their way in. I am personally not keen on insecticides, as I am not convinced about their safety. A reader has also suggested that painting the brickwork around the windows with Jeyes Fluid every autumn seems to act as a deterrent. Electric flykillers can be good solution, although the large numbers of dead flies can sometimes build up in the catch tray and create a fire hazard.

If you want to use an electric flykiller to kill cluster flies in an unoccupied area such as a loft, then choose one that is open at the bottom, so that when the catch tray is removed, the dead flies fall through into a separate metal container positioned underneath. I have tried several of these flykillers, and I have to say they are of variable quality. The main point to bear in mind is that the ultra-violet (UVA) lamps need to be changed regularly. Although the lamp may appear bright to the human eye, it loses its attraction to insects quite quickly; after 5,000 hours (thirty weeks of continuous use) the output will be down to only 50 per cent of the original. Also, normal UVA lamps are not as effective as more specialist insect-attractant lamps. 'Insect-o-cutor' make a special UVA-green lamp, in sizes to fit all insect killers, which they claim attracts more species of insects, and is longer lasting than a normal UVA lamp [PESTS/ANIMALS].

House Martins.

BIRDS' NESTS

Q **Despite removing their nests after they've gone, the house martins continue to return and rebuild them again. Is there a solution?**

A House martins are migratory birds who return year after year to the same sites to build their nests and breed. The nests are made from mud, and are usually stuck up on the walls below overhanging eaves. Most people find house martins welcome summer guests, with their entertaining evening flights as they swoop in formation around the house. They also perform a valuable role in controlling insect populations – adult house martins catch around 600 flying insects per hour to feed their chicks. You don't say why you find them a nuisance, but if it is because of their droppings, then the answer is to collect these on a board fixed to the wall below the nests. This can be a DIY effort, or purpose-made droppings boards are available from Jacobi Jayne [PESTS/ANIMALS], who also sell artificial house martins' nests for people who would like to encourage these delightful birds to nest around their homes.

USEFUL CONTACTS

The following is a list of the various bodies and organizations mentioned in the book. Their inclusion does not mean that I endorse or recommend them, but they may be worth contacting for advice, or as a starting point in your investigation of a particular topic or problem.

ARCHITECTS, SURVEYORS AND ENGINEERS

Readers who have read my grumbles about surveyors and architects are sometimes confused when I then recommend that you engage one to plan and supervise your building work. But the fact is that while there are many ignorant and incompetent building professionals, there are also some very good ones. The problem is sorting the wheat from the chaff. If you call the following bodies, they will give you a list of members in private practice in your area. It is then a matter of interrogating them until you find one suitable for the job you have in mind.

ABE – Association of Building Engineers – 01604 404121

CIOB – Chartered Institute of Building (incorporates the Association of Architects and Surveyors – ASI) – 01344 630700

RIBA – Royal Institute of British Architects – 020 7580 5533

RICS – Royal Institution of Chartered Surveyors – 020 7222 7000

BRICKWORK

Brick Development Association – 01344 885651 (details of brick matching service)

Easy Raker from Prema Diamond Tools – 01273 677 776, www.prema-diamond-tools.co.uk

BUILDING ORGANIZATIONS

Chartered Institute of Building (Chartered Building Company Scheme) – 01344 630774, www.cbcscheme.org.uk

National Federation of Builders – 020 76085150, www.builders.org.uk

CHIMNEYS AND FIREPLACES

Chimney Balloon Company – 01252 319325

A good (American) source of advice on fireplace problems is Hearth Net – www.hearth.com

CONSERVATION

Society for the Protection of Ancient Buildings (SPAB) – 020 73771644, www.spab.org.uk

CONSTRUCTION LITERATURE

Building Research Establishment publications can be ordered online from www.brebookshop.com or by phone from CRC Ltd – 020 75056622

Construction Industry Publications – 0121 7228200 (supply the JCT Contract for the homeowner/occupier for £10.99 including p+p)

The Housebuilder's Bible, by Mark Brinkley, is available direct from 01223 290230, www.rodelia.co.uk

DAMPNESS

Cavity trays

Cavity Trays – 01935 474769 or freephone 0800 7311799, www.cavitytrays.com

Manthorpe Building Products – 01773 514200, www.manthorpe.co.uk

Drained membrane systems

Newlath from John Newton & Co – 020 7237 1217, www.newton-membranes.co.uk/newlath.htm

Platon from Triton Chemicals Ltd – 020 8310 3929, www.triton-chemicals.com

Dampness and timber surveyors

Abbey Independent Surveys – 01572 774398, e-mail abbeyis@talk21.com

Dampness Diagnosis Consultancy – 020 8657 3750, e-mail david.hewett@btinternet.com

ELECTRICS

Fire Safe downlighters – 01527 831794, www.electro-technik.com

Honda generators – 0845 2008000 or www.hondaenergy.co.uk, through which you can contact a local supplier

NICEIC – 020 7564 2323, www.niceic.org.uk

Tenmat downlighter fire protectors, 0161 872 2181, www.tenmat.com

GAS

CORGI – 01256 372200, www.corgi-gas-safety.com

HAZARDS

National Federation of Master Steeplejacks and Lightning Conductor Engineers – 0115 9558818

Proctor Group Ltd – 01250 872261 (radon gas protection)

LOFT CONVERSIONS

The Loft Shop – 0870 6040404, www.loftshop.co.uk

PAINTING AND DECORATING

British Coatings Federation (lead paint advice) – 01372 360660

Dulux Select Decorator Service – 0840 7697668, www.duluxdecorator.co.uk

Artex

Artex-Rawplug – 0115 945 6100.

Paint removal

Strippers Paint Removers (chemical paint strippers) – 01787 371524

PAVING

Geosynthetics (Geotextiles) – 01455 617139, www.geosyn.co.uk

Grass paving blocks

Hauraton – 01582 501380, www.hauraton.co.uk

Hoofmark Ltd – 0191 5845566

PESTICIDES

Pesticides victim support is provided by Pesticide Action Network – 020 7274 8895, www.pan-uk.org

PESTS/ANIMALS

Bat Conservation Trust – 020 7627 2629, www.bats.org.uk

   (send SAE to 15 Cloisters House, 8 Battersea Park Road, London SW8 4BG)

Insect-o-cutor (electric flykillers) – 0162 428 0622, www.insect-o-cutor.co.uk

Jacobi Jayne (bird care products) – 01227 714 314, www.birdcare.com/jacobijayne

Woodland Properties – 01344 886459 (bird repellers/flyscreens)

PLASTERING

British Gypsum – 08705 456 123, www.british-gypsum.com

Insulated Render and Cladding Association – 01428 654011, www.inca-ltd.org.uk

Tarmac – 01992 715155 (Limelight renovating plaster)

Lime mortars and plasters

The Building Limes Forum – Glasite Meeting House, 33 Barony Street, Edinburgh EH3 6NX UK.

   Send SAE for a list of suppliers, enthusiasts and tradesmen, or see website

www.buildinglimesforum.org.uk

PLUMBING, HEATING AND DRAINAGE

Ariston (undersink heaters) – 01494 755600

Betz Dearborn (Sentinel central heating additives) – 0151 4209595, www.gewater.com/index.jsp

Brannan pipe thermometers – 01946 816600, www.brannan.co.uk

British Water publish ten free fact sheets on all aspects of domestic water treatment on

   www.britishwater.co.uk or call 020 7957 4554

Dualstream water-pressurized storage systems – 01394 386699

Electroheat electric flow boilers – 01256 363417

Fernox Helpline – 01799 550811, www.fernox.com

Heatrae Sadia (undersink heaters) – 01603 420111, www.heatraesadia.com/hs/heatraes.nsf

Hoofmark plastic soakaways – 0191 584 5566, www.hoofmark.co.uk

Hudevad Radiators – 01932 247835, www.hudevad.co.uk

The Institute of Plumbing – 01708 472791, www.plumbers.org.uk

Polypipe (Pacific dual-flush valve) – 01709 770990

Plumbworld (online discount plumbing and heating supplies) – www.plumbworld.co.uk

Renubath – 0800 1382202, www.renubath.co.uk

Boiler parts

Curzon Components – 0870 510 3030

FMT Ltd – 01245 357993

HRPC – 01772 819671 (parts availability can also be checked on their website www.hrpc.co.uk)

Peter Porter Electronics Ltd – 01920 871711

RS Components – 01536 444222, www1.rswww.com

Thermagas – 01257 275080

Cast-iron guttering

Replacement sections from J. & J. W. Longbottom Ltd, 01484 682141

RAINWATER HARVESTING/RECYCLING

Aquarius Water Engineering – 01704 878786, www.aquarius-uk.com

Tank Exchange – 08704 670706, www.thetankexchange.com

ROOFING

Flat Roofing Alliance – 01444 440027, www.fra.org.uk/home.html

National Council of Master Thatchers' Associations – 0700 0781909

National Federation of Roofing Contractors – 020 7436 0387, www.nfrc.co.uk, email: info@nfrc.co.uk

SOUNDPROOFING

Soundproofing leaflet available from BRE website, www.bre.co.uk/pdf/soundins_homes.pdf

or send an SAE to BRE Bookshop, Garston, Watford WD22 9XX

TIMBER FLOORS

Pioneer Woodfloors – 01799 541144

Victorian Wood Works – 020 8534 1000, www.victorianwoodworks.co.uk

TIMBER REPAIRS

Nickerson Chemicals ('Timbabuild' timber repair system) – 01636 636369

TREES

The Tree Care Company – 01234 376254, e-mail treecare88@hotmail.com

WINDOWS AND GLAZING

Crittall Windows – 01376 324106, www.crittall-windows.co.uk

Fein MultiMaster; for stockists call 01327 308 730

Fenestration Associates (window surveyors) – 01676 523583, www.fenestrationassociates.com

Glazpart (window vents) – 01295 264533

James Hetley (leaded-light repairs) – 020 77802344

Reddiseals (dry glazing system) – 01905 791876, www.reddiseals.co.uk

Renson (window vents) – 01622 685658

Sapa Building Systems (Monarch secondary glazing system) – 01684 853500, www.sapabuildingsystems.co.uk

Selectaglaze (secondary glazing) – 01727 837271, www.selectaglaze.co.uk

Steel Window Association – 020 7637 3571, www.steel-window-association.co.uk

INDEX